Being Black, Living in the Red

Being Black, Living in the Red

Race, Wealth, and Social Policy in America

Dalton Conley

UNIVERSITY OF CALIFORNIA PRESS
Berkeley · Los Angeles · London

University of California Press
Berkeley and Los Angeles, California

University of California Press, Ltd.
London, England

© 1999 by Dalton Conley

Library of Congress Cataloging-in-Publication Data

Conley, Dalton, 1969–
   Being Black, living in the red : race, wealth, and
social policy in America / Dalton Conley.
      p.   cm.
   Includes bibliographical references and index.
   ISBN 0-520-21673-3 (pbk.: alk. paper)
   1. Afro-Americans—Economic conditions.
2. Afro-Americans—Social conditions—1975–
3. Social classes—United States—History—20th
century.   4. United States—Race relations.   5. United
States—Social policy—1980–1993.   6. United
States—Social policy—1993–   I. Title.
E185.8 .C77 1999
305.896073—dc21   98-49951
                                                              CIP

Printed in the United States of America

08   07   06   05   04   03   02   01
9   8   7   6   5   4   3

The paper used in this publication meets the minimum
requirements of ANSI/NISO Z39.48-1992 (R 1997)
(*Permanence of Paper*). ∞

Contents

Acknowledgments

I would like to thank the many people and institutions who helped to make this book possible. Its first incarnation was as a doctoral dissertation at Columbia University in the Department of Sociology. There I received extensive comments from my thesis committee members, including my sponsor Seymour Spilerman, J. Lawrence Aber, Neil Bennett, Hiroshi Ishida, and Kathryn Neckerman. I would particularly like to extend my gratitude to Neil Bennett, who worked closely with me at the National Center for Children in Poverty.

In addition to the intellectual support that made this study possible, I received much financial help as well. I would like to thank the Graduate School of Arts and Sciences at Columbia University for providing a generous Paul F. Lazarsfeld Fellowship in Sociology that allowed me to complete my graduate work in a timely fashion. I am also indebted to the Center for Young Children and Families, directed by Professor Jeanne Brooks-Gunn of the Teacher's College at Columbia. Additionally, I would like to express my gratitude to the National Science Foundation, whose doctoral dissertation research grant made the analysis presented here possible (Grant no. 95–21011). Also of note were two student paper awards (1994 and 1995) from the Community and Urban Sociology section of the American Sociological Association; these awards helped to defray the expenses of delivering parts of this work as papers at the annual meetings in Los Angeles in 1994 and in

Washington, D.C., in 1995. The feedback I received in these forums was extremely valuable in guiding the research process.

For help in making the transition from dissertation to book manuscript, I am indebted to the Robert Wood Johnson Foundation Scholars in Health Policy Program at the University of California at Berkeley. The two-year postdoctoral fellowship not only provided me with enough time to make the transition but also put me in contact with another group of very capable critics, including Mike Hout, David Kirp, Jane Mauldon, and Martin Sanchez-Jankowski. As the manuscript moved through the submission, acceptance, and revision process, reviews from several anonymous sources were quite helpful, as were reviews from Jennifer Hochschild, Susan Mayer, Neil Fligstein, and Virginia Olesen. At the University of California Press, I am particularly indebted to my editor, Naomi Schneider, who made this work accessible to a much wider audience; to Mary Renaud, who made it readable; and to Jan Spauschus Johnson, who made it all happen.

Additionally, I owe thanks to my agent, Sydelle Kramer, and her partner, Frances Goldin, who saw through the dissertation to find a book somewhere within. Finally, I would like to thank all those individuals in my life who helped to support me on a personal level while this project was coming to fruition. They include, but are not limited to, my parents, Steve and Ellen; my sister, Alexandra; my grandmother, Sylvia Alexander; my spouse, Natalie Jeremijenko; and last but not least, my daughter, E, to whom this book is dedicated.

CHAPTER ONE

Wealth Matters

Property is theft.
*Pierre Joseph
Proudhon,*
1809–65

If I could cite one statistic that inspired this book, it would be the following: in 1994, the median white family held assets worth more than seven times those of the median nonwhite family. Even when we compare white and minority families at the same income level, whites enjoy a huge advantage in wealth. For instance, at the lower end of the income spectrum (less than $15,000 per year), the median African American family has no assets, while the equivalent white family holds $10,000 worth of equity. At upper income levels (greater than $75,000 per year), white families have a median net worth of $308,000, almost three times the figure for upper-income African American families ($114,600).[1]

Herein lie the two motivating questions of this study. First, why does this wealth gap exist and persist over and above income differences? Second, does this wealth gap explain racial differences in areas such as education, work, earnings, welfare, and family structure? In short, this book examines where race *per se* really matters in the post–civil rights era and where race simply acts as a stand-in for that dirty word of American society: class. The answers to these questions have important implications for the debate over affirmative action and for social policy in general.

An alternative way to conceptualize what this book is about is to contrast the situations of two hypothetical families. Let's say that both households consist of married parents, in their thirties, with two young children.[2] Both families are low-income—that is, the total household income of each family is approximately the amount that the federal government has "declared" to be the poverty line for a family of four (with two children). In 1996, this figure was $15,911.

Brett and Samantha Jones (family 1) earned about $12,000 that year. Brett earned this income from his job at a local fast-food franchise (approximately two thousand hours at a rate of $6 per hour). He found himself employed at this low-wage job after being laid off from his relatively well-paid position as a sheet metal worker at a local manufacturing plant, which closed because of fierce competition from companies in Asia and Latin America. After six months of unemployment, the only work Brett could find was flipping burgers alongside teenagers from the local high school.

Fortunately for the Jones family, however, they owned their own home. Fifteen years earlier, when Brett graduated from high school, married Samantha, and landed his original job as a sheet metal worker, his parents had lent the newlyweds money out of their retirement nest egg that enabled Brett and Samantha to make a 10 percent down payment on a house. With Samantha's parents cosigning—backed by the value of their own home—the newlyweds took out a fifteen-year mortgage for the balance of the cost of their $30,000 home. Although money was tight in the beginning, they were nonetheless thrilled to have a place of their own. During those initial, difficult years, an average of $209 of their $290.14 monthly mortgage payment was tax deductible as a home mortgage interest deduction. In addition, their annual property taxes of $800 were completely deductible, lowering their taxable income by a total of $3,308 per year. This more than offset the payments they were making to Brett's parents for the $3,000 they had borrowed for the down payment.

After four years, Brett and Samantha had paid back the $3,000 loan from his parents. At that point, the total of their combined mortgage payment ($290.14), monthly insurance premium ($50), and monthly property tax payment ($67), minus the tax savings from the deductions for mortgage interest and local property taxes, was less than the $350 that the Smiths (family 2) were paying to rent a unit the same size as the Joneses' house on the other side of town.

That other neighborhood, on the "bad" side of town, where David and Janet Smith lived, had worse schools and a higher crime rate and had just been chosen as a site for a waste disposal center. Most of the residents rented their housing units from absentee landlords who had no personal stake in the community other than profit. A few blocks from the Smiths' apartment was a row of public housing projects. Although they earned the same salaries and paid more or less the same monthly costs for housing as the Joneses did, the Smiths and their children experienced living conditions that were far inferior on every dimension, ranging from the aesthetic to the functional (buses ran less frequently, large supermarkets were nowhere to be found, and class size at the local school was well over thirty).

Like Brett Jones, David Smith had been employed as a sheet metal worker at the now-closed manufacturing plant. Unfortunately, the Smiths had not been able to buy a home when David was first hired at the plant. With little in the way of a down payment, they had looked for an affordable unit at the time, but the real estate agents they saw routinely claimed that there was just nothing available at the moment, although they promised to "be sure to call as soon as something comes up. . . ." The Smiths never heard back from the agents and eventually settled into a rental apartment.

David spent the first three months after the layoffs searching for work, drawing down the family's savings to supplement unemployment insurance—savings that were not significantly greater than those of the Joneses, since both families had more or less the same monthly expenses. After several months of searching, David managed to land a job. Unfortunately, it was of the same variety as the job Brett Jones found: working as a security guard at the local mall, for about $12,000 a year. Meanwhile, Janet Smith went to work part time, as a nurse's aide for a home health care agency, grossing about $4,000 annually.

After the layoffs, the Joneses experienced a couple of rough months, when they were forced to dip into their small cash savings. But they were able to pay off the last two installments of their mortgage, thus eliminating their single biggest living expense. So, although they had some trouble adjusting to their lower standard of living, they managed to get by, always hoping that another manufacturing job would become available or that another company would buy out the plant and reopen it. If worst came to worst, they felt that they could always sell their home and relocate in a less expensive locale or an area with a more promising labor market.

The Smiths were a different case entirely. As renters, they had no latitude in reducing their expenses to meet their new economic reality, and

they could not afford their rent on David's reduced salary. The financial
strain eventually proved too much for the Smiths, who fought over how
to structure the family budget. After a particularly bad row when the
last of their savings had been spent, they decided to take a break; both
thought life would be easier and better for the children if Janet moved
back in with her mother for a while, just until things turned around economically—that is, until David found a better-paying job. With no
house to anchor them, this seemed to be the best course of action.

Several years later, David and Janet Smith divorced, and the children
began to see less and less of their father, who stayed with a friend on a
"temporary" basis. Even though together they had earned more than
the Jones family (with total incomes of $16,000 and $12,000, respectively), the Smiths had a rougher financial, emotional, and family situation, which, we may infer, resulted from a lack of property ownership.

What this comparison of the two families illustrates is the inadequacy of relying on income alone to describe the economic and social
circumstances of families at the lower end of the economic scale. With
a $16,000 annual income, the Smiths were just above the poverty
threshold. In other words, they were not defined as "poor," in contrast
to the Joneses, who were.[3] Yet the Smiths were worse off than the
Joneses, despite the fact that the U.S. government and most researchers
would have classified the Jones family as the one who met the threshold of neediness, based on that family's lower income.

These income-based poverty thresholds differ by family size and are
adjusted annually for changes in the average cost of living in the United
States. In 1998, more than two dozen government programs—including food stamps, Head Start, and Medicaid—based their eligibility
standards on the official poverty threshold. Additionally, more than a
dozen states currently link their needs standard in some way to this
poverty threshold. The example of the Joneses and the Smiths should
tell us that something is gravely wrong with the way we are measuring
economic hardship—poverty—in the United States. By ignoring assets,
we not only give a distorted picture of life at the bottom of the income
distribution but may even create perverse incentives.

Of course, we must be cautious and remember that the Smiths and
the Joneses are hypothetically embellished examples that may exagger-
ate differences. Perhaps the Smiths would have divorced regardless of
their economic circumstances. The hard evidence linking modest financial differences to a propensity toward marital dissolution is thin; how-

ever, a substantial body of research shows that financial issues are a major source of marital discord and relationship strain.[4] It is also possible that the Smiths, with nothing to lose in the form of assets, might have easily slid into the world of welfare dependency. A wide range of other factors, not included in our examples, affect a family's well-being and its trajectory. For example, the members of one family might have been healthier than those of the other, which would have had important economic consequences and could have affected family stability. Perhaps one family might have been especially savvy about using available resources and would have been able to take in boarders, do under-the-table work, or employ another strategy to better its standard of living. Nor do our examples address educational differences between the two households.

But I have chosen not to address all these confounding factors for the purpose of illustrating the importance of asset ownership *per se*. Of course, homeownership, savings behavior, and employment status all interact with a variety of other measurable and unmeasurable factors. This interaction, however, does not take away from the importance of property ownership itself.

The premise of this book is a relatively simple and straightforward one: in order to understand a family's well-being and the life chances of its children—in short, to understand its class position—we not only must consider income, education, and occupation but also must take into account accumulated wealth (that is, property, assets, or net worth—terms that I will use interchangeably throughout this book). While the importance of wealth is the starting point of the book, its end point is the impact of the wealth distribution on racial inequality in America. As you might have guessed, an important detail is missing from the preceding description of the two families: the Smiths are black and have fewer assets than the Joneses, who are white.

At all income, occupational, and education levels, black families on average have drastically lower levels of wealth than similar white families. The situation of the Smiths may help us to understand the reason for this disparity of wealth between blacks and whites. For the Smiths, it was not discrimination in hiring or education that led to a family outcome vastly different from that of the Joneses; rather, it was a relative lack of assets from which they could draw. In contemporary America, race and property are intimately linked and form the nexus for the persistence of black-white inequality.

Let us look again at the Smith family, this time through the lens of race. Why did real estate agents tell the Smiths that nothing was available, thereby hindering their chances of finding a home to buy? This well-documented practice is called "steering," in which agents do not disclose properties on the market to qualified African American home seekers, in order to preserve the racial makeup of white communities—with an eye to maintaining the property values in those neighborhoods. Even if the Smiths had managed to locate a home in a predominantly African American neighborhood, they might well have encountered difficulty in obtaining a home mortgage because of "redlining," the procedure by which banks code such neighborhoods "red"—the lowest rating—on their loan evaluations, thereby making it next to impossible to get a mortgage for a home in these districts. Finally, and perhaps most important, the Smiths' parents were more likely to have been poor and without assets themselves (being black and having been born early in the century), meaning that it would have been harder for them to amass enough money to loan their children a down payment or to cosign a loan for them. The result is that while poor whites manage to have, on average, net worths of over $10,000, impoverished blacks have essentially no assets whatsoever.[5]

Since wealth accumulation depends heavily on intergenerational support issues such as gifts, informal loans, and inheritances, net worth has the ability to pick up both the current dynamics of race and the legacy of past inequalities that may be obscured in simple measures of income, occupation, or education. This thesis has been suggested by the work of sociologists Melvin Oliver and Thomas Shapiro in their recent book *Black Wealth/White Wealth*.[6] They claim that wealth is central to the nature of black-white inequality and that wealth—as opposed to income, occupation, or education—represents the "sedimentation" of both a legacy of racial inequality as well as contemporary, continuing inequities. Oliver and Shapiro provide a textured description of the divergence of black-white asset holdings. They touch on some of the causal factors leading to this growing gap, such as differential mortgage interest rates paid by black and white borrowers. However, because they use a "snapshot" of families as their primary source of information—that is, cross-sectional data collected at one point in time (the 1984 Survey of Income and Program Participation)—they are limited in the scope of their investigation of the causes and consequences of black-white wealth differentials over time.

I hope to build on the work of Oliver and Shapiro by developing a formal model for the inclusion of assets into statistical models of socioeconomic attainment and family processes, thereby mapping out the role that wealth inequities play in the larger context of a cycle of racial inequality. Specifically, it is the hypothesis of this book that certain tenacious racial differences—such as deficits in education, employment, wages, and even wealth itself among African Americans—will turn out to be indirect effects, mediated by class differences. In other words, it is not race *per se* that matters directly; instead, what matters are the wealth levels and class positions that are associated with race in America. In this manner, racial differences in income and asset levels have come to play a prominent role in the perpetuation of black-white inequality in the United States.

This is not to say that race does not matter; rather, it maps very well onto class inequality, which in turn affects a whole host of other life outcomes. In fact, when class is taken into consideration, African Americans demonstrate significant net *advantages* over whites on a variety of indicators (such as rates of high school graduation, for instance). In this fact lies the paradox of race and class in contemporary America—and the reason that both sides of the affirmative action debate can point to evidence to support their positions.

THE RACE-CLASS DEBATE

A brief review of the discourse on racial inequality may help to put the thesis of this book in historical perspective. The concept of equality most often used in public discourse was inherited from the French Revolution: *equality of opportunity*. Under this concept, equality would be achieved if each individual in a society enjoyed the right to compete in a contest unimpaired by discrimination of any kind. This form of equality would clearly be incompatible with an active, "color-aware" form of racial oppression such as the refusal to serve someone at a lunch counter or the denial of a job to an individual based on his or her physiognomy. Further, this concept fits very well with the game-like image many Americans have of the capitalist system. If the game is fair, our whole society is bettered by it. By contrast, if the rules are stacked in favor of one group, society is not making maximal use of its human resources. For example, if African Americans are barred from higher education, society as a whole may be deprived of the skills of a great surgeon or engineer who could not attend a university because of skin color. With this premise, arguments for equality of opportunity can often be made on the basis of efficiency rather than equity.

Because of this ideological safety valve, equality of opportunity is perhaps the least threatening type of equality to many in the white majority, who see a place for all at the starting gate as an underlying premise of the capitalist system. Lingering conscious or unconscious ideas of white superiority may have additionally blunted fears. According to this logic, whites would not have much to lose by allowing blacks into the economic game; if whites are inherently superior, why should they fear the entry of blacks into the contest? The belief in white superiority that had formed part of the public discourse since the early days of Western imperialism, we can speculate, may have provided a sense of security to some of the more privileged whites who did not fear for their class position, particularly during the period of rapid economic growth after World War II.

For these reasons, equality of opportunity served as the underlying philosophy and rallying cry that drove the liberal political triumphs of the 1950s and early 1960s, capped by the 1964 Civil Rights Act and the Voting Rights Act of 1965. With such legislation, equality of opportunity—in name at least—had been achieved. In theory, after 1965, discrimination in hiring, housing, and other aspects of life was illegal. It was at this point, according to sociologist William Julius Wilson[7] and others, that an overt phase of racial oppression ended in the United States and was replaced by economic subordination.

While legal equality of opportunity might have been established and some income gains made, institutionalized racism persisted nonetheless, and the scars of centuries of overt repression remained. A second type of equality had yet to be realized: *equality of condition*—more progressive and less ideologically acceptable to the American public than equality of opportunity. According to political scientist Jennifer Hochschild, "Three-fourths or more of both races agree that all people warrant equal respect, that skill rather than need should determine wages, that 'America should promote equal opportunity for all' rather than 'equal outcomes.'" She adds that most Americans think that everyone should attempt to amount to more than their parents and that "trying to get ahead is very important in making someone a true American."[8] Clearly, upward mobility and socioeconomic success are fundamental to at least the rhetoric of what it means to be American. By such a definition,

African Americans may, in fact, be the most American of all, socioeconomic indicators, they have made incredible progre passage of civil rights legislation. By other measures, howe not so "American"—that is, for whatever reason, upward mobility has been more difficult.

Although as a group African Americans have made progress in a number of socioeconomic areas, the base from which they were starting in the 1960s was dismally low. For instance, in 1964, only 9.4 percent of blacks held professional or managerial positions, compared to 24.7 percent of whites.[9] The median family income in the black community was less than half that in the white community. By the end of the decade (1969), 41.2 percent of black children still lived in poverty, compared to only 9.9 percent of white children.[10] Even when we compare blacks and whites with similar educational credentials, African Americans suffered from lower incomes and worked in less prestigious occupations than their white counterparts.[11] Statistics aside, the televised ghetto riots of the late 1960s may have been evidence enough for many American observers that substantial racial inequities remained in the United States.

Overall, conditions were worse for blacks than for whites across America. In addition, the mechanism by which inequality was transferred from generation to generation was different in the African American community. In their classic 1967 study, *The American Occupational Structure*, sociologists Peter Blau and Otis Dudley Duncan observed that the relationship between the occupations of black fathers and the occupations of their sons was weaker than the similar relationship among whites: regardless of class origin, African American individuals seemed destined to end up in the lower, manual sector of the economy. Blau and Duncan called this condition "perverse equality." In the same vein, the higher an African American attempted to rise in the occupational hierarchy, the more discrimination the individual faced. "In short," wrote Blau and Duncan, "better educated Negroes fare even worse relative to whites than uneducated Negroes."[12]

Despite a lack of equality of condition, many sociologists and historians agree that the period of the 1950s and 1960s was a time of important gains for African Americans. For instance, between 1949 and 1969, the median income (adjusted for family size) increased by 173 percent among African Americans, in contrast to a 110 percent increase for whites. (Keep in mind, however, that blacks were starting from a base income that was slightly more than a third that of whites in

1949.)[13] Additionally, between 1940 and the early 1970s, the black middle class grew at a faster rate than the white middle class. Based on a definition of "middle class" as having a family income twice the poverty line (note the income-based conception of class), the percentage of African American households in this group rose from a minuscule 1 percent in 1940 to 39 percent in 1970.

The period since 1970—the era of "economic subordination," according to Wilson—has been difficult to interpret in terms of race. Some of the positive trends continue for middle-class African Americans; other statistics, however, tell a different tale, a story of poor African Americans getting poorer. In deciphering the current state of race in America, it may help to view racial inequality in the context of the life course, starting with birth. Black infants, for example, are much more likely than white infants to be born with a low (under 2,500 grams) or a very low (under 1,500 grams) birth weight. In 1994, medical complications associated with low birth weight were the primary cause of death among black infants and the third leading cause for white infants. Correspondingly, the mortality rate among black infants that year (15.8 per thousand) was well over twice that among white and Hispanic babies (6.6 and 6.5 per thousand, respectively).[14]

Looking beyond infancy, we find that over half of all African American children under the age of six live in poverty, three times greater than the proportion in the white community.[15] When we move up the age ladder, the news gets better before it gets worse again. In examining educational statistics, we find that the high school completion rates for blacks and whites are essentially the same among younger adults (ages twenty-five to thirty-four, the group for whom civil rights advances should have had an effect), with 85 percent of African Americans attaining at least a high school education, compared to 88 percent of whites. Even more encouraging is that the proportion of adults in this same age group who receive some college education (not necessarily a degree) is higher for blacks than for whites (32 and 28 percent, respectively). When we examine college completion rates, however, we find that African Americans are only about half as likely as whites to complete a bachelor's degree (14 and 28 percent, respectively). The college attrition rate for black students has become a major problem on American campuses.[16]

When we move out of school and into the labor market, the situation deteriorates. The black-white wage ratio has begun to widen

slightly for all education levels since the 1980s.[17] Labor force participation and unemployment differentials have also increased.[18] For example, in 1994, the unemployment rate for blacks was 13.9 percent,
whereas it was only 6.2 percent for non-Hispanic whites. The black unemployment rate has only rarely dipped below double digits since the
dawn of the civil rights era, and it surpassed 20 percent during the
1982–83 recession. Even when African Americans are able to land a
job, it is likely to be a less desirable position. In 1997, only 16 percent
of employed African Americans held professional or managerial jobs,
compared to 31 percent of employed whites. By contrast, black workers were overrepresented in the service sector, with its lower wages: 26
percent of employed African Americans worked in service industries in
1997, while only 15 percent of their white counterparts held jobs in this
sector.[19]

Income trends reflect the occupational position of black workers. In
1997, the median income for black families was 55 percent that of
white families ($26,522 compared to $47,023). In this same year, 26
percent of black families lived under the poverty line, whereas only 6
percent of white families did so. Educational differences do not explain
these income gaps. For instance, among individuals who are high
school graduates (but have not completed additional education), median incomes are $14,881 and $18,446 for blacks and whites, respectively. When we consider only men, the disparity widens. Black male
high school graduates earned a median income of $18,898 in 1997
compared to $26,028 for white males. In other words, in 1997, African
American male high school graduates earned 73 cents to the dollar
earned by white male high school graduates. For more educated
groups, wage ratios are not much better.[20]

The labor market difficulties that African American men continue to
face have repercussions further up the age ladder. As mentioned earlier,
the black-white wealth gap is even wider than the income difference.
Other areas of life are affected as well. For instance, in 1997, only 46
percent of black families consisted of a married couple (with or without children). This figure is 56 percent of that for whites (81 percent).[21]
Some argue that this dearth of marriage in the African American community is partly a result of a shortage of marriageable (read: well-
employed) black men.[22] There seems to be a causal loop in the logic of
the current discourse on race in the United States: if black families have
two full-time workers, they can maintain economic equity with whites,

but blacks face economic obstacles in getting and staying married (as Chapter Five discusses). Race, family, and life chances seem to be inextricably linked in a vicious circle of inequality over the life course.

Given all these trends, it is understandable why liberals and conservatives are constantly at odds on issues such as the impact and continuing value of affirmative action or the reasons for persistent gaps in socioeconomic attainment between blacks and whites. Both sides can point to statistics to support their arguments, and the debate reaches a stalemate.[23]

The most provocative thesis regarding the state of racial equality today remains that issued by William Julius Wilson back in 1978 in his book *The Declining Significance of Race*, which was championed and attacked by a variety of scholars from both sides of the political debate. Wilson argued that the civil rights victories of the 1960s led to a situation in which overt racial oppression is largely a thing of the past (equality of opportunity), but in which the socioeconomic (read: class) differences between blacks and whites disadvantage African Americans relative to their white counterparts in terms of their chances for success in life. In its most distilled form, his argument is simply that class has eclipsed race as the most important factor determining the life chances of African Americans. As Wilson himself puts it in the first sentence of his classic work: "Race relations in America have undergone fundamental changes in recent years, so much so that now the life chances of individual blacks have more to do with their economic class position than with their day-to-day encounters with whites."[24]

Understandably, Wilson's controversial argument about the declining significance of race has come under careful scrutiny. Many researchers have tested his hypothesis that class is more determinant than race of the life chances of black Americans. Support has been found for his claim in terms of occupational mobility both within and across generations,[25] although race still remains salient in predicting earnings for given education levels[26] and net worth.[27] Furthermore, many scholars have documented the continued importance of race in both the economic and the symbolic realms for many black Americans.[28] There is some disagreement about the exact mechanism by which race affects the life chances of black Americans: some claim that it has a direct impact net of socioeconomic background characteristics; others argue that it does not. Most are in agreement that race influences the way socioeconomic background (class) affects the outcomes of individuals (a sort of compromise in the race-class debate). In other words, a consensus seems to be emerging that blacks who come from middle-class backgrounds are doing better than ever before while poor, predominantly inner-city blacks are being left further and further behind. In other words, there is an "interaction" between race and class background.

The race-class debate is far from settled, however. At the time Wilson penned that provocative statement (1978), it had not even been fifteen years since the end of the era of overt, legally tolerated racial oppression. If class has eclipsed race for any group, it would have done so for those born since the 1960s. In this book, I hope to push the race-class debate further by examining this post-1960s cohort and by revising how we think about class by adding net worth to the measurement of socioeconomic status.

WHAT IS SOCIAL CLASS?

In the jargon of social theory, the concept of "class" implies fundamental economic cleavages in a society, such as those between laborers and capitalists, managers and workers, manual and nonmanual employees, skilled and unskilled workers, or even blue-collar and white-collar workers. In the practice of social research, however, categorical class measures such as these usually prove inferior in their predictive power to a more gradated approach such as measuring socioeconomic status (SES). Researchers generally use indicators of SES to gauge the influence of social background on a variety of outcomes. The three measures that usually constitute socioeconomic status are education, occupation, and income.

There are many theoretical and empirical reasons why these three measures have been used. Put simply, they work—that is, in combination, they explain a significant amount of variation in socioeconomic outcomes across and within generations. They are also fairly easy to measure. Education is usually measured as years of formal schooling or highest degree attained (high school, college, and so forth). Occupation is scored in terms of its social prestige (for instance, being a doctor is more prestigious than being a salesperson, which in turn is more prestigious than being a ditch digger). Income is fairly straightforward: the more one has, the better off one is. (Chapter Two provides a more thorough discussion of these variables.) What these three measures have in common is that they fit nicely with our image of a fair society in which everyone gets a shot to succeed according to his or her own merits. Educational attainment may be at least partly related to innate cognitive ability as measured by IQ; educational success often translates into a prestigious occupation, which may in turn yield a high income.

By contrast, wealth, which has been left out of empirical analysis thus far, has other connotations, such as inheritance. Wealth is much more stable within families and across generations than is income, occupation, or education. In short, we are less likely to have earned it and more likely to have inherited it or received it as a gift. Therefore, wealth does not fit neatly into our vision of the ideal, meritocratic society.[29] Yet, for this very reason, it is critical to consider wealth when addressing issues of intergenerational inequality. At the same time, the social prestige that accompanies the ownership of assets is often the end to which education, occupation, and income all serve as the means. In both these ways, wealth forms an important part of social class.

The University of California sociologists who authored the recent work *Inequality by Design: Cracking the Bell Curve Myth* offer a good summary of the importance of wealth to a sense of economic security and social class. "Being prosperous," they write, "may mean owning a vacation home, purchasing private security services, and having whatever medical care one wants; being squeezed may mean having one modest but heavily mortgaged house, depending on 911 when danger lurks, and delaying medical care because of the expense of copayments." They highlight the important interaction of assets, income, and class by stating that for average, middle-income Americans, "one missed mortgage payment or one chronic injury might be enough to push them into the class that has been left behind."[30]

These authors employ the image of a ladder to illustrate two conceptually separate questions of inequality that are worth investigating. Who ends up on which rung is one question (issues of opportunity); the other is how far apart the rungs are (issues of equity/distribution of rewards). Wealth in its most tangible form represents the rungs to which many aspire; however, its importance in the transmission of inequality reveals that how far apart the rungs are placed is not independent of the factors that determine who ends up on which rung. Thus, we must consider that wealth both represents class and determines class.

Through this dual nature, assets can serve to create or reinforce class identity. One mechanism by which property may help to cement a status group stems from its consumptive and conspicuous nature. For ex-

ample, a status group might be unified on the basis of its common ownership of summer residences in a "selective" area. Expensive luxury
cars might also signal status through what Thorstein Veblen called
"conspicuous consumption," in his book *The Theory of the Leisure
Class*.[31] Identity through consumption is not limited to elites, however,
as Veblen may have implied in 1899, when he wrote; consumption has
become (or may have always been) a realm of expression for the middle classes as well. In 1970, sociologist Edward Shils wrote about consumption under the rubric of "lifestyle," claiming that it is a basis for
social standing that follows a different conceptual logic than the prestige hierarchy located within the labor market (that is, the doctor/ditch
digger differential). He argued that "lifestyle is one of the most important bases of prestige because, like occupational role, it is among the
most continuous and observable of the various deference entitle-
ments."[32] In this manner, each investment decision—which house to
buy, which securities to own—is a lifestyle judgment that creates a
group status affiliation for the owner. This dynamic may be most apparent with visible investments—illiquid assets such as homes, vehicles,
and businesses. "In its permanence," writes Charles Abrams of the family home, "the owner sees the stabilization of his own values; in the
firmness of its foundation he follows his own roots into the community
. . . in its ownership, he sees release from the fears and uncertainties of
life."[33]

While wealth can create symbolic affiliations in the realm of lifestyle
differentiation, it also has the effect of determining group alliances
within the purely economic realm. At various times during the industrial history of the West, it may have made sense to speak of occupational categories as the prime, if not sole, locus of class identity. The
union-management dichotomy at one time served as the contested field
for group interactions within both the economic and the political
spheres, and group identity largely followed this dichotomy. As Richard
Sennett and Jonathan Cobb wrote in *The Hidden Injuries of Class*,
"The essential character of money power for most manual workers is
that it comes to them not individually, but collectively, through union
action. . . . The labor negotiator is fighting for categories of work to be
rewarded, not for individuals to be singled out."[34] In the case of union
contracts, the wages of co-workers (for instance, the two sheet metal
workers described earlier) directly affect each other since co-workers
often find themselves together in a collective bargaining situation.

Today, however, this is less often the case. Unionization rates have hit a low of 11 percent in the U.S. private sector. One is no longer tied to co-workers in the labor market to the same extent as yesteryear; rather, one is in direct competition with co-workers in an economy that relies increasingly on temporary and nonunionized labor. Skill differentiation has become more finely graduated within the work force even as its variance has increased (as is inevitable with the ceaseless division of labor); each worker is more an individual entrepreneur trying to protect his or her tenuous position through constant cultivation of "human capital." No longer—in a global, postindustrial economy—can workers stand united on the basis of occupational roles that are themselves in flux. Thus, we can speculate that class identity resulting from common economic interests may solidify less frequently in the labor market and increasingly in other areas of life.

The realm where one's own economic interest may remain directly tied to that of one's fellow humans is in the world of property relations. Property values offer a prepackaged measure of social worth. In a sense, asset values serve as a quantification of social structure defined through the law. For example, the price of a rare painting, a misprinted U.S. stamp, gold, or any security is determined collectively through the market and is "artificially" (by human action) propped up in the marketplace. The value of a Renoir, ten thousand shares of IBM stock, or a pork belly futures contract is wholly determined by the fact that these items are socially desired within the society. In this sense, property values are where culture meets economics.

Nowhere can this be seen more clearly than in the realm of housing, the most common form of property accumulation in America. While it matters little what wages one's next-door neighbors earn, it matters dearly how the neighbors want to decorate the outside of their house. The value of the neighbors' property directly affects one's own economic fortunes—manifested in the price of one's own home. If the neighbors choose to decorate their home garishly (as defined by the tastes of the collectivity through the market) or to let it deteriorate, their action will lower not only their own property values but also the property values of other homes in the neighborhood by making the entire block a less "desirable" spot to live. In this manner, housing property merges—in a very visible way—symbolic status interests with direct economic ones. The results of this marriage range from strict zoning laws and school redistricting to "white flight" and the converse phenomenon of "gentrification." In all these ways, inequality is mapped by ownership for this generation and the next.

RESEARCH STRATEGY

One of the guiding motivations of my research is that if class (that is, socioeconomic status) is reconceptualized, uncoupling it from its traditional reliance on labor market measures such as income, occupation, and education, the apparently muddled situation of racial inequality in contemporary America will become clearer. The strategy that I employ to clarify this situation is to analyze data from a survey that has been conducted every year since 1968. The uniqueness of this particular survey (called the Panel Study of Income Dynamics, or PSID) lies in the fact that it follows the same families over time. As long as the researchers can track them down, every family from the original 1968 sample of five thousand American households (and those that have been added since the original set of interviews) is sought out and reinterviewed each year.

An additional strength of this survey is that any time a new family forms out of one of the sample families, the new family is given its own identification code as well as a number that links it back to the original family. In the case of divorce, for instance, two new families are added to the PSID rolls and are tagged with a common identifier specifying how they relate to the original family. The same holds true for the children of sample families who grow up and move out on their own. It is these children, born since 1962, who will form the basis of my analysis.[35]

The PSID is even more appealing for a study of race and wealth because the assets and liabilities of each family are reviewed every five years (beginning in 1984). Thus, one can follow the dynamics of family wealth and fortunes over time. Given the richness of these data, I followed the strategy of investigating the role of the levels of wealth held by specific families in 1984 on the outcomes of children from those households (whether or not the children moved out of the parental home) in the early to mid-1990s.

By relying on an analysis of how parental wealth during an individual's adolescence affects that individual's later outcome, I hope to avoid the major pitfall of this type of research: reverse causality. If I were to measure wealth and its consequences at the same time—in a snapshot fashion—I could never be sure whether wealth was affecting education, for instance, or whether education was affecting wealth levels. I have tried to avoid the lion's share of reverse causation by taking care to temporally order my measurement of indicators, but I must stress from the outset that family economic dynamics are complex, and even the best efforts to carefully avoid such pitfalls as reverse causality are not foolproof.

For example, if parents were reasonably sure that their teenage son would succeed in school and thus would be able to support himself well into his old age, the parents might consequently decide not to save very much money, believing that the child would not need it for his future. This possibility would present a case where causality ran from child's education to parents' wealth level (with a negative relationship), even though the latter had been measured a decade prior to its determinant! Alternatively, parents might spend all their wealth on private, early childhood education for their child and thus have little left by the time the child was a teenager in 1984. While such a dynamic would not constitute reverse causation *per se*, it too would result in an underestimation of the effect of parental net worth, since the wealth would have already had its impact and would have vanished by the time it was measured in 1984.

With such complex psychological and economic decision-making going on within families, I stress that the purpose of this book is not to provide the definitive word on measuring the effects of wealth and its relationship to income or other SES dynamics. If, for example, the PSID measured assets and liabilities every year as opposed to every five years, such a goal might be more feasible. Additionally, if the PSID included questions on the motivations of respondents for their economic plans and documented each investment and consumption decision, such a study might be more tractable. In the end, however, a definitive study is probably not completely feasible within the context of survey research. Rather, it would be better suited to in-depth, anthropological methods that seek to understand the decision-making dynamics within the household unit.

The purpose of the current study is more modest: simply put, it is to show that before we attribute black-white differences in certain life outcomes to race *per se*, we must take a better accounting of the economic resources available to American families, by not limiting ourselves to income measures. Whether the effects I attribute to wealth are actually reflecting unobserved family differences or permanent income levels (life-time expected earnings), for example, is not my primary concern. My main consideration is what happens to black-white differences when we choose to compare families with the same wealth levels (and who are equal in other characteristics that I can measure). Undoubtedly, there will be many omissions of possible alternative explanations, ranging from the economic to the attitudinal; however, what I hope remains at the end of this story is a demonstration of the reduced significance of race alone in a variety of realms where race has previously been considered to be of great importance.

IS IT ALL BLACK AND WHITE?

Throughout this introduction, I have spoken only of blacks and whites when addressing the issue of race. America is no longer a biracial society, however. So why examine the impact of wealth and property issues with respect to blacks and whites exclusively? One reason for this strategy is technical. It is very difficult to find useful, longitudinal data on assets for the American population; this is particularly true for minorities who make up a small percentage of the population, even when their numbers are growing rapidly. The PSID survey used for this study began collecting information from five thousand American families in 1968, following them each year up through the present (and will follow them into the future). At the time the survey commenced, families of Asian descent and those of Hispanic origin did not make up nearly as large a percentage of the total population as they now do. Therefore, by today's standards, they are greatly underrepresented in the original group that was to be studied and followed over the years. (The survey team has, however, made recent efforts to add other minority groups to the sample population.) Given the underrepresentation of these and other groups who have grown as a percentage of the general population in the three decades since the survey began, it has not been possible to present reliable statistical analysis for these families.

That said, there are other reasons why this shortcoming should not be so troubling. Perhaps the most important is that on almost all measures—including property ownership—blacks and whites demonstrate the greatest disparities of all racial groups in the United States.[36] This holds true for indicators ranging from residential segregation to wages to academic achievement. In other words, what is true for Latinos in terms of hindered life chances appears even more true for African Americans. Further, within the Hispanic population, wide variation exists in wealth and other factors. Certain groups such as Cubans and Spaniards tend to fall close to whites for a variety of indicators, whereas other groups such as Mexicans, Puerto Ricans, and Dominicans more resemble the African American population by socioeconomic and family measures. In short, the Hispanic population demonstrates much variation but largely falls between blacks and whites (closer to African Americans on average). Even more interesting, skin color within the Hispanic population is a good predictor of where on the spectrum between blacks and whites an individual is likely to fall. In other words, the "blacker" a Hispanic person looks, the more likely he or she is to resemble the African American demographic profile; the "whiter" a Hispanic person appears, the more he or she will resemble the demographic profile of European ethnic groups.[37]

What about Asian Americans, the so-called "model minority" (that is, a group that has been socioeconomically successful despite its minority status)? At one time in American history, Jews were considered the "model minority" and were pointed to as an example of how "anyone can make it in America" (the implied question asking why blacks could not do the same thing). Interestingly, Jews today are no longer generally considered a separate race but instead form part of the white community. In fact, sociologist Andrew Hacker claims that there are only two races in America, white and nonwhite; therefore, for instance, Pakistanis with very dark skin can be considered symbolically "white" in his scheme. He argues that today Asian Americans fall under the "white umbrella" as an "in-group"—in other words, they are not systematically excluded from reaping the benefits of American capitalism, as are those under the "black umbrella," the "out-group." Correspondingly, today the role of model minority has been largely taken over by Asian Americans.[38]

The issue of entrepreneurship also comes into play when making comparisons. If many Chinese and Koreans, for example, can come to the United States with nothing and manage to excel in school and start businesses with little formal capital, why cannot African Americans do the same? The answer to this question may lie in a long cultural history of entrepreneurship among these Asian ethnic groups—or perhaps in their very status as immigrants. "Immigrants in the United States, Canada and Australia," write Ivan Light and Carol Rosenstein in *Race,*

Ethnicity, and Entrepreneurship in Urban America, "continued to manifest higher rates of self-employment than the native born, a proclivity
they have displayed for at least a century."[39] By definition, immigrants
are the world's overachievers, so they do not form a valid comparison
group for the native black or white communities. The act of migrating
itself is an important causal factor to be reckoned with before any judg-
ments are made about the relative proclivities of ethnic groups toward
entreprencurial activity.

Research has supported this immigrant exceptionalism argument, finding in one case, for instance, "that successive generations of white ethnics
[in Providence] evidence successively lower rates of self-employment."[40]
Another study found that when "human capital" (education) is held constant, Asian American and African American entrepreneurship rates are
essentially the same.[41] Other work contradicts this finding, however, finding a net lower rate of self-employment among blacks even after factoring
out a variety of other variables.[42]

Theories of entrepreneurship may offer some explanation. One theory holds that a group's rate of self-employment will be high when it
faces disadvantage in the rest of the labor market.[43] Thus, the fact that
Asian Americans get a "low" return on their educational credentials
could help to explain their higher rates of entrepreneurship. But what
about African Americans? As we have already seen, black Americans
receive lower wages than the majority group (whites) at the same education levels. According to the theory, we should then expect African
Americans to have a higher than average rate of self-employment; instead, the rate is lower (3.7 percent in 1993, compared to 9.0 percent
for whites). These rates may indicate that this theory of "labor market
disadvantage" is missing an important component: group resources
(that is, levels of human capital). It is one thing to have high levels of
education (as Asian Americans do) and not be adequately rewarded for
them. It is quite a different situation to have lower than average education levels (as African Americans do) and receive still lower returns
on these years of schooling. In other words, the labor market equilibrium will balance itself in favor of self-employment only when the resources are there to begin with.[44]

Consumer racism has also been shown to have a role in depressing
the rate of black entrepreneurship.[45] If nonblack consumers—who obviously form the largest part of the market—automatically prefer a
white electrician or barber to a black one, for instance, this discourages

African American self-employment. It is also important to realize that
the rates of entrepreneurial activity for one group are not independent
of the rates for other groups. While there has been no evidence to show
that Asian American businesses have "prevented" black ones from
forming, we do have evidence that rates of Asian entrepreneurship increase in communities with a high percentage of black residents (net of
the size of the Asian population).[46] In other words, Koreans, for example, may not be displacing black businesses, but they are filling a consumer need in black communities that otherwise would have gone un-
tended since African Americans may lack the financial and educational
resources to start such enterprises. Entrepreneurship is related to immi-
gration, labor market prospects, and wealth endowments in complex
ways. Thus, even if the data were available, comparing Asian immigrants with native-born black Americans is neither simple nor fruitful.
The clearer comparison, which I will make in Chapter Two, is between
blacks and whites, the vast majority of whom are native-born.

ORGANIZATION OF THE BOOK

Chapter Two presents the first statistical analysis, addressing the question of why blacks own so much less property than whites. Some scholars have argued that whites have merely enjoyed a head start in property accumulation as a result of the overt economic and political
advantages they have held for centuries. The other side of the debate
has claimed that contemporary issues such as residential segregation
and differential credit access are the major culprits in accounting for the
racial difference in property holdings. Results from an analysis that
links two generations show that among the youngest cohort of blacks
and whites, historical (that is, parental) wealth disadvantages are the
most salient factors, although contemporary dynamics may become important over the life course.

Chapters Three and Four demonstrate how this wealth difference affects the life chances of young blacks and whites. For instance, Chapter
Three shows that when we compare black and white individuals, while
factoring out the effect of blacks' lower average parental incomes and
wealth levels, we find that African Americans actually complete higher
levels of education than their white counterparts. Further, the much-
touted employment and earnings gap between blacks and whites is
largely explained by class dynamics, not by race *per se*, as Chapter Four

demonstrates. Wealth explains much, but it does not explain every racial difference: analysis in Chapter Five suggests that class accounts for some, but not all, of the black-white differential in premarital child-bearing. At the same time, however, when net worth is taken into consideration, we find that the risk of being on welfare is the same for blacks and whites.

All of this is not to suggest that culture does not matter. Rather, these findings suggest that the culture (the attitudes, values, and practices of daily life) that leads to welfare dependency, for example, or the culture that begets wealth accumulation or educational success is not something based predominantly in either our racial identity or our genes. Rather, such cultural practices constitute the manifestation of and reaction to the economic class conditions in which blacks and whites tend to find themselves. What this study tells us, in other words, is that, on average, whites and blacks without homes or savings act the same, just as those with many assets, a great deal of education, and so on tend to behave in a similar manner (which does not deny that there remain important—yet socioeconomically benign—differences between blacks and whites, just as there are between any pair of ethnic, national, or religious groups). Many of the behaviors and circumstances that we have come to so closely associate with blackness or whiteness are really more attributable to the class structure of American society. It just happens that this class structure overlays very well onto skin color, which is a lot more visible than someone's investment portfolio. By saying that class "just happens" to map onto skin color, I do not mean to imply that this fact is the result of random chance. The consolidation of race and class is the fundamental problem to which this work and thousands that have preceded it point.

Taken as a whole, these findings should have a significant impact on the conception of racial inequality, the affirmative action debate, and social policy more generally. For example, we may be applying affirmative action policies to certain areas (such as education and occupation) in which African Americans do not truly suffer from a "racial" disadvantage while we neglect the realm in which the real seed of racial inequity lies: class/wealth inequality. To address the race question in the United States today, the question itself must be rephrased—casting it in terms of stocks, bonds, business proprietorship, and real estate ownership rather than in terms of education and earnings. We may find that our public policy discussions on the linkages between race, unemployment, and welfare dependency are misplaced because they lack a key element: the consideration of assets and social class. Throughout the book, I hope to inform this debate over race and class with empirical analysis. Chapter Six concludes by offering a theoretical unification of the evidence that has been marshaled in the previous chapters and speculates on possible implications for issues ranging from the causes of urban riots to affirmative action policy, from welfare policy to the potential privatization of Social Security.

CHAPTER TWO

Forty Acres and a Mule

*Historical and Contemporary Obstacles
to Black Property Accumulation*

The loss of wealth is the loss of dirt.
    John Heywood, circa 1564

In 1865, at the time of the Emancipation Proclamation, African Americans owned 0.5 percent of the total worth of the United States. This statistic is not surprising; most black Americans had been slaves up to that point. However, by 1990, a full 135 years after the abolition of slavery, black Americans owned only a meager 1 percent of total wealth.[1] In other words, almost no progress had been made in terms of property ownership. African Americans may have won "title" to their own bodies and to their labor, but they have gained ownership over little else.

During the nineteenth century and at the start of the twentieth, this lack of assets was nothing remarkable, for the vast majority of Americans of all races owned little if any property. But over the course of the twentieth century, there has been a dispersal of wealth[2]—limited as it may have been—with the result that the typical white American family in 1994 had a nest egg of assets totaling a median of $72,000. With a median net worth of approximately $9,800 in that year, the typical black family had no significant nest egg to speak of.[3] Unlike income or education levels, wealth has the particular attribute of tending to reproduce itself in a multiplicative fashion from generation to generation. More colloquially, "it takes money to make money." As a result, the black-white gap in assets has continued to grow since the 1960s, when civil rights victories were won.[4]

Black people seem to have gained little that would encourage them to maintain a realistic belief in the "American dream." In fact, this growing wealth gap may help to explain a paradox that exists with respect to race and the American dream. As a group, poor African Americans—increasingly concentrated in inner cities and relatively worse off—maintain the same level of credence in the American dream as they did in the 1960s. By contrast, the black middle class, which has achieved more in terms of income, occupation, and education since the 1960s, has grown increasingly bitter and disillusioned with the idea of the American dream. "In combination," writes Jennifer Hochschild, "these paradoxes produce the surprising result that poor blacks now believe more in the American dream than rich blacks do, which is a reversal from the 1960s."[5] For middle-class blacks, perhaps the promise of their higher education, more prestigious occupations, and even greater incomes falls flat since they still face difficulty in achieving parity with their white counterparts in the most tangible manifestation of class identity: asset accumulation (the house, the car, the business, and so on).

WEALTH BY INCOME BRACKET

Differences in wealth between blacks and whites are not a result of lower earnings among the black population. As Figure 2.1 shows, the story does not get much better when the lower incomes of African Americans are taken into consideration. Even with data broken down by yearly income bracket, the median and mean net worths of blacks are dramatically lower than those of whites. In fact, Francine Blau and John Graham conclude that even after taking into account the lower average incomes of African American families, as much as three-quarters of the wealth gap persists.[6]

When we look at the PSID wealth distribution by race and income in Figure 2.1 (also see Table A2.1, in the Appendix), we find that, at every income level, blacks have substantially fewer assets than whites. Among the poorest group (annual income of $15,000 or less in 1992), whites have at least some wealth, with a median net worth of $10,000 (the mean figure is $47,214), whereas the typical black family has virtually no wealth (the median is zero, and the mean is $15,959). A full half of all poor African American families have zero (or less than zero) assets, while slightly less than 23 percent of poor whites find themselves

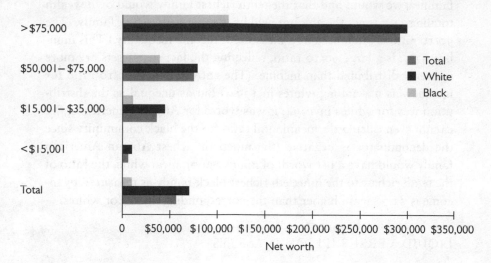

FIGURE 2.1. Median net worth in 1994, by race and annual income. At all
levels of annual income, African Americans have a lower median net worth
than whites. (See Table A2.1.)

in this situation. In the middle of the income distribution—the $35,001
to $50,000 range—whites have a median figure that is slightly more
than double that of blacks ($81,000 and $40,000, respectively; the
mean figures are $166,185 and $74,834). At the upper end of the income ladder, whites have on average almost three times the wealth of
blacks.

Examining the data graphically helps us understand the distribution
by race. When viewed in this format, it becomes clear that the rate of
increase of wealth as we move up the income ladder follows a curve for
both blacks and whites. At the lowest level, the percentage difference is
the greatest, but the absolute difference is the lowest, given the lower
amounts for both groups. The gap becomes smallest in percentage
terms among the middle-income group and then widens again among
the next two higher categories.

Because lower-income black families essentially have no assets, it becomes evident not only that African Americans suffer from lower asset
levels as a group but also that the distribution of wealth *within* the community is far more uneven.[7] For example, if we were to scale down the
entire white population of the United States to a total of one hundred

families, we would find that the tenth richest family would own wealth totaling 41.5 times the amount held by the ninetieth richest family. (The 90/10 ratio is often used as a measure of income inequality.) This number, 41.5, is a large 90/10 ratio, reflecting the fact that assets are more unevenly distributed than income. (The corresponding 90/10 ratio for income was 9.4 among whites in 1992.) But as unequal as the distribution was for whites in 1994, it was worse for African Americans. We cannot even calculate a meaningful ratio for the black community since the denominator is negative (the ninetieth richest African American family would have a net worth of minus $200); meanwhile, the ratio of the tenth richest to the ninetieth richest black family as measured by income is 12.7, again higher than the corresponding figure for whites.

LIQUID VERSUS ILLIQUID ASSETS

Although there is no absolutely clear line between liquid and illiquid wealth, many scholars do distinguish the two types of assets. As a general rule, liquid assets can be cashed in relatively quickly, as compared to illiquid assets. Liquid assets include stocks, bonds, and cash accounts; illiquid assets range from vehicles to real estate to business ownership. Liquid assets may prove more critical during times of crisis such as spells of unemployment, whereas illiquid assets such as a home, car, and vacation property may have more of an immediate psychological effect since they are consumptive as well as being investment instruments. A car, for example, might be necessary to commute to work, but it can also serve as a status symbol. Owning a valuable home may place a family in a better school district and a safer neighborhood while showing off economic power as well.

In a variation of the liquid-illiquid dichotomy, Melvin Oliver and Thomas Shapiro employ a similar distinction between net worth (NW) and net financial assets (NFA). They define net worth as total wealth minus liabilities; net financial assets are defined as net worth minus housing and vehicle equity. Employing this methodology, they demonstrate that in 1984 the black-white gap was greater for net financial assets.[8] When we jump ahead a decade and use a similar dichotomy with the PSID data, we find that, overall, median assets for blacks, excluding home equity, total $2,000; the corresponding figure for whites is $28,816 (see Table A2.2). The sum of $28,000 could provide substantial leeway in times of unemployment, medical crises, or other unex-

pected expenses. In comparison, $2,000 would not cover many mort-
gage payments or months of rent. The average (mean) white family,
with over $30,000 of fungible assets, could probably sustain itself for
quite a while through an income shock or other financial crisis.

SPENDING, SAVING, AND INVESTING: EXPLODING RACIAL STEREOTYPES

If African Americans saved less of their earnings than whites, this
would provide a relatively simple explanation for the wealth difference
by race. Certainly the popular stereotype is that African Americans are
more likely to display rampant consumerism. Popular culture is flooded
with images of the profligate urban black; films often depict an extreme
fashion consciousness among young African Americans. Since respect
and a sense of identity can be hard to come by through work in the
ghetto (and since jobs themselves are hard to come by), perhaps African
Americans resort to consumer spending more often than whites in
order to construct an identity in today's socioeconomic landscape.
Maybe African Americans react to feelings of oppression by indulging
in more escapist activities and thus spend a higher proportion of their
incomes. A heavier reliance on spending for consumer goods and en-
tertainment necessarily implies a lower savings rate and thus would explain racial differences in total wealth accumulation.

However enticing this explanation may be, a look at data over a five-
year period (1984–89) does not indicate that blacks save a lower percentage of income than their white counterparts. In the PSID data, we
find that African Americans saved an average of 11 percent of their annual income over this period, and whites saved 10 percent (not a statistically significant difference). This finding is consistent with other research that has examined black-white savings differentials (although
savings can be measured many different ways).[9] For example, economist Warren Hrung reports that when permanent income is taken into
consideration, there is no difference in the savings rates of blacks and
whites.[10] Others have found no significant "cultural" effects (such as
race might be) on savings at the individual level.[11]

Many other demographic factors, such as family size and structure,
education, age, and homeownership, affect savings levels. For instance,
female-headed households tend to save less than two-parent or male-
headed households. Families whose members have higher education

levels tend to save more. The relationship between savings and age is curvilinear: people tend to save more as they get older, until they hit a certain point—most likely, retirement age—when their savings decline and they may even move to dissaving (that is, spending down the capital).[12] Race, however, is not among the demographic factors that determine savings rates. Thus, we may conclude that the highly visible black consumerism witnessed through the lens of media stereotypes may be just that—a stereotype.

Alternatively, although it may be the case that African American adolescents disproportionately spend on particular consumer goods such as sneakers and movies, it may also be the case that these spending patterns are concentrated on very visible, recognizable consumer items that do not add up to much in figuring total expenditures and savings among the population as a whole. In other words, stereotypical "white" expenses might be less publicized but dearer in the final count.

Another stereotype is that African Americans have a lower propensity for entrepreneurship in the mainstream economy—that is, they are less likely to take on the risk of owning their own business or becoming self-employed. At the same time, blacks are more often depicted as "street hustlers," black-market or illicit entrepreneurs such as drug dealers, pimps, numbers runners, and so on. There is an obvious contradiction in portraying African Americans as averse to risk in the mainstream economy but willing to seek out even more dangerous gambles for profit in the underground economy. It is possible, however, that informal economic activities come to replace formal means of business development when attempts at legal business formation are repeatedly frustrated or when informal activities yield higher net profits.

It is beyond the scope of the data available in this study to analyze all the opportunities and activities available to African Americans and whites in the formal and informal economies (as well as the barriers). But it is possible to examine the data for an answer to the following question: are African Americans less likely than whites to be self-employed entrepreneurs in the mainstream economy? In the PSID data, the answer to this question is no. There is no significant racial difference in rates of self-employment. In fact, overall, African Americans have a slightly higher rate than whites (see Table A2.3).

This finding tends to obscure a more complex picture of a race-class interaction, however. When we examine the data more closely, we see that it is among the middle-income brackets that blacks are more likely to be entrepreneurs. At the highest income bracket, 10.6 percent of whites were self-employed, compared to only 2.6 percent of African Americans, a differential factor of 4. To a great extent, this group probably represents professionals such as doctors and lawyers—occupations to which blacks have only recently gained equal access. We should also keep in mind that self-employment can be defined in many ways, ranging from artisan work to business ownership to contract/temporary employee status. This variation may also explain the higher propensity of middle-income blacks to be self-employed, since those in this group may well be contract employees.

COMPETING EXPLANATIONS FOR BLACK-WHITE WEALTH INEQUALITY

If neither income differences, differential savings rates, nor propensity for entrepreneurship lead to racial inequalities in wealth accumulation, what is the source of the disparity? The reasons for the disparity may rest in the historical nature of race relations in the United States, in contemporary dynamics, or in both. Historically, low wages have meant a low savings rate in both absolute and percentage terms, while discrimination in the credit market has precluded African Americans from becoming business owners: "To a considerable extent [lack of wealth] can be traced to a long history of deprivation in this country," argues economist Andrew Brimmer. "This means that blacks have had much less opportunity than whites to earn, save or to inherit wealth. Because of this historical legacy, black families have had few opportunities to accumulate wealth and to pass it on to their descendants."[13] Whereas Brimmer attributes racial differences in wealth holdings primarily to the head start that whites have enjoyed, others claim that African Americans continue to face institutional barriers to converting their income to equity. Specifically, in their book *American Apartheid*, sociologists Douglas Massey and Nancy Denton document how black people continue to face discrimination in both housing and credit markets.[14]

The results of both these sets of forces are documented by sociologist John Henretta, who shows that during the 1970s blacks were much less likely than whites of similar incomes and ages to own their homes. Further, he demonstrates that even after accounting for a range of socioeconomic and demographic factors, the net worths of blacks were substantially lower than those of whites.[15] Additionally, Toby Parcel documents that, even among homeowners, African Americans face difficulty in converting their income to housing equity—that is, to net worth.[16] These data are quite dated by now, having been collected only half a generation after the passage of landmark civil rights legislation during the 1960s. Nonetheless, using simulation techniques, Oliver and Shapiro more recently estimate that "institutional biases in the residential arena have cost the current generation of blacks about $82 billion."[17] In *Assets and the Poor*, Michael Sherraden sums up the two forces leading to the black-white wealth difference:

> The most obvious answer is that blacks have always earned less than whites, and, over the years, these earnings shortfalls have resulted in less savings, less investment, and less transfers to the succeeding generations. Over time, less income can result in vast differences in asset accumulation. In addition, however, there is another dimension to the explanation: social and economic institutions have systematically restricted asset accumulation among blacks.[18]

Most scholars would agree with Sherraden that both current and past circumstances lead to racial differences in net worth. But the question remains: how much of the wealth discrepancy is linked to wealth inheritance and how much to contemporary conditions? The answer has important theoretical and policy implications. If it is the socioeconomic disadvantage of the parents of the current African American generation that matters, then the answer may lie in inheritance and property tax policy. But if the lion's share of the black-white wealth gap remains after parental socioeconomic status (including net worth) is taken into consideration, then an aggressive race-based policy in the housing and credit markets may be in order. Before we directly address this issue empirically, it will be helpful to review some of the historical and contemporary issues that may be at play.

THE HISTORICAL LEGACY OF DEPRIVATION

There is ample evidence to suspect that historical forces and their legacy of asset bequeathment play a role in explaining the current black-white wealth gap. While there has been a paucity of data on individual African American wealth holdings until very recently, we have ample evidence that, as a group, black people have endured a long history of asset deprivation, from the first days when Africans were wrested from their families, homes, and possessions in West Africa and brought to these shores in bondage, not "owning" even their bodies or their labor, let alone any tangible wealth. In fact, for the most part, slaves were legally prohibited from ownership of any form of wealth.[19]

Some theorists have argued that the social-psychological legacy of slavery prevented habits of savings and asset accrual among African Americans. "Using a cultural argument," write Oliver and Shapiro, "[conservative scholars] assert that slaves developed a habit of excessive consumerism and not one of savings and thrift."[20] Although there may be truth to the argument that individuals who lack an opportunity to accumulate savings would develop a more consumerist outlook, it is unlikely that such a legacy would persist a century later if blacks had not been continually prevented from accumulating assets in the postslavery era. It may even be the case that *especially* during the rough conditions of slavery, blacks had to be thrifty and resourceful in order to survive. Further, Oliver and Shapiro claim, "while slaves were not legally able to amass wealth, they did, in large numbers, acquire assets through thrift, intelligence, industry and their owners' liberal paternalism."[21]

During the antebellum period, some free black people did own property that totaled an estimated $50 million in 1860.[22] Historian Peter Kolchin has documented that even as early as the period between 1664 and 1677 (before the peak of slavery), in Northhampton County, Virginia, "at least 13 (out of 101) blacks became free landowners, most through self-purchase."[23] After the Emancipation Proclamation, rhetoric floated around regarding a potential and massive land redistribution. The Freedmen's Bureau, set up by President Andrew Johnson and administered by "good Christian" General Oliver Otis Howard, had the mission of promoting economic self-sufficiency among the former slaves. The agency, however, never delivered on its promise of dividing up plantations and giving each freed slave "forty acres and a mule" as reparation for slavery.[24]

The importance of the lack of land redistribution cannot be overstated. Historian Paul Cimbala writes, "Once established on property of their own, [the former slaves] believed, they would be truly free to pursue additional goals [such as wealth accumulation and political participation] without constantly worrying about offending those who otherwise would have been paying them wages."[25] W. E. B. Du Bois argued that if white America had made good on its promise of land repatriation to blacks, it "would have made a basis of real democracy in the United States."[26]

In many southern states where land redistribution did occur, it turned out to be only a temporary phenomenon. In Georgia, for example, Cimbala describes how land given to freed slaves by General Sherman "was restored [by General Howard] to its white claimants before the ex-slaves had even one full season to test their new status."[27] While Commissioner Howard "believed that the freedmen should have land and that the South could become reconstructed only if it became a land of small farms," according to Claude Oubre, Howard also clung to the notion that "freedmen should earn land and not receive it as a gift. He therefore encouraged freedmen to work and save money in order to pur-chase land." Never mind the argument that the slaves—through their servitude—had already earned the land. In the face of white southerners who refused to sell farms to blacks even if the whites could not afford to plant crops themselves, Howard "recommended that northerners, in-cluding bureau agents, purchase or lease farms to provide work for the freedmen."[28] In fact, P.S. Peirce writes that of the confiscated planta-tions, "the greater number went to northerners, who hired Negroes to cultivate them."[29] In this manner, the Freedmen's Bureau may have un-wittingly become a catalyst more for the enrichment of northern "car-petbaggers" than for the promotion of southern black entrepreneurship.

It was this hesitancy to "give" land to freed black slaves, combined with the wage labor/land-lease policy, that helped to foster the system of farm tenancy that dominated the South after the Civil War. Sharecropping (tenant farming) was an arrangement in which poor black farmers were provided with housing, seed, acreage, and provi-sions in return for cultivating the crop.[30] The black farmers did not own any of the capital (that is, the acreage or supplies) and thus were dependent on their white landlords, who kept them on the land at sub-sistence levels. While farm tenancy was politically different from slav-ery, in economic terms the end result was not much different. The rec-ollections of Moses Burge, the daughter of black sharecroppers in Georgia, attest to this fact: "We went barefooted. My feet been frost-bitten lots of times. My dad couldn't afford to buy no shoes. He'd get in debt and he'd figure every year he going to get out. . . ." But, she added, "[then] they'd tell you, 'You bought so and so.' They get through figuring it up you lacking $100 of coming clear. What the hell could you do? You living on his place, you couldn't walk off."[31]

While many southern blacks were trapped in a cycle of debt and no assets—denied the right to make deposits and get loans by banks across the region—whites were given low-interest loans to set up farms in the middle and far western United States. Those few black individuals who managed to escape sharecropping and join the westward migration with the promise of land grants found that their ownership status was "not legally enforceable" in, for example, the state of California.[32] A white person could come and lay legal claim to the land that a black individual had already settled, and the white person's title would be honored over that of the African American. "Thus," according to Oliver and Shapiro, "African Americans were largely barred from taking advantage of the nineteenth-century Federal land-grant program that helped result in an astounding three quarters of families owning their farms."[33]

In fact, the only major nineteenth-century institution that was somewhat successful in fostering wealth accumulation among African Americans was the Freedmen's Bank, part of the Freedmen's Bureau. This bank failed in 1874, however (after the Panic of 1873), largely as a result of "highly questionable no-interest loans from the bank to white companies" doled out by the white-controlled board of directors, according to Sherraden.[34] Despite its problems, the Freedmen's Bank did help some blacks acquire land and businesses. After its collapse, the rate of land ownership among black people did not rise as rapidly, and, furthermore, many blacks no longer trusted banks because many African American small investors lost all their savings when the institution failed.

Constraints on capital were not the only nineteenth-century barrier to asset accumulation for African Americans. Many southern states passed "Black Codes," laws that required blacks to have an employer or face arrest as a "vagrant." Manning Marable describes the result:

> Working independently for themselves, some Black artisans were fined, jailed and even sentenced to work as convict laborers. South Carolina's legislature declared in December 1865, that 'no person of color shall pursue or practice the art, trade, or business of an artisan, mechanic, or shopkeeper, or another trade employment or business . . . on his own account and for his own benefit until he shall have obtained a license which shall be good for one year only.' Black peddlers and merchants had to produce $100 annually to pay for the license, while whites paid nothing.[35]

Aside from such institutional and legal barriers, there always existed the not-so-subtle threat of lynching or other physical violence if an African American tried to open a business—particularly if the business might compete with white-owned franchises.[36]

Black ownership of wealth grew slowly during the latter half of the nineteenth century, and it continued to face obstacles in the twentieth century. The land holdings belonging to the majority of black title holders at the turn of the century were small, family-run farms; the advent of large-scale farming in the twentieth century hurt blacks disproportionately. The peak of farm ownership among African Americans was reached in 1910 at 218,000 units; this figure held steady until 1920. By 1930, it had dropped to 182,000, and to 173,00 by 1940. During this period of decline, which includes the Great Depression, many farmers, both black and white, were losing their land, but there appears to have been a net transfer of land from blacks to whites. August Meier and Elliot Rudwick estimate that the rate of land loss for blacks averaged 350,000 acres per year.[37] As the number of black-owned farms dropped over the course of the first half of the century, the numbers of African Americans who migrated to the northern industrial centers grew: between 1910 and 1970, 6.5 million black Americans moved from the South to the North; 5 million of this group made the transition after 1940.[38]

Meanwhile, Old Age Insurance (Social Security), established in 1935, "virtually excluded African Americans and Latinos, for it exempted agricultural and domestic workers from coverage and marginalized low-wage workers. . . . In 1935, for example, 42 percent of black workers in occupations covered by social insurance did not earn enough to qualify for benefits compared to 22 percent for whites."[39] Not receiving Social Security benefits meant that any savings that had been accumulated by retired or disabled black Americans most likely had to be spent during old age rather than being handed down to the next generation. Further, the lack of social insurance meant that many households had to care for and support indigent, elderly family members, directly diverting the next generation's resources away from savings and capital accumulation.

Perhaps the most dramatic barrier to black-white wealth equity in the twentieth century, however, has involved residential issues and institutions. For example, the Home Owners' Loan Corporation (HOLC), founded in 1933, helped many homeowners avoid default during the Great Depression. But it was the HOLC that institutionalized the redlining technique of associating estimated risks of loan default with neighborhoods. The HOLC invariably assigned black neighborhoods the lowest rating, ensuring that no HOLC-sponsored loans

went to black residents. Thus, African Americans could not as readily
refinance their mortgages during the Depression, and a greater proportion of black owners lost their homes when contrasted to their white
counterparts.

The story did not change after the Great Depression. The Federal
Housing Authority (FHA), established in 1937, in combination with
the Veterans Administration (VA) home-lending program that was part
of the Servicemen's Readjustment Act of 1944, made homeownership
possible for millions of Americans after World War II by guaranteeing
low-interest, long-term loans for first-home buyers. But African
Americans were systematically shut out of participation in these programs because loans were channeled to suburbs and away from the central cities where blacks predominantly resided. In fact, according to
Massey and Denton, with FHA financing, it became "cheaper to buy
new suburban homes than to rent comparable older dwellings in the
central city."[40]

"In the suburb-shaping years between 1930 and 1960," write David
Kirp, John Dwyer, and Larry Rosenthal, "fewer than one percent of all
mortgages in the nation were issued to African Americans."[41] The FHA
helped to facilitate this disparity. The *Underwriting Manual* distributed
to lenders by the FHA specifically prohibited lending in neighborhoods
that were changing in racial or social composition.[42] For example, "in
a 1941 memorandum concerning St. Louis, the FHA proclaimed that
'the rapidly rising Negro population has produced a problem in the
maintenance of real estate values.'"[43] In this manner, not only did FHA
policy prevent the emergence of a new, larger class of suburban black
homeowners, but the lack of loans to potential purchasers in the central city caused an accelerated decline in existing property values
among African Americans, since willing sellers could not find buyers.
All these institutionalized practices set the stage for the conditions of
racial segregation that are observable today and that may contribute, in
large part, to the black-white wealth disparity.

CONTEMPORARY BLACK-WHITE SEGREGATION

Over and above the historical forces that may be at work to depress the
wealth levels of African Americans relative to those of whites, there is
also evidence that race-based dynamics in the contemporary United
States play a major role in perpetuating this type of inequality. Owning

one's home is the prime method of equity accumulation for most families in the United States.[44] In 1997, the overall rate of homeownership was 65.7 percent, a record high (although, according to data from the Luxembourg Income Study, this rate still falls in the middle range among Western countries; the country with the highest percentage of homeowning households is Australia).[45] But the overall U.S. figure obscures differences by race and place.

Patterns of residential segregation that lead to a disproportionate concentration of minority households in central cities mean that African Americans are less likely than whites to own the homes in which they reside. In 1997, 28 percent of whites lived in central cities, compared to 55 percent who lived in suburbs. During that same year, the corresponding figures for blacks were almost a mirror image: 64 percent for urban residence and 31 percent for suburban residence. (These figures do not add up to 100 percent by race because they exclude rural residents.)[46] This spatial distribution is important because 72 percent of suburban residents owned their homes in 1997, compared to only 49 percent of their urban counterparts. The result of this combination is that in 1997 only 44 percent of blacks owned their homes, in contrast to 71 percent of whites, according to the Harvard Joint Center for Housing Studies.[47]

The issue of segregation is not economically benign. Housing in black neighborhoods has a lower rate of value increase (and in some cases may decrease in worth) when contrasted to similar units in predominantly white neighborhoods.[48] Therefore, not only do racially segregated housing markets hinder the efforts of African Americans to become homeowners, but also those individuals who do manage to buy a house may find that it is worth less than a comparable house owned by a white person purely because it is located in a black neighborhood. In this manner, the social-psychological realm (of racist ideology) may be directly linked to the economic arena (by determining the relative value of neighborhoods). As Chapter One discussed, property has the quality of picking up the social value conferred upon an object or idea. A rare stamp or a precious metal has no inherent productive value; rather, its value is socially conferred by the market. Likewise, black housing may be worth less because the majority group (whites) controls the market, and thus segregation is in this group's interest. White housing is worth more precisely because it is not black housing.

This dynamic is best illustrated by the process of "white flight." White flight usually occurs when the percentage of black residents in a community reaches a certain level (roughly 20 percent) and white homeowners begin to fear that their property values will drop. Why might they drop? Values fall because white flight creates a vacuum in the market—in other words, the anticipation of a market drop in housing prices becomes a self-fulfilling prophecy. This pernicious circle sustains racist residential ideology and directly links it to economics in the housing market. The property value/racial segregation dynamic affects the life chances of black Americans in many realms since, as a result of residential segregation patterns, poor minorities are more likely to find themselves living among other poor families (that is, concentrated) than impoverished whites are.[49] Minority families are also more likely to live in areas with abandoned buildings or in units that have multiple inadequacies.[50] In addition, because school budgets are financed through local property taxes, the issue of school quality is tied to the value of property.

The existence of such a dual housing market—a market segregated by race, where African Americans suffer limited housing selections as a result of institutional and overt discrimination—is well documented.[51] Furthermore, some researchers have used U.S. census data to demonstrate that levels of residential segregation have increased in the period since the 1960s,[52] although at least one study claims that residential segregation seems to have peaked in the 1970s and declined slightly since then—with the largest percentage decreases of segregation indices in newer southern and western cities.[53]

While there is a sizable literature tracking and documenting the importance of continued residential segregation, few researchers have addressed the issue of racial differences in rates of homeownership directly, in order to determine whether they result from class differentials or from racial dynamics. What researchers have shown is that racial segregation per se and the existence of dual housing markets cannot be explained by class; as Massey and Denton state, "Whereas segregation declines steadily for most minority groups as socioeconomic status rises, levels of black-white segregation do not vary significantly by social class."[54] Research by the U.S. Department of Housing and Urban Development (HUD) has shown that the dual housing market is maintained by a variety of practices such as overt discrimination on the part of real estate agents and institutional discrimination on the part of lending institutions.[55] A local study conducted in St. Louis by HUD found that African Americans paid 15 to 25 percent more than whites for similar housing.[56] Since housing quality was controlled in this study, any differences in price would be a result of race, not class. If this pattern were to hold across the entire country, we should expect a contemporary effect of race on wealth levels net of parental assets and other socioeconomic measures.

Most research documenting the effects of a dual market has focused on community-level issues such as neighborhood quality, spatial assimilation, or suburbanization.[57] Spatial assimilation is the process by which minority groups seek to convert income gains to social status through improved residential conditions, typically moving out from an urban ethnic enclave into a predominantly white suburb. African Americans have faced obstacles in making this transition, however. For instance, one study reports that blacks are less likely than Hispanics and Asian Americans to reside in the suburbs, even after accounting for differences in socioeconomic status.[58] When African Americans do manage to attain suburban residence, sociologist Emily Rosenbaum notes, the communities into which they "move tend to have lower income levels, higher unemployment, lower tax bases and more of the problems common to inner-city neighborhoods."[59]

This community-level focus of the literature is a result of the impetus for housing research. Stimulated by the urban riots of the 1960s, the Kerner Commission, appointed by the president, concluded that America was "moving towards two societies, one black, one white— separate and unequal."[60] Subsequent analysis was concerned with the nature of minority confinement to urban ghettos, the concentration of poverty, neighborhood-level effects, and the making of the underclass.[61] Massey and Denton write:

> Residential segregation is not a neutral fact; it systematically undermines the social and economic well-being of blacks in the United States. Because of racial segregation, a significant share of black America is condemned to experience a social environment where poverty and joblessness are the norm, where a majority of children are born out of wedlock, where most families are on welfare, where educational failure prevails, and where social and physical deterioration abound. Through prolonged exposure to such an environment, black chances for social and economic success are drastically reduced. . . . *The effect of segregation on black well-being is structural, not individual.*[62]

This focus on the macro-structural conditions that segregation creates
has neglected the mechanisms by which housing conditions affect the individual (and in turn contribute to the maintenance and continuation of
the structural conditions). One important way that housing segregation
may directly affect the individual family is through its impact on individual and family wealth accumulation. Little research has addressed the
role of segregation as it affects the economic well-being of individual
black family units.

Instead, individual-level research on race and housing usually takes
residential segregation as a given and looks at how black and white
families attain housing equity. For example, Rosenbaum reports that,
net of other socioeconomic and demographic characteristics, blacks in
the greater New York metropolitan area are less likely to own their
homes than whites (presumably as a result of spatial assimilation patterns).[63] Oliver and Shapiro analyze housing appreciation and find
that—net of inflation, year of purchase, mortgage rate, and an indicator of hypersegregation[64]—housing owned by blacks appreciates at a
significantly lower rate than housing owned by whites. These authors
also address credit issues, developing a statistical model that holds constant a number of factors (including household income and whether the
loan was financed through the FHA or the VA), and demonstrate that
blacks pay significantly higher mortgage interest rates than whites.[65]

In the PSID data, I find racial differences that point to the saliency of
current conditions in the housing and credit markets in determining
black-white wealth inequity. For example, African Americans who do
own homes and attempt to get financing against their equity (a second
mortgage) are much more likely to be turned down, with a 4.4 percent
rejection rate in contrast to a 1.1 percent rejection rate for whites (as
shown in Table A2.4). This may be related to the finding that 11.8 percent of white applicants have had previous business with the bank to
which they applied, in contrast to only 2.4 percent of their African
American counterparts. As a result, black homeowners are less likely to
have refinanced their mortgage (which often allows a homeowner to save
money by taking advantage of a drop in interest rates). On the other
hand, contemporary black homeowners are actually more likely (46.9
percent) than whites (21.7 percent) to have a government-sponsored
loan. Possibly as a result of this higher rate of government backing,
African Americans are less likely to have mortgage insurance (when an
institution other than the lender underwrites the loan, often because of a

small down payment). Some other aspects of credit financing, such as the propensity to have a fixed-interest mortgage and the likelihood of a mortgage tax, do not show sizable racial differences in the PSID data.

While these measures of credit access center around housing, they may imply that African Americans suffer from similar disadvantages when applying for business loans (for example, not having had previous business with the bank). Also important is that homeownership not only affects the quality of one's abode and neighborhood but also directly affects the amount of money left for other investing or spending.

Put simply, owning is cheaper than renting. The PSID data show that in 1996 the median rent for tenants was $400, while the median monthly mortgage payment for homeowners was only $279. Although other costs such as property taxes, insurance, and repair expenses are associated with owning, these costs are generally not enough to raise the typical owner's monthly cost over that of the median renter. The Harvard Joint Center for Housing Studies demonstrated that between 1982 and 1993, the proportion of income that went to mortgage payments in the average household declined from 34 percent to 20.2 percent, before rising modestly to 22 percent in 1996.[66] This increasing affordability of homeownership stands in contrast to rents, which have remained consistently high over the 1980s and 1990s. Thus, owning may actually free up more money for other expenses or investments. This may be part of the reason owners accumulate net worth much faster than renters.

RESOLVING COMPETING CLAIMS OF CAUSATION

All of this said, however, the issue of how much of the housing, credit, and business differences just discussed are a result of racial dynamics in the current generation and how much are the residue of family wealth differences from the previous generation has not been examined. Few researchers have enjoyed the benefit of longitudinal data that link generations; additionally, scholars have not focused exclusively on the post-1960s generation.[67] With a snapshot approach, previous researchers have not been able to determine whether it is lower rates of savings, a lack of parental assets, smaller inheritances, or poor investment performance that has led to the black-white gap in wealth in a given year.

With data that follow families over time and link generations, we can assess whether dynamics such as these explain racial inequalities in wealth or whether there remains a significant difference between the net worths of African Americans and whites even after factoring out these explanations. It is important to model the black-white wealth discrepancy in a multigenerational framework because it is not clear, for instance, how much differing rates of homeownership result from a lack of parental aid. Even the different interest rates paid by blacks and whites may be the result of the lower parental resources of black families, since the home buyer may be able to afford only a small down payment and thus may not qualify for the best loans. (The example of the two families described in Chapter One illustrates this dynamic.)[68]

We can address this debate by linking two generations of respondents (parents and their adult children). By focusing on the transmission of wealth across generations, it can be determined how much the lack of parental assets that are available to be passed on—the "sedimentation" of past racial inequity[69]—accounts for the current gap between the net worths of blacks and whites. It is important to note that in this discussion the term "historical" is used in a very specific sense, meaning the accumulation and transmission of wealth (assets) over the course of generations. This usage does not deny or negate that the historical dimensions of the economic and political oppression of African Americans have had other effects on the wealth accumulation of the current generation indirectly, through, for example, lower levels of human capital.

In order to explore this question, I will examine asset accumulation among African Americans and whites, factoring out a number of other measures that also have an impact on wealth and savings. First, however, we should look at the various demographic and socioeconomic factors that are being held constant in order to find the residual effect of race *in the filial (children's) generation.*

Permanent income: Obviously, families with higher incomes will tend to have higher wealth levels. We have already seen that when wealth levels are tabulated by annual income in a given year, a sizable gap remains between blacks and whites. I not only include income of the prior year in my statistical models but also hold constant the average income for the previous five years. This corrects for short-term income fluctuations resulting from shocks such as unemployment or a windfall. Such a five-year measure is often used as a proxy indicator of "permanent income" by economists. Permanent income represents the total income that an individual (or family) can expect to earn in a lifetime. In theory, if there were no constraints on credit, individuals could borrow on future expected earnings or save for anticipated income declines in order to maintain a more or less steady consumption level over the life course. Asset accumulation and spending down play an important role in this maintenance of lifestyle. While permanent income is a theoretical concept that could never actually be measured (except perhaps with income data on an individual for every year from birth to death), researchers who attempt to predict socioeconomic outcomes have found that adding more years to the five-year average does little to increase explanatory power.[70] Thus, I adopt the standard five-year proxy measure, averaged after being adjusted for inflation.

Age: Researchers have shown that age has a variable effect on wealth accumulation over the life course. During the prime working years of adulthood, wealth levels steadily rise as a result of savings, inheritance, and investment performance (a first-order effect). When individuals leave the labor market at the age of retirement, they generally start to dissave—that is, to spend down their capital (a quadratic effect). Some recent research suggests that this effect reaches an equilibrium (a cubic effect), that individuals do not spend down all their savings until death as the economic life-cycle model would predict.[71] Obviously, even if they wanted to, individuals cannot readily predict their own mortality, and they may keep some funds in reserve in case they outlive their own life expectancy. In addition, of course, there is the nontrivial issue of individuals' desires to pass on financial assets to the next generation. Blacks and whites demonstrate different age distributions (African Americans have shorter life expectancies), so it is important to take this into consideration when trying to analyze wealth differences.

Occupational prestige: In addition to parental "permanent income," I also include the occupational prestige score of the most recent job held by the head of the parental household. Professions with higher prestige (such as management positions) may lend themselves to greater wealth levels even when income is held constant. For example, individuals who are employed in high-status professions often receive a number of "perks"—such as expense accounts or company cars—that allow them to avoid certain household expenses. Even more critical, jobs in high-status professions are more likely to provide profit-sharing plans, matching-contribution retirement funds, or 401k plans, which directly increase the rate of family wealth accumulation. Because even at given ages and education levels African Americans are less likely to be currently employed and less likely to hold high-status positions if they are employed, we must account for these trends in trying to ascertain the net effect of race *per se.*

Gender and family structure: In comparing the wealth levels of blacks and whites, we must also consider the gender of the household head. Scholars have shown that female-headed households have lower levels of wealth (see Chapter Five for a thorough discussion). Since this is the case, and since African American families are more likely to fall into this category, we must hold the gender of the head of the family constant. Rather than simply using a snapshot approach, I include a measure of the gender of the head of household over time in much the same way I operationalize permanent income: over the same five-year period. A female head of household also acts as a very good proxy for a single-parent family unit.

Education: Education level affects a number of indicators, such as income, occupational prestige, and even family structure, and thus indirectly affects wealth through these factors. Even when we account for these indirect effects, however, education may still have explanatory power with respect to net worth. Better-educated individuals, for instance, may tend to make wiser investment decisions. Since African Americans tend to complete fewer years of education, I also hold this factor constant in making a net comparison of wealth levels. I include this indicator for the head of the parental household as well as for the respondent.

Parental net worth: I have factored out parental net worth in order to determine whether the effect of race in the current generation can be explained by the class status of the previous generation. Much of the effect of parental wealth is expressed through a variety of indicators such as education, income, family structure, and so on, which are all predicted by parental SES and wealth to a certain extent. Nonetheless, parental wealth may have a direct impact on filial net worth through gift giving, informal loans, and so forth. This is particularly true for a young cohort such as the one under investigation. Those individuals who have a substantial net worth in their twenties or early thirties are well positioned to accumulate a sizable nest egg as they enter their prime working years. As a rule, the earlier one attains wealth in the life cycle, the more one will attain in the end, since wealth begets wealth through returns on itself. Receiving $100,000 at age twenty yields a great deal more to an individual than the same amount received at age seventy (assuming that the twenty-year-old does not squander it).

STATISTICAL APPROACH

As I examine black-white differences in net worth (and in various other outcomes in subsequent chapters), I progressively complicate the model by factoring out possible explanatory factors (such as family structure or income) and examining how the effect of race changes when the model changes form. Of particular note is the effect of race (if any) when total wealth or its constituent parts are taken into consideration. In other words, by putting parental wealth into a model as a contributing factor, we can determine a "truer" net effect of race in determining net worth or other socioeconomic outcomes.

Of course, wealth may to a certain extent reflect underlying, unmeasured family differences in attitudes and values. But even if it is not parental net worth *per se* that explains, for example, asset accumulation or educational attainment, parental wealth is still an important factor to consider. For instance, if it is not the monetary value of assets that aids children's educational, occupational, or wealth attainment but rather the social-psychological characteristics of families who tend to accumulate high levels of wealth, it would nevertheless be important to factor out the effect of this dynamic in order to develop a cogent policy discussion of black-white differences in wealth, educational attainment, occupation, or family dynamics.

I begin with a simplistic, race-only model and then progressively "subtract" factors that may explain wealth differences, constantly monitoring what happens to the racial difference. With all these potential explanations factored out, any remaining effect of race on net worth may be a result of investment performance, institutional racism in the housing and credit markets, or some other "unobserved" factor that I have not measured—as is always the case in any research. It may even be possible that the effects of income, age, education, and so on are not really "true" effects themselves but rather reflect some underlying, unmeasured difference between families who also happen to vary on these axes. Such a dynamic could be related to values, attitudes, or even genetics. Such possibilities constitute a stimulus for future research, and I would hope that future scholars will readdress the findings I present in the following sections.

PASSING IT ON: PAST OR PRESENT INEQUALITIES IN WEALTH?

Let us now turn to an analysis of the source of black-white differences in net worth, focusing on the question of whether this gap is the result of the legacy of the past or the result of contemporary dynamics. In Figure 2.2, the first bar (simply contrasting wealth levels by race, the base model shown in Table A2.5) shows a significant, sizable difference in the wealth holdings of blacks and whites who were heads of households in 1994. (Data are presented in logarithmic form.) Looking at the second bar of the figure (corresponding to model B in Table A2.5), we see that if respondent characteristics such as level of education, age, gender, and even income two years prior are all equalized, blacks still suffer from an asset deficit. In other words, comparing a young African American family or individual to a white one with the same education level, income, age, and gender of the head of household, one would still encounter—on average—a sizable advantage for whites when it came to wealth levels.

When we add class measures of a respondent's parents, however, the racial difference disappears (see the third bar in Figure 2.2, model C of Table A2.5). In fact, when parental net worth is added to the measure of class background (the fourth bar), the black-white difference flips direction, though the difference is not statistically discernible from chance.

Further, Figure 2.3 (model D of Table A2.5) demonstrates that when we fully specify parental class by including wealth, the variables of parental education, occupational prestige, and income are not the ones that really matter. Income and occupational prestige mattered before wealth was included (model C of Table A2.5), but evidently this was only because of their association with wealth levels. In the wealth-inclusive class model, illustrated in Figure 2.3, parental wealth is the strongest predictor; race and other class variables are not statistically significant.

Trying to better understand the race-class dynamic, I broke out the parental wealth endowment into four components: liquid assets (stocks, bonds, certificates of deposit, and the like), the value of the family's primary residence if they own it, business and farm wealth, and

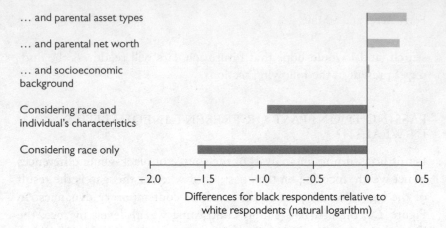

Differences for black respondents relative to
white respondents (natural logarithm)

FIGURE 2.2. The effect of being black on a respondent's net worth in 1994, by
model type. Darker bars are statistically discernible from zero; lighter bars are
statistically equivalent to zero. Young African Americans have levels of wealth
that are significantly lower than those of whites; however, this difference appears to be a result of class background, not race *per se*. (See Table A2.5.)

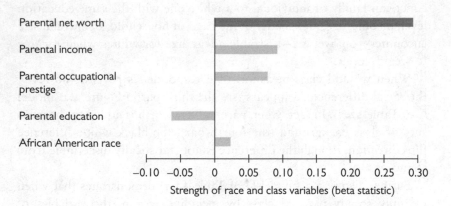

Strength of race and class variables (beta statistic)

FIGURE 2.3. The relative effects of race and class on a respondent's net worth
in 1994. Darker bars are statistically discernible from zero; lighter bars are
statistically equivalent to zero. Race is not significant in predicting the net
worth of young adults, and the only class variable that is significant is
parental net worth. (See Table A2.5.)

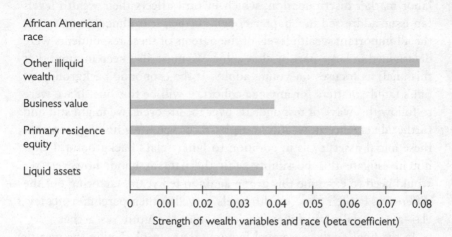

FIGURE 2.4. The effects of parental wealth on a respondent's net worth in 1994, by asset type. Lighter bars are statistically equivalent to zero. When parental wealth is broken out by asset type, all types lose significance; none are useful predictors. (See Table A2.5.)

other illiquid wealth (such as investment real estate, second homes, or vehicle equity). Each of these may demonstrate a different level of heritability. I would anticipate that liquid assets are the most important in predicting the wealth levels of young offspring since they are easily transferable; illiquid assets such as real estate and businesses may be more likely to be passed on at the time a parent dies. But, as Figure 2.4 (model E of Table A2.5) illustrates, in this instance when we break out parental wealth by asset type, we lose predictive power; none of its components are significant predictors on their own.

From the elimination of the black wealth deficit through statistical controls (and the reversal of its sign), one can deduce that the locus of black-white wealth inequality lies in the realm of class relations rather than reflecting racial differences *per se*. Race and class mirror each other with respect to the wealth distribution; however, in the end it may be the economically disadvantaged family backgrounds of young African Americans more than the color of their skin that hurts their efforts to accumulate wealth.

When I say that I find no effect of race on wealth accumulation, however, it must be kept in mind that I am speaking of a direct effect. It may be that skin color determines respondents' incomes through labor market discrimination, which in turn affects their wealth levels (an issue addressed in Chapter Four). Further, it is almost certain that the all-important wealth levels of the parents of these respondents were determined in large part by skin color. We must also keep in mind that this analysis focuses on young adults. If the economic background of one's family matters for any age cohort, it will be this one. If we were to follow this wave of respondents over the life cycle, we might still find further divergence in wealth levels by race even after holding constant these initial asset levels in addition to family class background. I cannot investigate this possibility with the data at hand, however; we would need to examine this group again in ten years, factoring out the differences in their 1994 wealth levels as well as their parents' 1984 levels—a potentially fruitful avenue of inquiry for future researchers.

In the final analysis, several factors matter in predicting the wealth levels of young adults, but race is not among them. Table 2.1 lists these factors in descending order of predictive strength.[72] The single most important factor for this age group is parental net worth. Among such a young group, parental net worth can have a very strong impact that dwarfs the individual's own labor market success as well as his or her own savings and investment behavior. Most likely, this effect represents the impact of parental gift giving in the form of trusts, down payments for first homes, and the like.

Alternatively, it could be the case that this variable is merely picking up shared attitudes and values between the two generations—that is, parents who tend to save and invest (and thereby attain higher net worths) may inculcate these values in their offspring, who also attain greater than average wealth without any direct financial help from their parents. Although this value-transmission dynamic is possible, it probably does not account for the lion's share of this effect, given how strong the effect is, net of many other factors that should have also absorbed the causal impact of such pro-wealth attitudes. In other words, the education and income of the respondent, for example, should also reflect the same learned values, leaving the parental net worth indicator to reflect more purely intergenerational financial transmission.

The second strongest effect is that higher income earned by the respondents themselves results in an increased net worth two years later. Obviously, the more income one has, the more one can save. But this effect may also be reflecting some reverse causality.[73] Since many investments produce income, net worth predicts current income to a cer-

TABLE 2.1

VARIABLES PREDICTING NET WORTH BY
DESCENDING ORDER OF PREDICTIVE
IMPORTANCE

1. *Parents' net worth[a]*
2. *Respondent's income*
3. Parents' permanent income
4. Parent's occupational prestige (head of household)
5. Parent's age (head of household)
6. *Female respondent*
7. Female-headed parental household (1980–84)
8. Parent's education (head of household)
9. Respondent's age
10. Respondent graduated from college
11. Respondent graduated from high school
12. African American race
13. Number of siblings
14. Parents received welfare in 1984

NOTE: Italic type indicates statistical significance at the $p < .10$ level; since the main argument of this book relies on the declining significance of the race variable, I chose to use this higher alpha instead of the more common .05 level. Appendix tables show four levels of significance along with standard errors. See Table A2.5. In similar tables throughout the text, I have in some cases presented the variables from the net worth model (as here, when the asset types do not add worthwhile information); in other cases, I have presented the asset type model. Readers should also note that the significance level depends on the standard error of the estimate and, thus, a variable with a weaker predictive value can be significant and another variable with a higher beta statistic (absolute value) can be "less" significant. Such is the case with the Female respondent variable in this instance.

[a]In the case of this model and all others where a continuous form of net worth (or its components) appears, I also included a dummy variable indicating whether the respondent had any wealth at all. In most cases, this indicator was either insignificant or worked in the opposite direction of the main wealth variable. It is included in order to account for the spike at zero net worth in the data. When it is significant in the opposite direction, it merely implies a nonlinearity in the effect of wealth rather than an actual negative effect of having wealth. When I run the data with only the dummy variable (i.e., without the continuous functional form as well), the negative effect goes away and in some cases becomes positive—that is, in the same direction as the main, continuous term.

tain extent just as income predicts net worth. Because one's income two years prior is strongly associated with one's income today, there may be a tinge of reverse causation picked up in this finding.

The only other factor that mattered significantly in predicting net worth among this young cohort was gender. Females who headed their own households tended to have lower net worths even after accounting for their lower incomes. This finding is consistent with past research and is examined more thoroughly in Chapter Five.

Several factors that did not matter are worth noting. Neither the level of education attained by the head of the parental household nor the level attained by the respondent had any effect—net of the respondent's income. The number of siblings had no effect (nor did an interaction term between the number of siblings and parental net worth), which is surprising. We might expect that with a given amount of wealth to aid one's children, the more children there are, the smaller each child's slice of the pie becomes. A number of other parental factors such as age, occupation, and welfare receipt had no significant effect. Finally, and most important, being black had no influence on the asset levels of this young group net of parental wealth and the respondent's own income.

This analysis demonstrates that several simple explanations of the racial gap in wealth—among them, differential savings rates and discrimination based on skin color—do not appear to account for the black-white wealth gap among the post-1960s generation of individuals. Rather, accounting for the historical legacy of asset accumulation (or the lack of it)—that is, the wealth of parents—appears to explain the gap in net worth between this cohort of blacks and whites. Other factors may of course be at work later in the life cycle, among them direct or institutional racism. For example, the respondent's own income is the strongest predictor of net worth; the lower incomes of African Americans may be a result of racism in the labor market that has a cumulative effect, resulting in lower levels of assets by the time this generation is ready to help out the next.

Also, initial differences in equity levels of a given generation may be exacerbated as the cohort matures through adulthood, in part by a difference in the way blacks and whites interact with their investments over the life course. As the cliché cited earlier states, "It takes money to make money." Those who begin with higher assets can take advantage of riskier investment instruments and higher rates of return. As Andrew Brimmer points out, blacks are much less likely to invest in the stock market (which can provide the greatest yields during certain periods);[74] this may be caused by a smaller parental head start or safety net. In addition, unstable income flows may lead to a "cashing in" of assets (or an accumulation of debt) over time, even if average income and savings rates are the same over the entire period. Finally, differences in the rates of homeownership and housing value accrual may lead to lower net worths in the parental generation, which in turn disadvantages the next in its efforts to secure the American dream. All these possibilities would lead to a ever-widening racial gap in wealth. When talking about wealth, it is impossible to isolate one generation from another, for initial endowments affect later returns, which determine initial endowments for the next generation.

These findings help to focus attention on the possible conditions that foster black-white differences in wealth accumulation. The historical legacy of asset poverty appears to play an important role in perpetuating this disparity. Designing policy to address the effects of the past on parental net worth in order to foster asset accumulation among the next generation of black Americans will not be easy, however. How does one redress past inequalities? Even if it is the legacy of the past that engenders racial differences in wealth today, by definition policy remedies must be directed at the newest generation. What these results indicate is that merely creating equal opportunity in the housing, securities, and credit markets will not do enough to rectify the racial imbalance because parental asset levels (which were presumably fixed in the past) engender advantages and disadvantages that are very important for the next generation.

The irony of this chapter (and to a certain extent, the book as a whole) lies in the fact that because there is no net racial effect that explains the black-white asset difference, policy must be more, not less, aggressive if it is to work toward the goal of racial equity in wealth. In other words, merely eliminating remaining discrimination—be it individual or institutional—will do little to alleviate the wealth gap, which has already been set into intergenerational motion. Only a radical, progressive, wealth-based policy will redress the issue. On the politically positive side, however, such policy need not be based on skin color. Class so mirrors race with respect to wealth levels that implementing an aggressive wealth-accrual policy for the "asset poor" would de facto help to ameliorate the racial gap, given that it is largely African Americans who constitute this group. Such policy possibilities will be addressed directly in Chapter Six.

CHAPTER THREE

From Financial to Social to Human Capital

Assets and Education

Base wealth preferring to eternal praise.
          Alexander Pope, 1688–1744

One of the most studied outcomes in sociology is educational attainment. As sociologists Peter Blau and Otis Dudley Duncan so cogently demonstrated in their classic book *The American Occupational Structure,* social stratification in the modern United States takes place largely within the educational system. This is not to suggest that the United States is a pure meritocracy. Rather, while the sorting of social positions may occur predominantly *within* the process of formal schooling, the socioeconomic endowments that each child brings to the educational system powerfully predict that individual's chances for academic success. The educational system, in the view of Blau and Duncan, serves as the link between family background and the occupational hierarchy.[1] Thus, in any examination of racial inequality, it is important to investigate the role that educational stratification plays in the reproduction of inequity across generations.

During the 1960s, researchers tried to examine the role of this system in the realm of racial inequality. In 1966, a report on education that had been commissioned by the U.S. Congress was published under the title *Equality of Educational Opportunity.* The "Coleman Report," as it later came to be known (after its principal author, James Coleman), concluded that school-based differences could not explain the differences in educational achievement between blacks and whites. Further, it asserted that, for all racial groups, family background (that is, class) mattered much more than school policies (such as curriculum, teacher-to-pupil ratios, and so on) in determining the success or failure of students. The Coleman Report has been reanalyzed by a host of scholars who—for the most part—came to the same general conclusion: in essence, the educational system did an excellent job of reproducing the same class differences that children brought to it in the first place.[2]

Given this perspective, it might make intuitive sense that the seed of racial inequality lies not in the educational system but rather in the differential endowments that blacks and whites bring to the process. Hence, we may see the educational system as a lens through which to view the reproduction of racial inequality rather than as the central agent of that inequality. This concept has important implications for the affirmative action debate, as I explain at the end of this chapter. In the meantime, we can peer through that lens at some of the educational trends among African Americans and whites.

Among the younger cohorts in American society, the levels of educational attainment for blacks and whites have steadily converged since the 1940s, through the period of school desegregation, until the middle 1980s. By 1982, the education gap between blacks and whites had declined to an almost insignificant level, particularly for women. But during the 1980s, some of the educational gains achieved by blacks eroded.[3] By 1997, 13 percent of African Americans between the ages of twenty-five and thirty-four had not completed high school, compared to 6 percent of whites.[4]

The higher up the education ladder we look, the wider the differences become. The gap between the races in college enrollment rates narrowed until the late 1970s, when it reached convergence among those aged eighteen to twenty-four, and then widened steadily during the 1980s and 1990s. By 1994, the college enrollment rate for whites in this age group was 43.6 percent, while the rate for African Americans was 35.5 percent. Data on students who moved directly from high school to college show that, in 1994, the college enrollment rate for black students who graduated from high school that year was 50.8 percent; the corresponding figure for white students was 64.5 percent, a gap that had also widened from statistical parity in 1977. Making the transition directly to college is important because the earnings possible with a high school degree are significantly lower than those possible with a college education; thus, anything that delays completion of education reduces earnings during that period. Between 1976 and 1986, black female college enrollment increased, but the percentage of college-aged black males enrolled in college declined from 35 percent to 28 percent over this ten-year period.[5]

The differences just described are certainly significant, but the real story is in racial differences in college completion data, measured in both absolute rates and time to degree. In 1997, 14 percent of African Americans between the ages of thirty-five and forty-four held a bachelor's degree. The comparable figure for whites was approximately double, at 29 percent.[6] For those African Americans who do get degrees, the time it takes to complete the degree is substantially longer than the time it takes for whites: the mean duration of time from initial enrollment until completion of the bachelor's degree is 7.19 years for blacks, compared to 6.24 years for whites, almost a full year's difference by race. This is a substantial opportunity cost for black students to bear in terms of lost postgraduate earnings.[7] This longer period of time, combined with the finding that blacks are less likely to start college right after high school, makes the mean age at college completion higher, perhaps making these graduates less attractive to potential employers. The story is even worse when we consider graduate and professional degrees: African Americans hold only 3.1 percent of doctoral degrees, about a quarter as many as one would expect, given the population percentages.[8]

As the analysis in this chapter indicates, however, educational differences are largely a result of socioeconomic inequalities between blacks and whites rather than a result of racial differences *per se*. In fact, previous research has already shown that the black-white gap in educational attainment is a reflection of underlying differences in socioeconomic status and family structure.[9] These findings do not preclude the possibility that assets also play an important role with respect to race and education, as the following sections discuss.

ASSETS AND THE FINANCING OF EDUCATION

Over and above traditional measures of socioeconomic status such as income and occupation, parental asset levels may affect several dynamics that have importance in explaining who succeeds educationally and who does not. Wealth (net worth) may reflect long-term family legacies that have been discounted by the usual analyses of income or occupational data. For example, parents who are professionals, who come from a long line of professionals, and who have inherited substantial wealth might be better able to solidify their children's educational outcomes than another set of parents who are professionals and who have an equivalent income but who are burdened by debt from student loans and thus cannot play as large a role in aiding their children's education. In other words, two families with the same household income might have vastly different resources at their disposal to provide advantages to their children. These advantages can be as tangible as extracurricular and private education, financial support during college, or in-kind aid such as supplying educational materials.

In the contemporary United States, perhaps one of the more costly and important material goods that parents can provide to better their children's educational prospects is a home computer. This is the sort of extracurricular expense that can be paid for out of wealth holdings (liquid assets). In 1993, 32.8 percent of white students used a computer at home, compared to only 10.9 percent of African American students, a full two-thirds fewer.[10] About half of these students of each race use their home computers for school work. Thus, although blacks and whites are just as likely to use a computer "educationally" when they have one at home, blacks are much less likely to own the hardware. Put another way, the difference between the races does not lie in the attitude toward education and technology; rather, it more likely rests in the financial obstacles associated with obtaining a computer. While there is as yet no evidence on the importance of computers in the home for eventual school performance, substantial research does support the importance of the overall home environment in determining cognitive development and educational success. A major component of this Home Observation and Measurement Scale (HOME), as it is called, is the availability of educational toys and the like.[11]

While "extras" such as a computer at home may help to engender racial differences in educational outcomes, perhaps the greatest role that wealth could play is in the financing of postsecondary education. Given the enormous cost of a university or college education, income level may not adequately represent the ability of a family to infuse its children with the human capital that is increasingly critical for success in the labor market. Although many schools do provide financial aid (particularly for minority students), this assistance generally does not cover the entire cost of college attendance. For the academic year

1992–93, the average net cost (after financial aid awards) for students attending four-year public institutions was $7,326; the corresponding cost for private schools was $11,552.[12] These costs are slightly less for low-income students, but not that much less: among pupils coming from low-income families, the average net costs were $5,070 per year for four-year public institutions and $5,872 for private four-year colleges and universities.[13] Since private schools generally have larger endowments and fewer poor students, they can afford to be more progressive in their aid policies, which makes the gap between the net costs of private and public colleges less among low-income students than among their middle-class and wealthy counterparts.

Any way we look at the numbers, however, it is clear that families are burdened with substantial costs and that these costs may not be adequately addressed by annual income. Could the two poor families described in Chapter One afford to pay $5,000 toward educating one of their children? Certainly the African American parents, who were renting a home, could not have done so. The white parents, however, who had substantial home equity, might have been able to draw down on that resource (through a second mortgage, for instance) in order to send their child to college. Similarly, it is unlikely that the average middle-income household—black or white—can afford to pay $10,000 a year out of family paychecks for each child in college. But the parents may have assets that they have accumulated, saved, or inherited that will do the job.

Given these net cost figures, it is not surprising that some research reports that individuals from low-income families tend to enroll in less selective colleges, net of academic ability, achievement, or educational expectations, since there is an association between selectivity and cost.[14] Since families are more likely to pay for college expenses out of wealth than out of current income (because of the enormous costs associated with postsecondary schooling), assets should have a similar—if not stronger—effect on predicting the selectivity of educational institutions attended (which may, in turn, determine the continuation of schooling past college). Further, studies have shown that, over the long term, owning one's home is cheaper than renting;[15] thus, homeowners can free up more funds to finance their children's educational expenses.

Other research has already implied but has not directly shown causal pathways by which asset differences may affect educational financing and, ultimately, racial differences in attainment. For example, holding income constant, sociologists Francis Goldscheider and Calvin Goldscheider found that young African American adults receive less from and contribute more to their parents than their white counterparts during the period immediately following high school, implying a substitution of work for schooling.[16] This interpretation is supported by other research claiming that extensive work involvement leads to a lack of study time.[17] Further, in their 1991 study, Goldscheider and Goldscheider also found that parental financial contributions to their children's educational expenses had a very strong effect on the children's educational expectations—such that the effect of income is eliminated. The implication is that if African American teenagers received more financial support directly from their parents (and the parents had the wealth to share), the young people might harbor higher expectations for educational attainment and might have a much easier time realizing their aspirations.

While studies such as the one just described have not directly considered wealth in their analysis, they may be implicitly detecting the importance of assets and uncovering one of the mechanisms by which assets affect educational attainment. It may be that among black teenagers, extensive work involvement (out of financial necessity) hurts their studies and substitutes for additional schooling; further, the lack of capital provided by parents, combined with the family's need for additional income from adult children, may depress young African Americans' educational expectations and ultimately their success. In fact, according to education researchers John Kane and Lawrence Spizman, although many colleges and universities make extensive efforts to recruit black students, parental resources and geography are the determining factors leading to lower educational attainment for African Americans.[18] While Kane and Spizman were referring to state and region of residence when they invoked the issue of geography, the issue of *local,* neighborhood geography is another very important mechanism by which asset differentials may lead to differences in educational attainment for blacks and whites.

ASSETS, SOCIAL CAPITAL, AND SCHOOL DISTRICTS

In many senses, wealth may have very direct effects on educational attainment even if it is not specifically translated into educational financing. Housing assets, for instance—the modal form of wealth holding for American families—may produce (or may act as proxy for) "neighborhood effects." Since William Julius Wilson argued in 1987 that the plight of the inner-city poor largely results from a lack of "social capital" (role models, connections, and so on) in the neighborhoods where they reside, extensive research has attempted to test his thesis with respect to success in the educational system.[19] A variety of researchers have found support for Wilson's thesis and for the salience of the social capital of neighborhoods to the issue of race and schooling.

One study of northern California high school students reported that community socioeconomic status was the only factor related to grade point average for both racial groups.[20] A number of studies have looked at educational attainment as an outcome, finding that, net of family characteristics, higher levels of community socioeconomic status raise the odds of high school graduation and the number of years of schooling ultimately completed.[21] One of these studies even reports that—factoring out the income level and other characteristics of one's own family—living among a greater proportion of neighbors with incomes over $30,000 positively affects the cognitive development of five-year-old children (in addition to reducing the risk of dropping out of high school among adolescents).[22]

Why should community characteristics make a difference? Neighborhoods matter for economic as well as social reasons. Economically, neighborhoods matter in the United States because schooling is funded at the local level by property taxes. Thus, wealth not only has the effect of freeing up money for private school attendance but also has very direct consequences for the quality of public schools attended by children in the community. Higher property values mean a bigger tax base and almost inevitably translate into greater per-pupil expenditures by the school district; financing differences are reflected in teacher-to-pupil ratios as well as in the presence or absence of educational items such as computers in the classroom.

One study of first-graders showed that learning opportunities for African American students were inferior compared to those afforded their nonblack counterparts and that these differences arose largely from inequalities between school districts in the availability of technological resources.[23] In 1993, 29 percent of white kindergarten (and pre-K) students used computers in their school, while only 16 percent of their African American counterparts did so (slightly more than half as many).[24] This gap narrows as we ascend the educational ladder until it reaches equity in college; by then, however, many black students are disadvantaged with respect to their white counterparts who learned how to use computers at a much younger age.

Clearly, owning a home in a high-value neighborhood directly affects the amount of public resources devoted to each child. As long as schools remain financed at the local level by property taxes, enormous differences in quality by district will remain, differences associated with the housing wealth in that community.[25] Although the Coleman Report asserted that "school quality" as measured by financing and teacher-to-pupil ratios matters less than the socioeconomic backgrounds of students, school quality nevertheless has an impact: this effect explains at least 10 percent of variance in test scores (and perhaps more in the educational attainment of students). This is not to mention the "unmeasurable" economic resources that a wealthier community can provide. In fact, economist Susan Mayer found that students attending schools with a greater proportion of students from well-off families had a significantly higher likelihood of completing high school, net of the students' own backgrounds. Further, this effect of a school's socioeconomic composition was much stronger for those students who were from disadvantaged backgrounds themselves.[26]

Even if we could compensate for economic differences by implementing magnet schools, busing, and other special programs that create a better socioeconomic and racial mix in schools, important socially based neighborhood effects on educational attainment might nonetheless remain. Local communities matter because they represent the next outer developmental shell after the household/family. Anthropologists and sociologists have demonstrated time and time again in a variety of settings that social capital in the form of role models and peer influences has important consequences on individual behavior and ultimate life chances for success—particularly for children and adolescents.[27] Robert Haveman and Barbara Wolfe write that those children "who grow up in a neighborhood where young high-school dropouts are prevalent . . . are likely to have a different assessment of the stigma costs attached to this decision than are other teenagers."[28] Not only may the stigma of dropping out be lessened, but such life choices may also have a contagious effect.[29]

Finally, poor children who live in poor neighborhoods are more likely to be exposed to a variety of environmental hazards such as violence, crime, and drug abuse, all of which can have a damaging impact on the academic efforts of children and adolescents.[30] These risk factors and their relation to the increasing concentration of poverty are particularly relevant to the issue of racial differences in education, for African Americans not only are more likely to be income-poor but also are more likely than their poor white counterparts to live among other poor families in urban environments. This concentration of black poverty is directly related to the dynamics of housing, wealth, and racial segregation, as we saw in the previous chapter.

ASSETS AND ACADEMIC ORIENTATION

In addition to its role in reflecting the dynamics of educational financing and differences in neighborhood and school quality, wealth may also influence educational achievement in intangible ways. Although the gap in educational attainment between blacks and whites has narrowed slightly, a wide gulf remains between the two races in the basic academic and informational skills they command.[31] In their best-selling book *The Bell Curve,* Richard Herrnstein and Charles Murray argue that deficits on the part of African Americans are a result of genetic differences in IQ—that is, of their inherent ability to learn. These authors claim that if the IQ deficit of African Americans could be statistically eliminated, the data would show that blacks actually complete high school and college at higher rates than whites[32]—a difference Herrnstein and Murray attribute to policies such as affirmative action. They assume, however, that IQ is determined at birth and not shaped by social and economic forces throughout childhood and beyond; this assumption is belied by a long tradition of research on intelligence testing that these authors overlook (and by the fact that the IQ gap between whites and blacks is greater for adults—after years of inequality—than it is for children).[33] A more plausible explanation is that both the skill and IQ deficits from which African Americans suffer result from social dynamics, which may, in turn, be affected by wealth and social class.

For example, some theorists have suggested that blacks achieve less than whites in school because of an "attitude problem." African Americans, according to this logic, frequently have less motivation to succeed in school and do not view the educational system as the primary ladder for upward mobility; instead, they equate academic success with "selling out" or "becoming white." The best account of this dynamic comes from anthropologist John Ogbu, who generates a theory of "oppositional culture." According to his paradigm, involuntary minorities such as African Americans (those who did not come to this country by choice) can be characterized by a "low-effort syndrome." This condition is an oppositional response to subordination and oppression and hinders black academic achievement. Ogbu describes this syndrome as a coping mechanism and argues that it leads to what many white Americans see as a black "attitude problem."[34]

While some analysis from survey data has suggested that blacks remain "committed to social mobility via education,"[35] such research has focused on adults who most likely completed their educational careers long ago. At least one study that focused on high school seniors in particular areas (in this case, Louisville, Kentucky) has shown that, on the whole, academic identity has the same meaning for all groups of respondents except black males—the least educationally successful and perhaps the most likely to manifest the "oppositional culture" to which Ogbu refers.[36] Assets, however, may play a role in shaping the view of education as a vehicle for upward mobility (versus a view of education as a means of selling out). The best illustration of this is perhaps provided by an "accidental" social science experiment.

In 1980, the multimillionaire businessman and philanthropist Eugene Lang was asked to give a speech to sixth-graders at a school in Harlem. As he was driving through the poor, primarily black and Hispanic neighborhood on his way to deliver a prepared text—exhorting the students to stay in school by highlighting the virtues of hard work and education as vehicles for upward mobility—he was struck by the utter devastation of the area, which had been his own childhood neighborhood, although he had not visited for twenty years. As he tells the story, in the face of such poverty, he thought that his words sounded ridiculously naïve, and he tore up the speech. Instead, when he confronted the sixty-one sixth-graders, he told them that if they finished high school, he would pay the tuition necessary for them to attend the colleges of their choice. In a school district with a drop-out rate that ranged between 50 and 75 percent, and in a neighborhood where few students ever made it to college, fifty-four of the sixty-one students graduated from high school. Of that number, thirty-two went on to college.[37] Clearly, Lang did not change the children's neighborhood, the quality of their school, their family structures, the education or income levels of their parents. What he provided these children was in essence an asset.

This asset—in the form of a promissory note—served a role that many white middle-class adolescents take for granted: it brought college within the realm of possibility. By changing expectations, this asset improved school performance. It is important to note, however, that it was not the expectation of financial help alone that helped these schoolchildren. The foundation Lang set up to administer his promise also provided extensive tutoring. Without this other, more tangible manifestation of Lang's financial commitment, many of the students would not have made it as far as they did. All the same, his efforts demonstrate two important ways in which assets can help: by changing expectations and by providing the extracurricular assistance that those heightened expectations require. In discussing his 1988 welfare reform bill, Senator Daniel Patrick Moynihan (whom we will encounter again in the discussion of family structure in Chapter Five) said as much by claiming that wealth "can be used to nurture children for whatever success is said to require, be it tuition or orthodontia. With it is an insurance policy that gives not only physical but psychological comfort to a developing child."[38]

HOUSING AND EDUCATION

Housing has been shown to be one of the prime determinants of social status.[39] As Emily Rosenbaum writes, "In addition to providing physical shelter, housing provides the family with privacy and stability, and it serves as an outward sign of social status."[40] Particularly for adolescents, the social status conferred by having the best house in the neighborhood may instill confidence that could translate to success in an academic setting. Conversely, living in conditions that are inferior to those of one's peers may cause anxiety and a lack of confidence in one's family and oneself. Since underlying conceptions of poverty often rely on a notion of relativity, housing quality may be the most visible way that relative poverty (or affluence) manifests itself in the lives of adolescents and with respect to their primary group affiliations.

The housing unit itself—especially its spaciousness and quality—can also have an important effect. Ever since the days of Malthus, demographers have periodically worried about the possible detrimental effects of overcrowding. In the 1960s, interest in crowding was stimulated by Calhoun's study of laboratory rats, which linked high population density with aggressive behavior, disruption of mating patterns, and higher

rates of illness.[41] Calhoun's findings led researchers to look for detrimental effects of higher population density in the human species.
Population density became a particularly hot topic of study in the
1970s, when increased population growth and urbanization led to concerns about overcrowding in the world's cities.

Despite the common perception that urbanization, and the higher
population density that accompanies it, leads to increased crime, higher
rates of mental illness, and a general decline in health, researchers have
concluded that "while density at the macro-level probably has some
minor 'pathological' effects, it is not a variable of major substantive importance."[42] Instead, research interest has shifted to the micro-level—
that is, to the household level. Evidence suggests that objective crowding within the household—measured as the number of persons per
room—has more observably detrimental effects, including irritability,
withdrawal, weariness, and poor mental health.[43]

Researchers have studied the effects of household density (crowding)
on a variety of dependent measures. They report that the number of
persons per room is a good objective measure of crowding and that this
variable significantly predicts physical and psychological withdrawal
among family members, poor mental health, poor physical health, and
poor social relationships both within and outside the home.[44] These effects may represent a primary mechanism by which economic hardship
and housing constraints (particularly those faced by minorities) exhibit
their negative effects on the educational attainment of children.
Crowding is particularly salient to issues of race and education because
African Americans have consistently lived in more crowded conditions
than have whites.[45] Further, household density is linked to housing
wealth, as those families who can buy a house usually enjoy more space
than their renting counterparts.

Household density's positive association with poor physical and mental health is likely to indirectly depress educational achievement; ab-
sences from school increase because of higher rates of illness, and, as a
result, academic performance and learning can suffer. Further, these
health handicaps may combine with a lack of privacy in crowded households. No matter what a child's educational aspirations are, the child
will suffer academically if there is no quiet space to study, away from the
noise of other children. In addition, those who live in more crowded
households may sleep less or endure irregular sleep patterns. All these
factors can result in a lack of concentration both in the home, when a

child attempts to study and do homework, and in school, when the child tries to pay attention to lectures and participate in class discussion.

Crowding may have other indirect effects on children's academic achievement as well. The stress that household crowding engenders can cause parents to be irritable or psychologically withdrawn, as Irwin Altman suggests in his research.[46] A crowded household may thus result in a lack of constructive social interaction between parents and children. Since parental involvement is important for a child's cognitive development,[47] anything that depresses constructive interaction is likely to be detrimental to children's educational attainment. Through these and other possible mechanisms, household density may affect educational progress. In fact, research has shown that household crowding does have a detrimental effect on the educational attainment of both blacks and whites.[48]

Another household-level factor that affects educational attainment is the actual physical quality of the housing unit.[49] A decaying dwelling can be detrimental in many ways.[50] Primary among such considerations is the danger of exposing a child to a variety of environmental health hazards. The most damaging hazard is ingestion of lead paint. Poor children demonstrate higher blood lead concentrations than nonpoor children.[51] One report concludes that "the highest prevalence of lead poisoning has been recorded for poor black children living in decaying inner-city neighborhoods; the lowest, among non-poor children living in suburban areas."[52] Other health hazards that may be posed by an old or decrepit housing unit include the presence of asbestos, the less well-documented but more common risk of infection posed by decaying insects such as cockroaches, and danger from the presence of rodents such as mice and rats (or even bats). In short, anything that can be detrimental to the health of a developing child will be directly or indirectly deleterious to the child's mental health, cognitive development, and, ultimately, academic success.

All of these mechanisms by which wealth may affect educational attainment are speculative at this point. The sections that follow will first determine the magnitude of the wealth effect, then examine how this affects the relationship between race and educational outcomes, and, finally, investigate what it is about wealth that matters, by breaking it up into its constituent parts. I will attempt to determine how the wealth of an individual's parents in 1984—when he or she was a child residing in the parental household—affected that individual's educational outcomes a generation later, in 1995. By following this strategy, we can be relatively certain of the direction of causality. (For a more thorough discussion of possible caveats, see Chapter One.) The logic of inquiry is the same as it was for modeling net worth in Chapter Two: examining the changing effect of race when we take into consideration class variables.

ARE DIFFERENCES IN EDUCATIONAL ATTAINMENT A RESULT OF RACE OR CLASS?

Keeping in mind all these reasons why wealth could matter, we can directly address the question of whether differences between African Americans and whites in educational attainment are in fact racial differences or whether they are a statistical artifact of class differences. The first bar of Figure 3.1 indicates that when blacks and whites are compared only by race, without any class considerations, black students are no less likely than whites to complete high school. When the most basic statistical controls are introduced (the second bar of Figure 3.1, model B of Table A3.1), blacks actually demonstrate a slight advantage with respect to high school completion, although it is not statistically significant. When the traditional measures of parental socioeconomic status (income, education, and occupational prestige) are taken into consideration, the African American advantage becomes strong and significant: blacks are 2.60 times more likely than whites to complete high school, all else being equal. When we add net worth to the model, this difference increases slightly, to a ratio of 2.67 to 1; when wealth is broken out into its constitutive parts, the odds ratio drops slightly, to 2.56 to 1.

Table 3.1 presents important effects (and noneffects) in the asset type model. As the table indicates, the age of the respondent matters: the older respondents are, the more time they have had to complete schooling. Among a much wider band of respondents (this sample ranges in age from eighteen to thirty years old), one would find that age is negatively associated with educational attainment because average levels of schooling were lower earlier in the century. But within the current sample, which consists of a young, relatively narrow band of respondents, many may not have completed their educational careers (though none are currently enrolled in school). Thus, there is a positive effect for age. Also, females attain higher levels of education than their male counterparts. This is consistent with trend data that show female educational progress outpacing that of males.

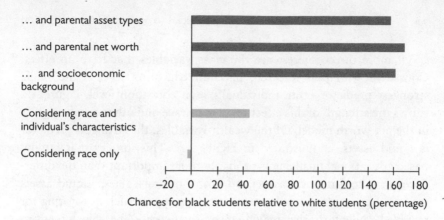

... and parental asset types

... and parental net worth

... and socioeconomic background

Considering race and individual's characteristics

Considering race only

-20 0 20 40 60 80 100 120 140 160 180

Chances for black students relative to white students (percentage)

FIGURE 3.1. The effect of being black on the odds of high school graduation, by model type. Darker bars are statistically discernible from zero; lighter bars are statistically equivalent to zero. When the high school graduation rates of blacks and whites are contrasted only by race, they are statistically equivalent. When class differences are factored out, however, African Americans have higher net rates of high school completion. (See Table A3.1.)

TABLE 3.1

VARIABLES PREDICTING HIGH SCHOOL
GRADUATION BY DESCENDING ORDER
OF PREDICTIVE IMPORTANCE

1. *Parent's education (head of household)*
2. *Respondent's age*
3. *Parents' liquid assets*
4. *Female respondent*
5. *African American race*
6. *Net value of parents' business*
7. Parents' permanent income
8. Female-headed parental household (1980–84)
9. Parent's age (head of household)
10. Parent's occupational prestige (head of household)
11. Equity of parents' primary residence
12. Net value of parents' other illiquid assets
13. Number of siblings
14. Parents received welfare in 1984

NOTE: Italic type indicates statistical significance at the $p < .10$ level; see Table A3.1.

Of more direct interest are the class variables that have an effect. Consistent with past research, parental education level is the single strongest predictor of an individual's own education level. Figure 3.2 shows the strength of this effect relative to race and other class variables in the net worth model. Of the wealth variables, the strongest predictor is liquid assets, as illustrated in Figure 3.3. This implies that family-based educational financing is probably more important than the differences in school districts associated with housing values. Liquid assets may help parents to afford extracurricular support such as tutoring for troubled students, or they may finance private schooling, which tends to yield lower drop-out rates. The value of parental business also seems to have an effect, although it is barely significant at the 10 percent probability level and may be due to chance, since there does not appear to be a direct causal link between business value and educational outcomes (unless this reflects the tendency of new immigrants—whose children generally do well in school—to own small businesses).

Table 3.1 also shows that when assets are incorporated into statistical models, a number of effects that have previously been noted disappear, possibly artifacts of asset differences. For example, female-headed family structure becomes unimportant when wealth levels are taken into account. In other words, those factors that have been shown to matter (and those that matter in my own nonwealth models in Table A3.1) most likely have their influence because of their association with wealth levels. It may not be the gender of the head of household *per se* that counts but rather that female-headed households are less likely to have accumulated significant wealth holdings to aid their children. This finding is relevant to current discussions of race, for single parenthood and female-headed families are often used as racial code words in the debate over poverty and welfare. In fact, parental welfare receipt itself does not seem to have any impact whatsoever. (Neither does parental age, although youthful parenthood has been another hot-button topic in political discussions.)

We may also be surprised to learn that neither the occupational prestige nor the income level of parents appears to matter in predicting high school graduation. When we do not account for wealth levels, income matters—but when we employ a fully specified statistical model, taking into consideration assets as well as income level, my earlier speculation finds support, namely, that parents most likely finance education out of liquid assets rather than out of yearly earnings. That income appeared to matter before wealth was included in the analysis is again an artifact

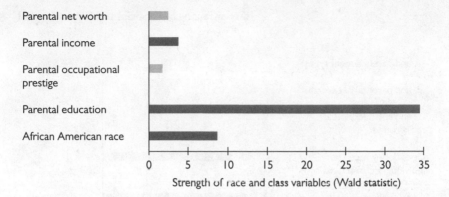

FIGURE 3.2. The relative effects of race and class on the odds of high school graduation. Darker bars are statistically discernible from zero; lighter bars are statistically equivalent to zero. African American race has a significant and positive impact on the odds of completing high school; parental income also has a significant and positive effect. By far the strongest factor, however, is the level of parental education. (See Table A3.1.)

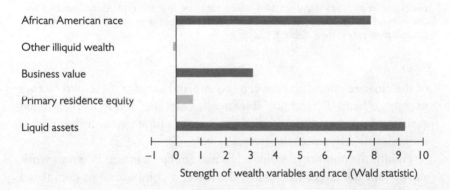

FIGURE 3.3. The relative effects of wealth by type on the odds of high school graduation. Darker bars are statistically discernible from zero; lighter bars are statistically equivalent to zero. Among the wealth variables, parents' liquid assets have the strongest positive impact on rates of high school graduation. Race is almost as strong a predictor as liquid wealth, and the value of a parental business has an impact as well. (See Table A3.1.)

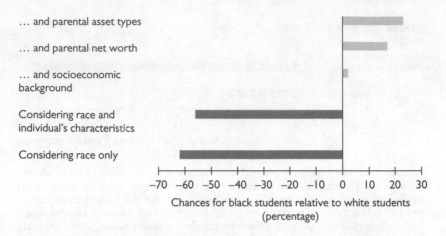

... and parental asset types

... and parental net worth

... and socioeconomic background

Considering race and individual's characteristics

Considering race only

−70 −60 −50 −40 −30 −20 −10   0   10   20   30

Chances for black students relative to white students
(percentage)

FIGURE 3.4. The effect of being black on the odds of college graduation, by model type. Darker bars are statistically discernible from zero; lighter bars are statistically equivalent to zero. African Americans demonstrate a decreased chance of completing a bachelor's degree when the sizable class differences between black families and white families are not considered; net of social class, however, blacks and whites are no different in regard to college completion rates. (See Table A3.2.)

of the close relationship between income and wealth; these two factors usually go hand in hand (are statistically correlated). But, as mentioned earlier, they are analytically distinct, and it is liquid wealth that makes a significant difference, not income level.

Finally, the number of siblings has no significant effect. Previous work shows that the larger the family, the lower a child's level of completed education.[53] Because the "pie" is divided among a greater number, children from larger families enjoy fewer economic and psychological resources than those from similar small families. There has been debate over the extent to which this negative effect of large families stems from parental attention being split among a greater number of children or from the increased division of parental economic resources; my findings, though preliminary, weigh in on the side of family economics.

Moving on to the realm of higher education, we find that African Americans are only 38 percent as likely as whites to have completed a bachelor's degree when race alone is considered. Accounting for social class eliminates this dramatic difference, however. Figure 3.4 shows that in a fully specified class model African Americans actually demonstrate

TABLE 3.2

VARIABLES PREDICTING COLLEGE
GRADUATION (RECEIPT OF A
BACHELOR'S DEGREE) BY DESCENDING
ORDER OF PREDICTIVE IMPORTANCE

1. *Parent's education (head of household)*
2. *Respondent's age*
3. *Number of siblings*
4. *Equity of parents' primary residence*
5. *Parents' liquid assets*
6. *Parent's age (head of household)*
7. Net value of parents' other illiquid assets
8. Parents' permanent income
9. Parent's occupational prestige (head of household)
10. African American race
11. Female-headed parental household (1980–84)
12. Parents received welfare in 1984
13. Female respondent
14. Net value of parents' business

NOTE: Italic type indicates statistical significance at the $p < .10$ level; see
Table A3.2.

an advantage in the odds on college completion relative to whites, although this advantage is not significantly different from zero (see also Table A3.2). As Figure 3.5 illustrates, parental education itself is the strongest predictor of college completion, as it is for high school graduation. More than anything else, having a parent who went to college seeds the aspirations and expectations necessary for an individual to finish college. Of the other class variables, only parental net worth is significantly associated with college graduation.

When we break out wealth by type, as in Figure 3.6, primary residence equity (somewhat surprisingly) proves to be the best predictor, followed by liquid assets. Perhaps, given the enormous cost of college tuition, many parents cannot afford to pay for college out of income or even liquid assets alone but must take out a second mortgage to defray their children's expenses. Other researchers may do well to examine in more depth the decision-making processes involved in college financing and their relation to homeownership.

With respect to college completion, Table 3.2 presents more or less the same pattern as that for high school graduation, with a couple of notable exceptions. The number of siblings does matter for college completion, whereas for high school completion it became insignificant when class

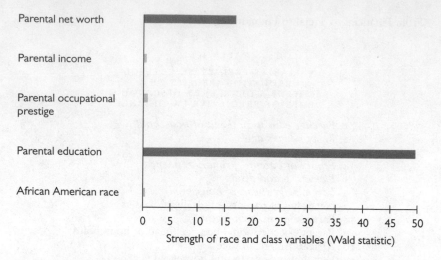

FIGURE 3.5. The relative effects of race and class on the odds of college graduation. Darker bars are statistically discernible from zero; lighter bars are statistically equivalent to zero. The only race or class variables that matter in predicting the completion of a bachelor's degree are parental education and parental wealth. (See Table A3.2.)

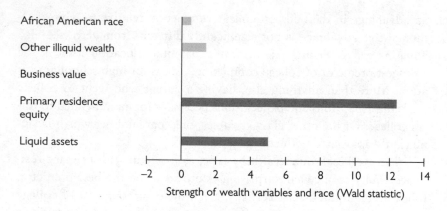

FIGURE 3.6. The relative effects of wealth by type on the odds of college graduation. Darker bars are statistically discernible from zero; lighter bars are statistically equivalent to zero. Of the various asset types, the value of a family's home has the largest positive impact on college completion rates, followed by liquid assets. (See Table A3.2.)

was held constant. The greater number of siblings an individual has, the lower the odds that the individual will finish college. This effect may be related to financing issues: with a set amount of economic resources, the amount that parents can contribute to each child's college education declines as their number of offspring increases. Parental age is positively associated with college completion as well. Gender has no effect at this educational stage, however. Given the female advantage in completing high school and the lack of a similar effect at the college level, where money matters more, one may speculate that a financial bias against girls exists within some families that eliminates the advantage. (Previous research has also suggested such a dynamic.)[54] This speculation needs to be investigated further, however.

When we contrast the findings of the college and high school analyses, we are left with an interesting puzzle. It may make sense that there is no net racial difference at the college level: either affirmative action is working, or it has never been necessary, when class is taken into consideration. But what are we to make of the rather strong positive effect of being black on the odds of completing high school, especially since there is no formal affirmative action program at the high school level?

There appear to be two possible explanations of this advantage that black students seem to hold in secondary school completion. The first is that, net of social class, the schools that African Americans attend are on average "easier" than the comparable schools that white students attend. Evidence that black high school graduates from the inner cities are less well prepared on average than whites in terms of test scores and other cognitive measures would suggest this interpretation. We must keep in mind, however, that most of the data presented concerning racial differences in test scores and the like do not account for permanent parental income, let alone wealth. The second possible interpretation is that, when we cut through the disadvantages of class, African Americans actually demonstrate a greater level of commitment to education than their white counterparts, despite anecdotal or ethnographic evidence to the contrary. In other words, the "oppositional" culture to which John Ogbu refers is in fact common to a certain socioeconomic stratum, and within comparable strata African Americans behave in much the same way that many other ethnic, national, or religious minorities do: they put great stock in education as a route to upward mobility.

In order to add greater texture to these findings, I examined two other educational indicators: the odds of being held back a grade, and

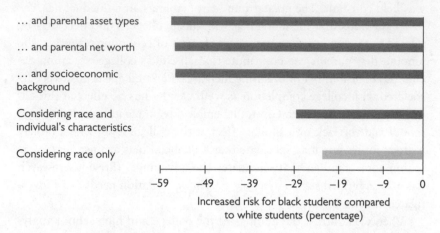

... and parental asset types

... and parental net worth

... and socioeconomic background

Considering race and individual's characteristics

Considering race only

−59   −49   −39   −29   −19   −9   0

Increased risk for black students compared
to white students (percentage)

FIGURE 3.7. The effect of being black on the risk of being held back a grade, by model type. Darker bars are statistically discernible from zero; lighter bars are statistically equivalent to zero. When only race is considered, there is no significant difference between blacks and whites in being held back a grade. But when social class (including wealth) is equalized, African Americans have a reduced risk of being held back. (See Table A3.3.)

the risk of being expelled or suspended from school.[55] In theory, not advancing a grade with one's cohort is an indication of poor academic performance. Likewise, being expelled or suspended is a loose indicator of behavioral or disciplinary problems—that is, an oppositional attitude. Both of these measures, however, like graduation itself, can be affected by a whole host of other factors, not the least of which are the standards maintained by the individual school.

That said, Figure 3.7 (Table A3.3) looks at the effect of being African American on a child's risk of being held back a grade. Simply comparing blacks and whites yields no significant racial difference in this indicator. When social class (with or without wealth) is factored out, however, African Americans are only 44 percent as likely as whites to be held back (43 percent when assets are broken out by type). As in the case of graduation, the education level of parents is the strongest class variable (higher parental education reduces the risk), followed by net worth (higher parental wealth levels lower the odds of being left back), as Figure 3.8 illustrates. The only other significant predictors are the gender of the respondent, with females less likely to be held back (this is, in fact, the strongest predictor overall) and the age of the respondent (older respondents are less likely to have been held back). When we break out

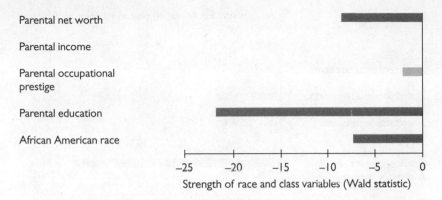

Strength of race and class variables (Wald statistic)

FIGURE 3.8. The relative effects of race and class on the risk of being held back a grade. Darker bars are statistically discernible from zero; lighter bars are statistically equivalent to zero. Being African American reduces the risk of being held back a grade, as does higher parental net worth. Parental education is the strongest predictor of grade repetition, however: the higher the level of parental education, the less the risk. (See Table A3.3.)

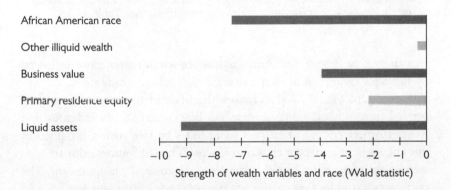

Strength of wealth variables and race (Wald statistic)

FIGURE 3.9. The relative effects of wealth by type on the risk of being held back a grade. Darker bars are statistically discernible from zero; lighter bars are statistically equivalent to zero. Of the various types of parental wealth, greater liquid assets and greater business worth significantly reduce the odds of being held back a grade. The effect of liquid wealth is slighter larger than the effect of African American race. (See Table A3.3.)

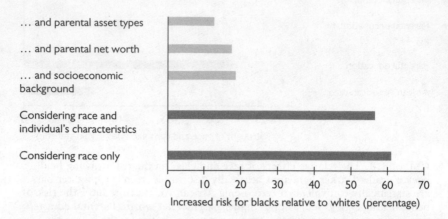

... and parental asset types

... and parental net worth

... and socioeconomic background

Considering race and individual's characteristics

Considering race only

0   10   20   30   40   50   60   70

Increased risk for blacks relative to whites (percentage)

FIGURE 3.10. The effect of being black on the risk of expulsion or suspension from school, by model type. Darker bars are statistically discernible from zero; lighter bars are statistically equivalent to zero. The heightened risk of being expelled or suspended that African American students face is really a result of class dynamics; the effect of being black declines to insignificance when socioeconomic status and wealth are equalized. (See Table A3.4.)

wealth by type (Figure 3.9), liquid assets are what matter most, followed by business value, just as in the case of high school graduation.

Figure 3.10 (Table A3.4) examines the odds of being expelled or suspended from school. Simply comparing blacks and whites indicates that African Americans are 61 percent more likely to face such a penalty. But this finding is an artifact of class differences. When SES and wealth are considered, the racial effect becomes smaller and statistically insignificant. The only class variables that matter are parental education and wealth, and these both reduce the likelihood of expulsion or suspension as they increase (see Figure 3.11). Gender is the only other factor that matters at all; women are less likely to have been expelled or suspended during their educational careers. Figure 3.12, which breaks out wealth by type, shows that only liquid assets appear to matter in predicting the risk of expulsion or suspension from school. It is not entirely clear why this is so. Perhaps liquid assets finance private schooling or emotional support (counseling or a psychologist) when a student is having behavioral difficulties. Or it may be the case that families with liquid assets have households that are much less stressful and therefore have fewer disciplinary problems among their school-aged children. Such speculation offers grist for future research endeavors.

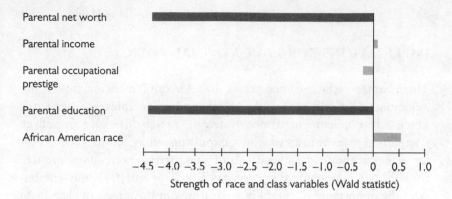

FIGURE 3.11. The relative effects of race and class on the risk of expulsion or suspension from school. Darker bars are statistically discernible from zero; lighter bars are statistically equivalent to zero. Of the race and class variables, the only ones that are significant in predicting expulsion or suspension are parental education and parental net worth. Race is not a factor. (See Table A3.4.)

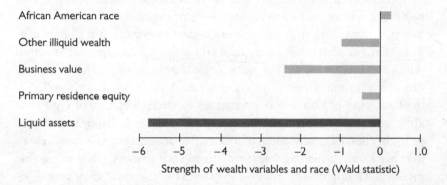

FIGURE 3.12. The relative effects of wealth by type on the risk of expulsion or suspension from school. Darker bars are statistically discernible from zero; lighter bars are statistically equivalent to zero. Of the wealth variables, only parental liquid assets significantly reduce the risk of expulsion or suspension. (See Table A3.4.)

IMPLICATIONS FOR EDUCATIONAL POLICY

This chapter—which demonstrates that African Americans hold a net advantage over whites in high school graduation rates and academic grade advancement but demonstrates no racial difference in college completion rates or rates of school expulsion—may set off a social policy alarm in the reader's head. All of these trends are counterintuitive to what one may observe in everyday life. This situation only emphasizes the importance of carefully separating out the effects of class from those of race. Overall, blacks do worse than whites (the result one expects from anecdotal information and summary statistics), but when the differences in economic endowments that African Americans and whites bring to the educational system are taken into consideration, blacks do better than whites in some measures and the same as whites in others. Perhaps in this changing race coefficient lies the seed of the virulent debate over affirmative action that is going on today.

Specifically, proponents of affirmative action in education argue that previous evidence justifies the continuance or expansion of affirmative action programs. African Americans are underrepresented at the upper echelons of the academic hierarchy, plain and simple. When affirmative action policies are removed, as they were in California in 1996, the results are disastrous for minorities: in 1997, only one African American enrolled in the University of California's prestigious Boalt Hall School of Law after affirmative action was eliminated (and he had deferred from the previous year). In contrast, many critics of affirmative action as it now stands claim that blacks are benefiting "unfairly" from such policies. They argue that race-based affirmative action initiatives lead to "reverse discrimination"—that is, they lead to less qualified blacks receiving preference over more qualified whites in college and graduate school admissions.

What this chapter has shown is that both sides may be right. Blacks are disadvantaged with respect to their white counterparts. But when black and white students have the same socioeconomic backgrounds, blacks enjoy some advantages. This is because the differences in average levels of educational attainment between blacks and whites are not about race *per se*. They are about socioeconomic status. Blacks are not disadvantaged in the educational system; rather, they are disadvantaged in the resources they bring to the system. Race matters, but only indirectly—through the realm of class inequality. Hence the perception that affirmative action benefits the African Americans who need it least: it is race-based when it should be class-based. (Chapter Six addresses the issue of designing class-based affirmative action policies.)

For now, the importance of assets in the process of educational stratification should be reiterated. For instance, net worth is the second most important predictor of attaining the increasingly important college degree (after parental education level). This central importance of assets in financing higher education in an increasingly technical economy shoots a hole through the enticing account of inequality offered by Herrnstein and Murray in *The Bell Curve*. They argue that universalism—that is, equal opportunity—has ironically led to a new, more intractable form of inequality based on cognitive ability as reflected by IQ. The story they recount goes something like this: America as a land of equal opportunity has given rise to a situation over the past few generations in which the smartest people succeed as a result of their *natural* talents, freed from the social barriers to opportunity that once existed. At the same time, the smartest people mate with the smartest people and engender the brightest offspring. Thus, the biological process of reproduction writ large mimics the social hierarchy. The increasingly hierarchical child-producing process complements the technical, postindustrial economy, where the diversity of occupational skill requirements has become greater. (One only need think of the different knowledge bases required to work as an assembly-line worker and an aeronautical engineer, a difference of a magnitude that may not have existed a hundred years earlier.) But if knowledge of aeronautical engineering does not follow automatically from great cognitive ability but rather requires an increasingly expensive and drawn-out formal education, the financial endowments of parents (independent of their cognitive endowments, since less of the educational process now takes place in the home) may matter increasingly and not less, as *The Bell Curve* would imply.

With the data available for this study, I can only speculate as to the multiple ways in which wealth matters for educational attainment. The tasks that remain for future researchers include adjudicating between the relative importance of educational financing, social capital, and household conditions as mechanisms by which assets have their effects, for such differences have important implications not only for educational and racial policy but for our understanding of how educational differences interact with class to produce labor market outcomes.[56] It is to this next stage in the cycle of stratification—labor market outcomes—that the following chapter turns.

CHAPTER FOUR

Up the Down Escalator

Wealth, Work, and Wages

All this wealth excludes but one evil—poverty.
                    Samuel Johnson, 1709–84

Each year *Business Week* magazine publishes a list of the chief executive officers (CEOs) of the thousand largest corporations in the United States. Of those one thousand top jobs, African Americans held exactly two of the slots in 1994. "Unfortunately," writes sociologist Andrew Hacker, "there are no serious signs that the other 998 firms are grooming black executives for eventual top jobs."[1] Obviously, the better jobs in America are not held by African Americans. As a result, only 9 percent of black men made more than $50,000 in 1997—in contrast to 24 percent of white men.[2] At the other end of the economic spectrum, blacks are also faring much worse than whites. In 1997, the unemployment rate for whites was 4 percent, whereas for blacks it was almost triple that rate, at 11 percent. In other words, one out of every nine African Americans was actively looking for work (not to mention those who had become discouraged and dropped out of the labor market entirely).[3] During the thirty-four years between 1960 and 1993, the black-white unemployment ratio dipped below 2 to 1 in only six of those years.[4] This unemployment gap is not explained by different education levels; in fact, it is among male college graduates that the unemployment gap is the greatest. These racial differences form the basis of investigation for this chapter, which addresses black-white differences in employment patterns and earnings.

yes!

POVERTY AND UNEMPLOYMENT

The earliest attempts to explain black-white differences in unemployment were rooted in a cultural argument. The "culture of poverty" thesis argued that poverty combined with a persistent lack of opportunities to cause individuals (African Americans, in this case) to adopt alternative practices from those of mainstream society. Such practices range from the pooling of resources across households as a kind of informal insurance to informal, off-the-books work to welfare use and even to criminal activity.[5]

According to this theory, such life practices can serve to aid survival at certain times, but by the time structural conditions change (for example, a loose labor market tightens up), the "culture" of being poor has been socialized into certain groups.[6] This culture prevents individuals from taking advantage of new, more lucrative mainstream opportunities when they arise and, in a sense, keeps them from realizing their full potential in the traditional labor market. In short, it is the lifestyle and coping mechanisms of the poor that actually keep them poor. Although such arguments were made about the poor in general, they became useful to conservative scholars who wanted to explain why African Americans were persistently disadvantaged.[7] By the end of the 1960s, however, such cultural arguments were dismissed by liberal scholars who claimed that these conservative explanations were akin to "blaming the victims" for their own economic problems instead of acknowledging the larger, structural constraints that prevented black people from achieving the same occupational and earnings success as their white counterparts.[8]

One liberal alternative to the culture of poverty argument relied on the imagery of a line of people waiting for work. The "job queue" theory envisions a symbolic line of job seekers in which people are in order from first to last according to the human capital (the education and skills) that they bring to the labor market.[9] Those at the front of the queue, with high levels of human capital, will enjoy relatively continuous employment and receive high financial and prestige returns for their participation in the world of work. Those at the tail of the queue tend to have erratic employment prospects, since they are needed only when the economy is in full swing and experiencing a labor shortage. Given the lower quantity and quality of education that African Americans receive in this country, the lack of social capital they enjoy (in the form of personal connections that can provide jobs), and the discriminatory practices of many employers, it is no surprise that they find themselves at the end of the long line of job seekers.[10]

By the 1980s, conservative arguments were once again ascendant. In his controversial book *Losing Ground,* Charles Murray (also an author of *The Bell Curve*) resurrected the culture of poverty thesis with a new twist. Murray argued that it was not poverty *per se* that fostered socially undesirable practices such as welfare dependency or criminal behavior as alternatives to traditional employment. Rather, he claimed that the "perverse incentives" of liberal government programs caused alternative practices to be adopted by those at the bottom of the income distribution. For example, according to Murray, the rise in joblessness among black men could be explained by a rise in welfare benefits (that provide an alternative to wages) and the proliferation of other government programs that resulted from Lyndon Johnson's Great Society initiative. Before the War on Poverty, Murray wrote, parents had little economic choice but to marry and participate in the world of work. But with subsidized food, medical care, housing, and even income transfers, it becomes possible to have children out of wedlock, live on the dole, and so on; such an arrangement may even become preferable. Under Murray's paradigm, the unemployed poor are not following a different set of norms and values than the rest of America follows; quite the contrary they are acting rationally, in their own best interest.[11]

Following this logic, Murray's solution to the problem of black joblessness would be simple: cut off benefits to "force" people to work. A host of scholars challenged *Losing Ground* on both methodological and theoretical grounds. For example, when adjusted for inflation, welfare benefits that have risen in absolute dollars have actually declined in value.[12] More important, Murray assumed that there would be jobs to fill, ignoring the fact that major restructuring has occurred in the American economy (perhaps as a result of globalization), shifting employment bases out of the cities, where blacks predominantly live, and into the suburbs. As a result, unemployment and poverty have become increasingly concentrated, as demonstrated by William Julius Wilson in *The Truly Disadvantaged.* To make matters worse, according to Wilson, well-employed residents of urban neighborhoods have been leaving in droves over the past three decades.[13] This middle-class migration to the suburbs leaves the remaining, unemployed residents of these impoverished neighborhoods with little information about job opportunities that may exist. Such spatial and social dynamics cannot be explained by Murray's account and cast doubt on his simplified causal story.[14]

ECONOMIC SEGMENTATION AND RETURNS TO SCHOOLING

For those African Americans who are employed, the situation does not get much better. In the second quarter of 1998—a period of "full" employment—black men who worked full time made 78 cents for each dollar earned by their white counterparts, while black women made 85 cents to each dollar white women earned.[15] Overall, trend figures give no signs that black-white ratios in income are going to get any better in the near future; furthermore, any optimistic numbers that are cited usually result from declining wages for whites (a more or less steady trend since the oil shock of 1973).

Thus, although American society may be moving closer to educational parity between blacks and whites (at least in terms of *quantity* of schooling), for some reason this progress is not translating into occupational (and earnings) success for blacks relative to whites. Even black men with bachelor's degrees earn 76 cents on the dollar of white men with similar educations.[16] College-educated black women do better (97 cents on the dollar) relative to white women, but this is largely a result of depressed wages among white females. In the wage distribution, we again find a paradox: "Twice as many well-off as poor African Americans describe insufficient pay or challenge as the feature of their job that bothers them the most," writes Jennifer Hochschild of a respondent poll in *Black Enterprise* magazine.[17] It is the more highly educated who feel racial inequality the most acutely.

In trying to explain why African Americans earn less per year of schooling, some scholars have focused on understanding the distribution of black and white workers in both the country and the economy.[18] Researchers in this tradition have found that while blacks tend to be more concentrated in the South—where wages are significantly lower than in the rest of the nation—this factor alone does not account for income differences or the wage differential by education group.[19] Another approach, the "dual labor market" theory, argues that there are two relatively distinct labor markets in which individuals compete.[20] These are not regionally distinct labor markets (for instance, the

South and the non-South); rather, they are conceptually different and socially segregated. The first—called the primary sector—contains well-paid jobs that offer the possibility of upward, intragenerational career mobility. This sector includes professionals such as doctors, lawyers, and teachers as well as technical workers such as computer programmers. By contrast, the other sector, the secondary labor market, provides low-paying, low-prestige employment that may be irregular and docs not allow for substantial upward mobility within a lifetime; this sector is best embodied by service industry occupations such as those in fast-food chains, retail sales, and domestic work.[21]

Within such a framework, blacks tend to be trapped within the secondary labor market, perhaps as a result of racially segregated job networks and the preclusion of African Americans from "internal labor markets"[22]—that is, blacks are at a disadvantage since firms tend to hire from within, thus perpetuating exclusion.[23] In a systematic analysis, one study estimated that at least 14 percent of black-white earnings differentials are attributable to the distribution of blacks and whites across labor market divisions.[24] In other words, without altering individual worker characteristics at all (skills, credentials, experience, and so forth), one-seventh or more of the wage gap would be eliminated if African Americans had the same proportional representation as whites in the various industry and occupational categories.

Also intriguing in this regard is sociologist Eric Olin Wright's analysis of the Panel Study of Income Dynamics (PSID) data, which demonstrated that, within occupational class positions (with the exception of managers), income returns to education were the same for blacks and whites.[25] For example, when one compares black and white sheet metal workers, doctors, or retail salespeople, the wage by education level is the same. What Wright did not address in his research was the question of how people arrive at their occupational class positions—that is, knowing that black electricians earn the same as white electricians only narrows down the problem to the question of why there are not more black doctors or engineers.

In this way, Wright's findings highlight the importance of career lines. Individuals do not arrive at their occupational positions by random paths but rather through a series of life and work events, starting with their education and entry into the labor market. If African Americans become disproportionately stuck in the secondary labor market or the public sector when they start out, their future earnings will suffer. According to sociologist George Wilson, this is in fact what happens. He claims that a number of ethnographic and quantitative studies have shown that blacks are "channeled into 'race conscious' job functions that are geared to delivering services to low-income African Americans and are removed from mainstream intra-firm career ladders."[26]

Given the importance of career starts, it behooves us to examine the cohort of entrants to the labor market in order to better understand the dynamics of racial inequality in earnings and employment. In fact, it is all the more important to examine younger black workers because they are the ones who have presumably benefited from the civil rights gains of the 1960s. Overall figures may obscure the reality of the situation because they include many older African Americans who launched their careers before the days of "equal opportunity." Among this post-1960s group, research has shown that black women have reached equity with white women, whereas black men have not equaled the earnings and labor market success of their white counterparts (at equivalent levels of schooling).[27]

In trying to explain the labor market difficulties experienced by young African Americans, some theorists have posited that while the quantity of education attained by blacks and whites has more or less equalized, the quality of that education still betrays racial disparities, resulting in a *skills mismatch* between the educational preparation of young African Americans and the increasingly technological nature of the economy.[28] Quality of education is notoriously difficult to measure. One study using expenditures per pupil as an indicator found that the returns to quality of education were similar for blacks and whites among a young cohort (ages seventeen to twenty-six in 1969) in the National Longitudinal Survey of the Labor Force (NLSLF).[29] Using PSID data, another study reported racial differences in the returns to quality of education for the age group thirty to fifty-five (though this research largely examined workers whose careers started in the pre–civil rights era).[30] Some scholars assert that when cognitive skill is accounted for, the effect of race disappears; others, however, dispute this claim.[31] It may also be the case that employers overtly or *statistically* discriminate against African Americans in the hiring process—betting that a white applicant with the same level of educational attainment has enjoyed better schooling and is thus better prepared for the work environment.[32]

Still other theorists argue that in addition to (or in lieu of) a skills mismatch, there exists a *spatial mismatch* between African Americans—who are predominantly concentrated in the inner cities—and the primary-sector job base that is increasingly located in the suburbs. These employment opportunities are not only beyond the geographic reach of most African Americans, who often lack transportation, but also beyond their informational reach.[33] As Christopher Jencks writes in his collection of essays entitled *Rethinking Social Policy,* "Suburban manufacturers do not advertise their vacancies in places where inner-city blacks would learn about them (major metropolitan dailies or the state employment service, for example)."[34] This argument resembles the dual labor market theory, though with a more geographic, spatial flavor. Under this paradigm, residential segregation has a direct impact on the labor market fortunes of African Americans. Evidence has been marshaled showing that part of the earnings gap can be explained by the concentration of black people in central cities[35] or the percentage of black residents in a particular community.[36] A higher percentage of African Americans in a community hurts earnings opportunities for *blacks* more than it does for whites, suggesting not only that companies leave the central cities to search for "whiter" pastures but also that those who remain may statistically discriminate, preferring white residents.

The premise of this chapter is that including assets in the concept of socioeconomic status will help to clarify some of the issues surrounding racial differences in employment and earnings. I anticipate that whites and blacks with equivalent family backgrounds in terms of income and assets (as well as other demographic characteristics) will receive more or less the same rewards from the labor market. Before examining this analysis and its implications, we should first review some of the important mechanisms through which wealth may affect the labor market fortunes of blacks and whites.

WEALTH AND LABOR MARKET FORTUNES

With few exceptions,[37] researchers investigating inequality have focused on the extent to which occupational status and income are inherited, ignoring wealth.[38] Estimates of the heritability of economic status range between 3 and 20 percent, on the low side.[39] If this were the case, it would imply a great deal of upward and downward mobility in

American society: we would be able to explain only 3 to 20 percent of the variation in socioeconomic outcomes for a given generation by examining where the parents of each member of that cohort fell in the distribution of rewards. These initial figures, then, seem rather low, given the general perception about how much socioeconomic background affects our life chances.

In the cause of refining these heritability estimates, researchers have tried to account for all sorts of unobserved variance such as measurement error,[40] response variability,[41] genetic factors,[42] and multiyear income fluctuation.[43] These studies yield intergenerational income correlations of .3 to .5. In short, by focusing on income, researchers have found a maximal inheritance factor of one-half. How can this finding be reconciled with the intergenerational, historical nature of poverty among African Americans in the United States? It may simply be the case that by not incorporating wealth into their paradigms, the authors of the literature on status attainment and human capital have missed a significant amount of variation in families' levels of economic resources. These resources can translate not only into future wealth both within and across generations[44] but also into advantages in employment prospects and labor market earnings.

HOUSING AND VEHICLES

One recent study of a large retail bank showed that, net of many other factors, job applicants who were referred by an individual who already worked for the bank did better at both the interview and job-offer stages of the hiring process.[45] Obviously, it helps to know someone in the loop. But where do such connections come from? In 1973, sociologist Mark Granovetter made a convincing argument that they do not come from intimates such as close friends and family; rather, they come from weaker connections outside the immediate group or "clique."[46] His "strength of weak ties" argument boils down to this: Individuals do not hear about new opportunities from those people with whom they have strong, intimate connections and with whom they interact on a daily basis, since they are all sharing the same information and life experiences. Rather, new opportunities come from those connections that are not reinforced on a regular basis. It may be that cousin in the next county whose business is expanding and who has a job available. Or it could be a woman at a party who talks about a local start-up company that has just begun hiring. In the movie *The Graduate,* the main character gets career advice from a friend of his parents in the form of one word: plastics. In the documentary film *Hoop Dreams,* one of the young men living in urban Chicago lands a position working for the company that produces the *Encyclopedia Britannica.* He learns about the job possibility from the donors of his brother's basketball scholarship, hardly intimate connections.

What is the connection between wealth, racial differences in employment patterns, and this discussion of weak ties? The social networks of weak ties that provide job opportunities may often be spatially organized. Much of the discussion of racial inequality in work and wages has focused on the notion of a spatial mismatch between employers and potential employees. This spatial mismatch matters for two reasons: accessibility of job networks, and accessibility of the jobs themselves. In short, the good jobs and the information about them are increasingly located in the suburbs, while the majority of black individuals reside in urban centers.

Job information can be formal in nature, such as advertisements that are not aimed at inner-city residents, or informal, such as word of mouth. When families own the homes in which they reside, they are most likely live in the suburbs. In turn, living in the suburbs may translate into access to richer networks of weak ties (for example, more word-of-mouth information). For this reason, the transition to homeownership in one generation may be key to solidifying the employment prospects of the next generation. By contrast, if black professionals are not able to purchase homes in the suburbs, their high levels of human and financial capital may do their children less good since the neighborhood social networks to which they enjoy access cannot provide much in the way of useful information and connections for their children's employment prospects. Even for African Americans located in the suburbs, their racially segregated, lower-value areas may provide social networks that yield fewer and less lucrative job opportunities.

In addition to the issue of hearing about a job, there is the issue of getting to it. Given the dispersed nature of suburban sprawl and the lack of adequate public transportation, reaching a job in the suburbs generally requires a car. To a certain extent, this holds true whether the potential worker lives in the city or in the same suburb where the job is located. Where public transportation is a possibility, such commutes may take up several hours a day.[47] Therefore, in addition to home ownership, vehicle ownership may make a difference in labor market outcomes.

The counterpart to the spatial mismatch hypothesis is the skills mismatch hypothesis (and the statistical discrimination corollary). If blacks and whites have similar amounts of education but not similar quality of education, employers would be quite rational—given the limited information with which they have to work—to statistically discriminate against hiring African Americans. They do not even have to do it on the basis of skin color. It is just as easy to assume that an individual who attended an elite private school (more than likely predominantly white) is better qualified than one who attended an inner-city public school. Even the levels of academic training between two public schools may vary greatly depending on where they are located. While the Coleman Report (discussed in Chapter Three) cast doubt on the role of school funding, educational materials, and teacher-to-pupil ratios as explanations for achievement differences between blacks and whites, it did not question the existence of differences in performance between schools— whether or not they are accounted for by these crude measures of quality. Furthermore, differences between school districts with respect to the academic quality of instruction may not matter in the end. As long as employers *think* that the education in a white, suburban neighborhood is better than the education in a black, inner-city one (or even in a black suburban community), it remains rational for them to discriminate against blacks on the basis of schools attended. Again, geography and housing wealth interact to disadvantage African Americans in the labor market.

BUSINESS AND FARM WEALTH

If young adults cannot get jobs through the informal networks of their community, who is their employer of last resort? Among African Americans, it turns out to be the government (which might be the employer of first resort as well). Among other ethnic groups that enjoy a long tradition of small-business ownership, however, it may be the family itself. When children complete their educational careers and cannot find work immediately, they may opt to move back in with their parents (or remain there if they have never left). During the transition from schooling to the wider world, family-based employment may provide an important income source for young adults. Alternatively, working in a family business may be the best employment opportunity that many individuals enjoy. Thus, one would expect children of a family that owns a farm or a business to be less likely to be unemployed, even if working for mom or pop is not their first choice.

But a family cannot provide work to its dependents if it does not have work to provide. Examining small-business ownership, one finds that 425,000 business enterprises were owned (primarily) by African Americans in 1990.[48] This amounts to only 2.4 percent of the total for the nation, meaning that blacks are about one-fifth as likely to be business owners as we might expect, given their numbers in the population. "By and large," writes Andrew Hacker, "black businesses are local concerns, with annual receipts averaging around $50,000."[49] This level of economic activity hardly leaves much room to give children a break by taking them into the business at a reasonable yearly wage. To make matters worse for the employment prospects of young African Americans, only 70,000 of the 425,000 establishments owned by blacks have *any* paid employees.[50] Clearly, African American parents generally lack the business resources to hire their children (or nieces and nephews, for that matter). This, too, should help explain the black-white gap in employment prospects.

LIQUID ASSETS

Liquid assets also may reflect quality differences at the higher levels of education that translate into differential employment and earnings prospects. Since parents are more likely to pay for postsecondary schooling out of assets than out of current income, higher wealth levels may act as a proxy for differences in college quality and prestige. Clearly, someone with a bachelor's degree from Yale or Harvard has greater earnings potential in today's society than someone whose degree is from a lesser-known state school, for instance (whether or not this income differential is justified). To get that elite degree, assets are required. Thus, wealth may affect not only the quantity and perhaps the quality of instruction but also the *perceived* quality of college and graduate schooling.

School prestige, while difficult to measure, may be very important in the eyes of employers making hiring and promotion decisions.

Sociologists Hiroshi Ishida, Seymour Spilerman, and Kuo-Hsien Su offer three possible reasons for this importance: "(1) the graduates of high quality institutions [may] have higher cognitive and noncognitive skills, (2) employers [may] use college quality as a 'signal' of higher productivity, and (3) the graduates of prestigious institutions [may] enjoy advantageous networks and political alliances among alumni."[51] Although these three reasons matter to varying degrees, each would help to explain the black-white employment and earnings gap among college-educated workers, since African Americans tend to attend less prestigious schools than whites (possibly as a result of the financial dynamics discussed in Chapter Three).

With the available PSID data, we cannot gauge the prestige and investment value of the schools attended, but we can assume that higher parental wealth (and particularly liquid assets) may reflect greater opportunities for more elite education. While this is not a direct effect of wealth on employment, it may be a very important indirect effect of assets on employment and earnings prospects.

Additionally, liquid assets may in fact have some direct effects on the occupational fortunes of young adults. For instance, liquid wealth provides an economic cushion against the uncertainty of an increasingly volatile labor market. As researchers John T. Cook and J. Larry Brown explain, "Assets provide a form of insurance against uncertainty, and a way of preparing for future expenses. . . . Assets are a key factor in achieving economic self sufficiency, an essential part of the American value of putting aside resources to protect the family against financial disasters, and preparing children for education and future employment."[52] If a family holds significant levels of liquid assets, it can make these resources available to children in times of need—for instance, as they search for a first job.

The connection to wages is that the longer a person can afford to wait before taking a job, the higher the "reservation wage" that individual can maintain. A reservation wage is the pay rate at which an individual chooses to enter (or exit) the labor force—that is, the minimum price of that person's labor. For instance, suppose that someone is looking for work and is offered a job at $8 an hour and does not take it. Another company then offers this person a comparable job at $9 per hour, and he or she decides to accept the work. We can estimate that this individual's reservation wage is somewhere between $8 and $9 per hour.

Obviously, we cannot estimate a particular individual's reservation wage accurately, but statisticians can approximate it for various groups in society. It may be the case that those young adults with parents who have substantial liquid assets are able to maintain a higher reservation wage. (Of course, raising the reservation wage in this manner would also depress labor force participation, lowering the overall employment rate for the group.) For example, if someone who has just completed school benefits from an informal parental loan to pay the rent, this individual might be able to wait out a rough period in the economy and hold out for a desirable job—a job that might pay substantially more than the first available employment opportunity. Alternatively, having the economic support of parents (provided out of parental assets) might allow an individual to pursue a highly risky career path with potentially great economic rewards—acting, for instance, or starting a business. Because middle-class African American families are more likely to be burdened by debt than to enjoy a comfortable cushion of cash on hand, taking into account levels of liquid wealth may help to explain the black-white wage gap.

DO WHITES WORK MORE FOR HIGHER WAGES?

The strategy followed by this chapter's analysis is to break down the overall earnings discrepancy between blacks and whites into three parts. The first part tackles the question of whether African Americans are more likely than whites to be unemployed or out of the labor force. The second part looks at rates of underemployment—that is, the number of hours worked by those who are working at least sometime during the year. The final part compares wages among those who work full time, addressing the question of whether whites earn more because of the color of their skin.

DIFFERENCES IN UNEMPLOYMENT AND LABOR FORCE PARTICIPATION

In this set of analyses, I confine the comparisons to those individuals who come from families defined as low-income in 1984—that is, who had an annual income in 1984 that was less than 185 percent of the poverty threshold for a typical family of four. This definition is not

arbitrary; rather, it is a line that the government often uses to determine eligibility for programs such as Medicaid insurance.

Lack of monetary need is not likely to be one of the reasons that individuals in this group are not working. Thus, we can avoid confusion
about the direction of the effect of parental class variables such as income and wealth. Among the entire population, by contrast, those
with higher parental wealth may be less likely to work, simply because
they do not have to. Among the poor, with their more limited assets,
wealth would probably have a more positive impact on the tendency
to work. If one already has some stake in the American dream, one is
more likely to participate in the labor market in order to preserve that
stake.

For the outcome measure, I use the dual term "unemployment/labor
force nonparticipation," since it is difficult to tell whether an individual is actively seeking employment (defined as being "unemployed") or
is simply not participating in the labor market at all. Those not participating in the labor force may be doing so out of choice, or they may
be frustrated with repeated attempts to find work. Either way, the end
result is the same: they have not worked all year.

Figure 4.1 shows that, among the offspring of this low-income population, none of the models exhibit any significant racial differences in
the likelihood that one will not be working. While race does not matter, Table 4.1 lists other factors that do have a significant impact. For
example, women are more likely to be out of the labor force or unemployed. Among the class variables (whose relative strengths can be seen
graphically in Figure 4.2), parental wealth lowers the likelihood of un-
employment/labor force nonparticipation,[53] as do higher levels of
parental education (also see Table A4.1). Another factor that appears to
matter—though the causal mechanism may not be apparent—is the
parent's occupational prestige. In this case, the effect is counterintuitive:
the higher the parental prestige, the less likely the respondent is to be
employed.

Two other factors matter in predicting unemployment/labor force nonparticipation status. The first, which has important policy implications, is
parental welfare status. Evidently, coming from a low-income family that
had used welfare in a given year (1984) reduces the likelihood of a young
adult being employed. This finding shows that the conservative line of reasoning regarding perverse incentives may have some validity. Welfare receipt is, however, a much less powerful predictor than other, class-based

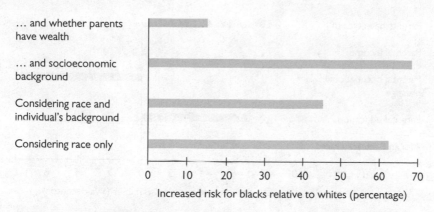

FIGURE 4.1. The effect of being black on the risk of unemployment/labor force nonparticipation in 1992 for sons and daughters of 1984 low-income families, by model type. Lighter bars are statistically equivalent to zero. No model has a significant effect. (See Table A4.1.)

TABLE 4.1
VARIABLES PREDICTING UNEMPLOYMENT/
LABOR FORCE NONPARTICIPATION
BY DESCENDING ORDER OF
PREDICTIVE IMPORTANCE

1. *Female respondent*
2. *Parents had assets in 1984*
3. *Parent's occupational prestige (head of household)*
4. *Parent's education (head of household)*
5. *Parents received welfare in 1984*
6. *Number of siblings*
7. Respondent graduated from high school
8. Parents' permanent income
9. Parent's age (head of household)
10. Female-headed parental household (1980–84)
11. African American race
12. Respondent graduated from college

NOTE: Italic type indicates statistical significance at the $p < .10$ level; see Table A4.1.

variables. (Meanwhile, coming from a female-headed parental household does not seem to matter directly.) The other significantly predictive factor is number of siblings; coming from a larger family reduces the odds of being out of the labor force or unemployed. This may be a result of the greater financial responsibilities that individuals from larger families face

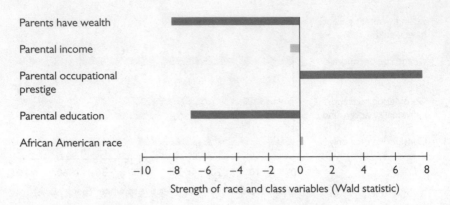

FIGURE 4.2. The relative effects of race and class on the risk of unemployment/labor force nonparticipation in 1992 for sons and daughters of 1984 low-income families. Darker bars are statistically discernible from zero; lighter bars are statistically equivalent to zero. If low-income parents have some assets, their offspring are less likely to be unemployed or out of the labor force. Higher levels of parental education among this group also reduce the risk of being without a job, although higher parental occupational prestige increases it. (See Table A4.1.)

if they are needed to help to support their siblings. Alternatively, those persons from larger families may have wider job networks.

DIFFERENCES IN UNDEREMPLOYMENT

This set of analyses focuses on those of both races who are employed, examining how much they work in a given year. If measuring employment status during a given period provides a "snapshot" of a person's economic trajectory, measuring the level of work activity over the course of an entire year provides something akin to an entire "videotape." Many workers, particularly those on the margins of the labor market, may shift in and out of employment on a seasonal or cyclical basis. They might work full time during certain periods, part time during others, and not at all at still other times. This fluid conception of work status jibes well with the visual imagery of the job queue theory of employment discussed earlier in the chapter. Census data has shown that African Americans are more likely than whites to be unemployed in a given week and that those black workers who do have jobs are

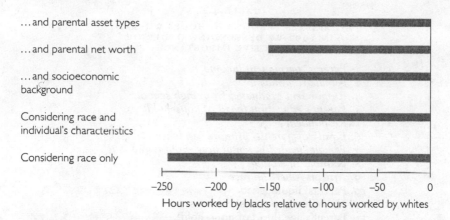

...and parental asset types

...and parental net worth

...and socioeconomic background

Considering race and individual's characteristics

Considering race only

-250   -200   -150   -100   -50   0

Hours worked by blacks relative to hours worked by whites

FIGURE 4.3. The effect of being black on hours worked in 1992, by model type. Darker bars are statistically discernible from zero. African Americans were employed for significantly fewer hours than whites when compared only by race. Considering class reduces this effect, but blacks are still underemployed even when background differences (including wealth) are factored out. (See Table A4.2.)

likely to be employed for fewer hours ("underemployed").[54] These two phenomena are not unrelated: low wages in combination with underemployment may lead black workers to become discouraged and drop out of the labor market.

In light of the fluidity of work status, I chose to examine those individuals who worked at least one hour in the year, thus indicating at least a minimal commitment to the labor force. Among this group, young African Americans worked significantly fewer hours than young whites when compared solely on the basis of race. This difference is on the order of 245 hours per year, or more than seven fewer weeks of work (based on a 35-hour work week). This difference is statistically significant and is represented graphically by the base model in Figure 4.3 (also see Table A4.2). When socioeconomic background differences (as traditionally conceived) are equalized, this gap in work hours narrows slightly, but not by much, to about 183 hours per year. This black-white differential remains statistically significant (see the third bar of Figure 4.3).

When parental wealth forms part of the measure of social class, the deficit among blacks in hours worked drops even more, to just over 150 hours. In the final bar of Figure 4.3, the asset type model, the

TABLE 4.2

VARIABLES PREDICTING HOURS WORKED
IN 1992 BY DESCENDING ORDER OF
PREDICTIVE IMPORTANCE

1. *Parents' permanent income*
2. *Female respondent*
3. *Respondent graduated from high school*
4. *Parent's education (head of household)*
5. *Respondent's age*
6. *Equity of parents' primary residence*
7. *Female-headed parental household (1980–84)*
8. *Number of siblings*
9. *African American race*
10. Parents' liquid assets
11. Net value of parents' business
12. Parent's age (head of household)
13. Net value of parents' other illiquid assets
14. Parent's occupational prestige (head of household)
15. Parents received welfare in 1984
16. Respondent graduated from college

NOTE: Italic type indicates statistical significance at the $p < .10$ level; see
Table A4.2.

racial difference increases slightly. In the full model, as indicated in
Table 4.2, females work less. Older respondents (within the relatively
narrow age band considered) work more hours, presumably because
of greater work force experience, as do respondents who have completed high school. Coming from a large family tends to increase the
number of hours an individual works (for the same reasons elucidated
in the preceding section), whereas coming from a female-headed
household reduces the number of hours worked (perhaps because of
greater time commitments to the family of origin, in the form of help-
ing out a single mother at home).

As Figure 4.4 illustrates, parental income actually has a negative effect on hours worked when asset levels are taken into consideration,
whereas net worth has a positive effect. Ways in which wealth might
have a positive impact on the number of hours worked have already
been suggested. But what to make of the negative effect of parental income? Throughout this book, I have emphasized that income and
wealth are conceptually distinct, a tenet that holds true here, where they
act in opposite directions. With this in mind, we might speculate that the
negative effect of income reflects attitudinal differences. Given that we
are comparing families with similar education, age, and family structure,

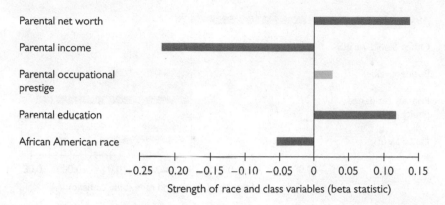

FIGURE 4.4. The relative effects of race and class on hours worked in 1992. Darker bars are statistically discernible from zero; lighter bars are statistically equivalent to zero. Those respondents with better-educated parents and those with higher parental net worth tend to work more hours; African American race and higher parental income both reduce the number of hours worked. Income and wealth, therefore, work in opposite directions. (See Table A4.2.)

it may be that those individuals whose parents have high income flows do not need to work as much themselves. This effect would appear to be distinct from the opportunity-enhancing effects of assets and perhaps even the greater work/savings ethic implied in families that have accumulated sizable wealth holdings. Also, a sizable number of the younger respondents may still live at home. In such a situation, a lower family income might serve as an incentive for them to contribute more to the household and thus work more hours. This account is circumstantially reinforced by the analysis of wages in the next section; however, it should be reiterated that this causal account is speculation and requires direct testing.

Besides income, other class variables that matter include parental education (positively associated with hours worked), again implying the possibility of attitudinal dynamics. When we break out wealth into asset types, shown in Figure 4.5, we find that primary residence equity has a positive impact on hours worked, suggesting the importance of spatial dynamics in the labor market, as discussed earlier in the chapter. In the end, however, being black does have a net negative effect on the amount of employment, though it is much smaller than the class effect (and the effect of other background factors) and is only marginally statistically significant ($p < .10$).

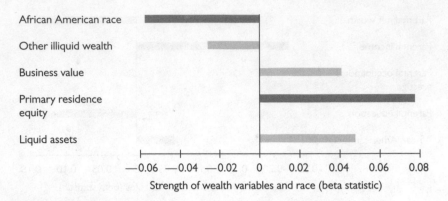

FIGURE 4.5. The relative effects of wealth by type on hours worked in 1992. Darker bars are statistically discernible from zero; lighter bars are statistically equivalent to zero. Of the various types of parental wealth, the value of a family's home positively affects how much offspring work when they become adults, suggesting support for spatial (neighborhood) dynamics. (See Table A 4.2.)

DIFFERENCES IN WAGES

The earnings gap between blacks and whites can be broken down into the likelihood of being employed at all, the number of hours worked by those who are employed, and the wage rate. There does not seem to be a significant racial difference among low-income individuals in the likelihood of being employed, although there does appear to be a net difference in the number of hours worked. This analysis focuses on the third question: do the group of post–civil rights African Americans who are employed full time earn less per hour? Initially, the answer seems to be an obvious yes. Other researchers have already documented that the incomes of African Americans are significantly lower than those of whites. This difference cannot be entirely accounted for by the lower number of weeks that blacks are able to work per year. In fact, in *Rethinking Social Policy,* Christopher Jencks presents the black-white ratio of weeks worked and that of "income per adult." Combining these ratios yields the statistic that blacks still earned only 72 cents per adult per dollar earned by whites for the weeks worked in the given year (1989).[55] Jencks's work and other researchers' analyses do not break out the youngest cohort of workers, however, which may be important if much of the wage gap is a result of differences among older workers.

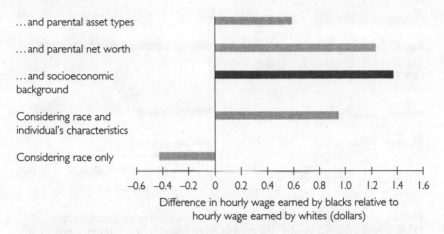

FIGURE 4.6. The effect of being black on 1992 hourly wages, by model type. Darker bars are statistically discernible from zero; lighter bars are statistically equivalent to zero. When socioeconomic background is equalized, young African Americans who work full time enjoy a wage advantage over their white counterparts; this advantage becomes insignificant, however, when the depressive effects of parental wealth are taken into consideration. (See Table A4.3.)

The data presented here confirm this. In the first bar of Figure 4.6 (the base model), young African Americans who were employed full time earned less than whites per hour worked, but this difference is not statistically significant (also see Table A4.3). When parental socioeconomic status is held constant, however, this effect actually flips direction, becoming significantly positive: when SES is factored out, African Americans earn almost $1.42 more per hour than their white counterparts. This finding that African Americans who are employed full time may earn more per hour than whites (depending on the model) provides a possible explanation for the net negative effect of being black on hours worked. Classic economic theory predicts that when an individual or group receives higher wages, part of this wage benefit will be used to "buy" leisure time—that is, to work fewer hours.

When we control for assets and asset types, this African American advantage ebbs and loses significance. This is because parental wealth actually has a negative effect on wages, contrary to the prediction that it facilitates access to higher-paying jobs. Perhaps coming from a family that has greater wealth obviates the need to take the highest-paying job

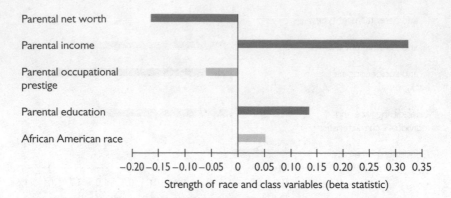

FIGURE 4.7. The relative effects of race and class on 1992 hourly wages. Darker bars are statistically discernible from zero; lighter bars are statistically equivalent to zero. Higher levels of parental education and parental income increase the hourly wages of young full-time workers, whereas parental net worth reduces wages. (See Table A4.3.)

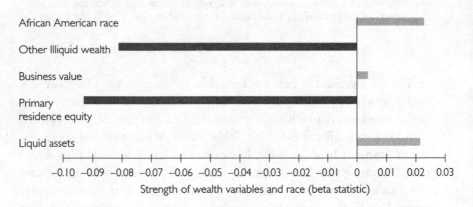

FIGURE 4.8. The relative effects of wealth by type on 1992 hourly wages. Darker bars are statistically discernible from zero; lighter bars are statistically equivalent to zero. Of the wealth variables, primary residence equity has the strongest effect in depressing wage levels. (See Table A4.3.)

and allows a young adult to pursue a less traditional, less well-paying career path such as that of artist, writer, teacher, and so on. Figure 4.7 shows that parental permanent income has the strongest positive impact on wages. Parental education is also positively associated with the wage rate, whereas parental occupational prestige is negatively associated.

TABLE 4.3

VARIABLES PREDICTING HOURLY
WAGES AMONG FULL-TIME WORKERS
IN 1992 BY DESCENDING ORDER
OF PREDICTIVE IMPORTANCE

1. *Parents' permanent income*
2. *Respondent's age*
3. *Respondent graduated from college*
4. *Female respondent*
5. *Parent's education (head of household)*
6. *Equity of parents' primary residence*
7. *Net value of parents' other illiquid assets*
8. *Respondent graduated from high school*
9. *Parent's occupational prestige (head of household)*
10. Parent's age (head of household)
11. Parents received welfare in 1984
12. African American race
13. Number of siblings
14. Parents' liquid assets
15. Female-headed parental household (1980–84)
16. Net value of parents' business

NOTE: Italic type indicates statistical significance at the $p < .10$ level; see Table A4.3.

Finally, Figure 4.8 shows that among the manifestations of wealth, primary residence equity is what matters most in depressing wages of the next generation, while other illiquid wealth also has a deleterious effect, albeit smaller in magnitude. Among the respondent's own characteristics listed in Table 4.3, the strongest predictor is age: older individuals, who have spent more time accruing experience in the labor market, have higher earnings. Female respondents earn less than male respondents. Graduating from college provides a significant wage boost, as does high school graduation.

SUMMARY

Let us piece together these three sets of findings. African Americans from low-income families are no less likely than whites—overall or net of class variables—to be employed. Those who work at least one hour in a given year tend to work a lot fewer hours than whites do, even when class is taken into consideration. This may in part be a response to African Americans' higher net wage rate, through what economists call a "substitution" effect, substituting leisure for additional income.

The bottom line with respect to race is that there is no bottom line: higher wages for African Americans are certainly a surprising finding and may indicate the effects of affirmative action policy. Future researchers with larger datasets should examine the question of which groups of African Americans are enjoying this wage benefit net of class background—for example, those with higher educations who come from well-off families or those who do not enjoy these socioeconomic advantages. In fact, in his book *Markets and Minorities,* conservative economist Thomas Sowell has argued that if affirmative action helps at all, it aids well-off minorities.[56]

Fewer work hours may reflect this higher wage, or they may reflect racial differences in the ability to attain full employment. Further clouding the issue is the fact that the causal mechanisms of certain SES and wealth variables are not entirely clear. Work is a difficult topic to predict and analyze, since individuals may *want* to work (or not) or, alternatively, they may *have* to work (or not). Parental economic resources may have opposite effects on each of these tendencies. It is important to keep in mind, however, that the magnitude of any racial effect is dwarfed by the effects of social class indicators.

In sum, the analysis presented in this chapter shows that young African Americans start their careers at a sizable disadvantage in comparison to their white counterparts. It also demonstrates, however, that this disadvantage may not be entirely racial in nature but instead may contain a significant economic component. The title of this chapter is a reasonable analogy for the situation of young African Americans: they are going up the down escalator—that is, although occupational differences are more attributable to class than to race, they are persistent nonetheless, given the distribution of parental income, wealth, and other forms of socioeconomic status. Because the jobs held by this set of respondents are likely to be the first career-line jobs of these individuals (who have recently entered the labor market), they are particularly important in predicting later occupational and earnings outcomes.

There remains much room for future researchers to examine the mechanisms by which higher parental social class helps offspring to get off on the right start toward a successful career in the primary labor market. Deeper understanding may require in-depth, qualitative methodology to uncover how advantages are provided in the transition from the educational system to the occupational system. For now, however, certain implications are becoming clear. As suggested by the previous chapter's analysis of education, we must question whether race-based social policy in hiring may be misguided, for it is the economic disadvantage of African American families that dominates over purely racial effects. Chapter Six gives detailed attention to the issue of affirmative action in the context of the race-class debate. But first, Chapter Five addresses two other realms of life that are not unrelated to economic well-being: family structure and welfare dependency.

CHAPTER FIVE

It Takes a Village?

Premarital Childbearing and Welfare Dependency

> . . . Get place and wealth—if possible with grace;
> . . . If not, by any means get wealth and place.
> *Ben Jonson, 1573–1637*

In the 1990s, two-thirds of African American children are born out of wedlock. Not unrelated to this fact, more than half of all black families are headed by women—that is, there is no male adult "officially" present in the household. Andrew Hacker writes that these percentages "are from three to five times higher than those for white households and markedly higher than those recorded for black Americans a generation ago."[1] Why do such statistics matter? Maybe being officially wed makes little difference to the well-being of African American individuals; perhaps having a mother and a grandmother as caregivers is no worse than the duo of a mother and a father. Or perhaps it is the case that—as some anthropologists claim—African American men are consistently undercounted in household surveys. Even if such speculations were to prove true, however, statistics regarding single parenthood and female-headed families would remain important for two reasons.

First, researchers have consistently shown that young women, either black or white, who bear children out of wedlock or raise them without a husband are more likely to have deleterious life outcomes. Further, the children raised by single mothers face the same increased risks as their mothers and also have a greater likelihood of becoming single parents themselves, thus perpetuating the "cycle of illegitimacy."[2] Demographers Neil Bennett, David Bloom, and Cynthia Miller summarize the research literature by stating that "a long line of academic research has documented strong associations between non-marital teenage childbearing and low levels of completed schooling, earnings and family income, increased likelihoods of being poor or on welfare, and future marital instability."[3] There is some debate as to whether the effects of nonmarital childbearing are artifacts of unmeasured, confounding socioeconomic differences—that is, the group of women who have children as teenagers and out of wedlock may be those who face a greater likelihood of being undereducated, poor, or on welfare in any case, regardless of the birth of their children.

Researchers Arline Geronimus and Sanders Korenman are the most vocal proponents of the hypothesis that the apparent relationship between negative life outcomes (for both the mother and the child) and marital status at the time of childbirth is an illusion. They use sister comparisons to document that much of the statistical relationship between these two factors is eliminated when family characteristics are taken into account. By comparing sisters from the same family—one who had a child when she was unmarried and young and one who had a child when she was older and married—they are better able to factor out unobserved differences in the population and determine the "true" effect of being older and married when having a child. When this technique is used, the negative impact of nonmarital childbearing is reduced, although it is not eliminated.[4] Others dispute these results, finding a larger negative effect when using the same strategy of sister comparisons with data from the Panel Study of Income Dynamics.[5] Regardless of whether the link between out-of-wedlock childbearing and deleterious socioeconomic outcomes is causal or merely associative, premarital fertility remains an important social indicator, a proxy, for negative life outcomes.

Second, statistics on single parenthood and female-headed families are important for political reasons. These statistics are particularly charged because of their relationship to the issue of welfare (whether they are truly causal or merely correlated). Single mothers are more likely to be on welfare than are married couples with children; in addition, the offspring of single parents have a greater chance of being on welfare themselves when they become adults.[6] For example, among a sample of recipients of Aid to Families with Dependent Children (AFDC) who were less than thirty years old, Robert Haveman and Barbara Wolfe report that "three-quarters first gave birth as a teenager, in most cases out of wedlock."[7] Still other costs, such as food stamps and Medicaid health insurance, are also associated with single parenthood. In 1990, the Center for Population Options estimated that "about $22 billion is paid annually through AFDC, food stamps, and Medicaid to [unwed] teenage mothers. Each family that began with a birth to a teenager will cost the public an average of about $17,000 in some form of support over the next 20 years."[8]

Because these figures may seem large, they add fuel to the political fire over welfare spending. The truth is, however, that AFDC always constituted only a small portion of overall social spending, as does its current successor, Temporary Assistance to Needy Families (TANF). "Even though low-income public assistance programs accounted for less than 18 percent of federal social spending, far less than the proportions for Social Security and Medicare," according to Theda Skocpol, "these welfare programs took the brunt of the Reagan efforts to trim the 'social pork barrel.'"[9] When we view these cost-cutting efforts in light of the fact that African American women are more likely than white women to have an out-of-wedlock birth as a teenager and also to experience more frequent and longer periods of reliance on welfare, it should be no surprise that discussion about the "safety net" becomes the most heated—yet the most veiled—area of debate about race and poverty.[10]

RACIAL DIFFERENCES IN FAMILY STRUCTURE

THE HISTORICAL VIEW

Research about racial differences in family structure has been highly politicized from its onset. Scholars of various disciplines have attempted to explain why African American marriage rates are lower than those of white Americans, why nonmarital births as well as divorce are more common among African Americans, and why African Americans are more likely to live in extended households (that is, with individuals who are not members of their immediate family).

Since the turn of the century, many historians and social theorists have described how centuries of slavery disrupted the traditional kinship structure of formerly African families. Writers such as W. E. B. Du Bois, in his books *The Philadelphia Negro* and *The Negro American Family*, argued that white slaveowners had stripped the black man of his familial authority, and the result was the disruption of black family units.[11] In other words, the humiliation and emasculation that male slaves faced at the hands of plantation owners destroyed the corner-stone of the family: the patriarch. According to the logic of Du Bois and other scholars such as E. Franklin Frazier, Stanley Elkins, and Gunnar Myrdal, this destruction of traditional kinship ties in the antebellum South is the key factor that led to the "disorganized" kinship patterns observed among African American families in the twentieth century.[12] (Recently available census data suggests that sizable differences in family structure between blacks and whites go back at least as far as the beginning of this century.)[13]

Perhaps the most famous rendering of this historical legacy thesis is that of now-Senator Daniel Patrick Moynihan, whose 1965 report at the U.S. Department of Labor asserted that slavery had caused the development of a matriarchal community in which the strong personalities of black women (an adaptation to slavery conditions) contributed to the erosion of the male role in the family structure.[14] As a result of this "matriarchy," according to Moynihan, few stable nuclear families could form, and a "tangle of pathology" developed. This version of the slavery story placed the black matriarch in the role of determining African American family structure. Further, an underlying assertion of the Moynihan report was that the socioeconomic conditions faced by African American families in late-twentieth-century America were the result of this disjointed family structure—and in particular the role of black women.

Now largely discredited, Moynihan's report received immediate criticism from scholars who contended that he had reversed the causal order—that in fact it was the ongoing effect of the disadvantageous socioeconomic circumstances of black Americans that caused the organization or disorganization of their family units. In addition, these scholars criticized the social-psychological component of the Moynihan argument, which attributed black family structure to the temperament of African American women.

To support their attacks on Moynihan's thesis, social historians of the 1970s documented the fact that stable nuclear households did exist during slavery, contrary to the assertions of Moynihan, Frazier, and others. For example, Robert Fogel and Stanley Engerman argued that such households were tolerated and perhaps even encouraged by some plantation owners in order to facilitate more efficient production by slaves.[15] Eugene Genovese asserted that the "matriarchy" Moynihan ascribed to the slavery era is more accurately characterized as a situation of relative sexual equity.[16] Perhaps the most persuasive counterargument was offered by Herbert Gutman's *The Black Family in Slavery and Freedom,* in which he analyzed plantation birth records, marriage applications, and census data for the period between 1880 and 1925. Gutman concluded that the dual-parent household was the dominant family type during slavery and that a majority of postslavery African Americans lived in nuclear families.[17]

Another piece of evidence suggesting that a historical dynamic cannot explain contemporary black-white differences in family structure is the finding that the intergenerational transmission of divorce is greater among white families than among African American ones[18]—that is, whether or not one's parents are divorced matters more for whites than for blacks in predicting one's own risk of divorce. If the kinship patterns of the nineteenth century explained the higher rates of family instability among African Americans today, one would expect the reverse dynamic: a stronger intergenerational legacy, or inheritance, of family patterns among blacks than among whites. The evidence that intergenerational transmission of family structure is actually weaker among black families (at least in the case of divorce) by no means eliminates the possibility that history matters, but it does weaken the case.

Further, if there is a cultural legacy of the slavery experience that impedes the formation of stable marriages and nuclear families, it certainly is not showing up in the attitudes or intentions that black Americans are expressing to survey researchers in late-twentieth-century America. Family researcher and social commentator Robert Staples finds that African Americans tend to report more conservative, more traditional views of family life than do whites.[19] Other scholars have found that black subjects are most likely to rate their families as their greatest source of life satisfaction.[20]

During the same period in which historians and social psychologists were attacking the legacy of slavery thesis, sociologists and anthropologists were reexamining the causal ordering that Moynihan and others had implied. In the 1970s, some researchers asserted that racial differences in family structure are greatly reduced when socioeconomic characteristics are held constant. Specifically, scholars argued that economic pressures—not cultural patterns—caused African Americans to form nonnuclear family arrangements.[21] For example, sociologists Ronald Angel and Marta Tienda demonstrated that it is during specific times of acute economic hardship that many poor African Americans (and whites) extend the borders of their households, taking in extended family members or unrelated individuals.[22] If a historically based dynamic accounted for a propensity to live in nonnuclear settings, we would not expect living arrangements to be so responsive to the temporary economic fortunes of the family. In her ethnography of poor black women in a midwestern city, Carol Stack documented how such family strategies work to aid survival. When income flows are uncertain, as they are for poor African Americans, a wider informal insurance network is needed—that is, the risk pool must expand; hence the development of nonnuclear kinship structures. Within these kinship structures, individuals can "swap" time (for child care), goods (such as food, clothes, or furniture), and cash. "This powerful obligation to exchange," writes Stack, "is a profoundly creative adaptation to poverty."[23]

Given the overrepresentation of African Americans among the ranks of the poor throughout the history of the United States, it would make sense that racial differences in family patterns may be related more to socioeconomic circumstances than to cultural legacies. Nevertheless, racial differences persist even after socioeconomic background (as traditionally conceived) is equalized. But are these remaining racial differences the result of slavery-induced culture? In an apparent compromise in the debate over historical forces versus socioeconomic characteristics, demographer Steven Ruggles used a newly developed census dataset (the Integrated Public Use Microdata Series, or IPUMS) to show that the most dramatic changes in African American family structure have occurred since 1960. He writes that "among blacks, the percentage of single-parent households was relatively stable from 1880 through 1960, and then it increased sharply." Meanwhile, "the percentage of extended households among blacks was also fairly stable between 1880 and 1960, but has dropped significantly since then." Ruggles concludes that "from 1880 through 1980, divergence between black and white household composition increased. . . . Thus, although the origins of the characteristic pattern of black household composition can be traced to the nineteenth century, race differences have become far more pronounced over the course of the twentieth century."[24]

THE CURRENT DEBATES

Most scholars agree that racial differences in family structure have increased most dramatically over the past thirty years. To account for these changes, many conservative theorists, such as Charles Murray, blame changes in welfare policy. In *Losing Ground*, Murray tried to demonstrate that an increase in welfare payments generated "perverse incentives" for low-income women not to marry, in favor of having children on their own.[25] Prior to welfare changes in the 1960s, Murray argued, the economic benefits associated with out-of-wedlock child-bearing were slim in contrast to the stigma costs that accompanied it. But by the end of that decade, he claimed, the scales had tipped the other way.

Murray cited two specific developments in welfare policy. First, the sixties saw a loosening of restrictions on who was eligible for benefits. In 1968, for example, the U.S. Supreme Court struck down the "man in the house" rule, ending the practice of having welfare workers pay surprise visits to AFDC recipients in order to determine whether they were living with a man (who was assumed to be a potential source of support). With this change in policy, women no longer had to choose between receiving welfare and having a male partner; they could have both as long as the man was not legally responsible for raising the woman's children (that is, as long as they were not married)—hence the legal incentive for low-income individuals not to wed. Second, Murray asserted that, as a result of the War on Poverty, the dollar amounts of welfare benefits increased over the 1960s and 1970s, even when adjusting for inflation. This rise in the financial attractiveness of welfare accompanied—and, according to Murray, caused—a simultaneous rise in out-of-wedlock births. In Murray's scheme, the connection to race is the following: because African Americans are more likely to be at the bottom of the income distribution, where such calculations about welfare and marriage matter, they are disproportionately affected by the incentives for having children outside marriage that are engendered by the increased welfare benefits and the revised regulations.

Some circumstantial evidence can be marshaled to support Murray's claim. For example, demographers Zenchao Qian and Samuel Preston found that the declines in marriage among the poorly educated, a group in which African Americans are overrepresented, "reflect a substitution of cohabitation for formal marriage." Further, "most of the decline in marriage rates in the 1972 to 1987 period would be eliminated if cohabiting couples were included in the numerator . . . of marriage rates."[26] In other words, people in general are increasingly living together rather than getting married, and this is particularly true among

African Americans. The link to welfare policy does not necessarily follow, however. It may be that welfare is driving this substitution of cohabitation for marriage, but the fact that this substitution is occurring in all socioeconomic groups (not only among low-income couples) suggests that it also reflects some wider cultural change that extends beyond the issue of welfare—for instance, the sexual revolution or the widespread use of birth control pills.[27]

Staying within Murray's logic, however, we might expect that what goes up should come down: if rising welfare benefits led to higher rates of cohabitation and out-of-wedlock births, then lower benefit levels should lead to the reverse trend. The 1980s were a period of retrenchment in government spending. Correspondingly, inflation-adjusted welfare benefits dropped in value, and eligibility restrictions were tightened. "By 1991, average benefits available to a mother and two children had fallen to $7,777, down from about $10,600 in 1972," note Haveman and Wolfe; however, rates of single parenthood failed to fall below 1972 levels.[28] Further eroding Murray's case, David Ellwood and Mary Jo Bane compared welfare benefit levels across states and found no relationship between the generosity of welfare payments and the rate of out-of-wedlock births.[29] In light of both these findings, Murray's line of reasoning seems weak at best.

Other researchers have cited demographic differences between the African American and white populations as an explanation of differences in family structure. Research has demonstrated that the sex ratio in a community can have an impact on the rate of marriage formation (as opposed to nonmarital childbearing). The sex ratio is expressed as the number of males per 100 females; studies have shown that a balanced ratio (somewhere between 95 and 105) leads to more frequent and more stable marital unions than a ratio that is skewed in either direction.[30] One analysis of census data found that, after accounting for the traditional difference in age between men and women at time of first marriage (men usually being two years older than women), the black population contained relatively fewer eligible black men per 100 women.[31] In part, this is because African American men experience the highest mortality rates (and shortest life expectancy) of any racial or gender group. Further, they also face the highest risk of incarceration or institutionalization, and they are more likely to have joined the military than their white counterparts, making participation in the civilian marriage market difficult at best.

While there is no doubt that these demographic differences do exist between the black and white communities, the sex ratio approach has yielded mixed results. One study that examined Louisiana parishes (counties) and also looked at the 1980 National Survey of Black Americans reported that the sex ratio was predictive of women's—but not men's—rates of marriage and divorce.[32] Researchers Daniel Lichter, Diane McLaughlin, George Kephart, and David Landy, who directly addressed the issue of black-white differences in the propensity to marry, demonstrated that while the sex ratio is a strong predictor of marital unions, "racial differences in mate availability account for a relatively small share of existing racial differences in marriage."[33]

William Julius Wilson and Kathryn Neckerman combined the work of demographers with their own study on the economic transformation of the inner city to construct a marriageability index, counting only civilian men who are gainfully employed per 100 women. Their premise is that, within the contemporary American social landscape, the male partner must be employed if a stable marriage is to form. Following this line of reasoning, Wilson and Neckerman cited a decline in the number of available blue-collar jobs in the inner cities as a cause of the increased divergence between black and white family structure over the past thirty years.[34]

Other researchers who have tested the effect of black male employment rates on the incidence of marriage (and, by inverse association, the rate of out-of-wedlock births) report mixed results. Mark Testa and Marilyn Krogh, in a study of inner-city Chicago, found that although black male employment is positively related to the likelihood of marriage, "increases in black male joblessness . . . do not fully explain declines in the incidence of marriage. The hypothesis of stable marriage rates, controlling for employment status, is rejected."[35] Testa also reported similar results in a study of a nationally representative sample.[36] Likewise, work using data from the state of Wisconsin showed that marriage rates for black individuals were lower than those for whites even when labor market compositional effects were held equal.[37] Assessing the impact of community characteristics such as the sex ratio is difficult, however. For instance, it is hard to know what the relevant marriage market is. Is it the local neighborhood as indicated by census tract or zip code, or is it the greater metropolitan area? Or does assortive mating take place on a national level? The answer probably varies depending on the subgroup under discussion.

Given the limitations of the demographic and employment approaches in explaining contemporary racial differences in family structure, perhaps property ownership is an additional factor worth considering. In fact, family structure has repeatedly been shown to be an important determinant of wealth accumulation and receipt of private transfers (gifts).[38] On average, married couples have greater asset levels than single-parent families, extended-family households, or couples who are cohabiting. Of all family types, those headed by single mothers have the lowest net wealth holdings; of this group, never-married women with children have the lowest net wealth. Of all families with children, single-mother families have the lowest median wealth level: zero—that is, at least half of all single mothers with children have no net assets or are in debt. Even when we break down these statistics by income bracket (thus accounting for the lower income levels of female-headed households), sizable differences in average wealth levels by family type remain.[39] While this is strong evidence that family structure may help to determine wealth levels, the converse may be true as well: (parental) assets may predict family structure. Given that the large differences in net worth by race appear to overlay onto wealth disparities by family type, it is reasonable to suspect that assets may be playing a causal role in generating black-white differences in family structure. The following sections explore several specific reasons why wealth may help to explain racial differences in marriage formation and nonmarital childbearing.

ASSETS, MARRIAGE, AND PREMARITAL CHILDBEARING

What does it take to get married? At the most basic level, it probably requires only a few dollars for a license, a witness, a judge or religious figure, and of course two willing participants. In practice, however, marriage is a time of transition from the family of origin to the family of destination. It involves not only forming new kinship bonds but also setting up a new household. Setting up a household, in turn, requires resources. Indeed, American families rely on informal transfers and assistance from a wide range of sources.[40] As stated earlier, wealth is the stuff transfers are made of. Whereas income goes to maintain a given level of consumption, wealth serves as the reserve stock from which generous parents, grandparents, aunts, and uncles draw to provide a prospective new family with a no-interest loan to finance an engagement ring, for example, or a wedding, or even a home. In theory, none of this is required for a marriage, but social norms are strong. Living in the parental home as a single, teenage mother is one thing, but living with one's parents as a married family unit is quite another. Therefore, anything that helps to facilitate the formation of independent household units, such as parental wealth, should encourage marital unions (and thereby discourage nonmarital births).

In addition to the role that parental wealth and private transfers may play in promoting marriage, assets may also have an effect by discouraging teenage, or premarital, childbearing. (I use the term "premarital childbearing" to refer specifically to unwed teenage mothers, as distinguished from the more general issue of nonmarital childbearing by women of various ages.) When we view family choices from the point of view of a rational teenage girl, we assume that she knows the extent to which she gains and loses by having a baby before she is married. But, as Haveman and Wolfe note,

> the full opportunity costs associated with the foregone earnings and marriage possibilities attributed to the nonmarital birth are likely to be understated. On the other hand, the potential psychological benefits of having a child of one's own may be glamorized and exaggerated. Because the information available to teenagers is likely to be poor and asymmetrical, their decisions may tend to be biased toward conceiving and bearing children out of wedlock.[41]

By acting as the tangible manifestation of potentially foregone opportunities, parental wealth may help a teenager to more easily recognize the costs associated with bearing a child out of wedlock. By contrast, a teenager who sees in her own family few material benefits for which to strive or which she might want to provide to her own offspring has less reason to wait for marriage before having children. In other words, the dream of a marriage, a house, and a car may be a lot less attractive without the house and the car. Further, parental assets can also *reflect* parental attitudes that emphasize responsibility. This sense of responsibility may result from, or be indicated by, savings behavior and wealth accumulation. In turn, research has shown that parental values that emphasize responsibility reduce the risk of teenagers bearing children out of wedlock.[42]

An alternative to the rational choice model of premarital childbearing is the contagion theory. This approach suggests that teenagers are more likely to behave in a certain way if they see this behavior enacted among their peers. For instance, in one of the first quantitative studies

of the determinants of premarital childbearing, Dennis Hogan and
Evelyn Kitagawa found that having a sister who had borne a child out
of wedlock significantly increased one's own odds of doing the same.[43]
Other studies report that, net of individual characteristics, adolescents
who live in disadvantaged neighborhoods (areas with low average levels of socioeconomic status and high rates of teenage childbearing) are
more likely to have a child as an unmarried teenager.[44] The link to
parental wealth is the same as it was for education: housing wealth is
strongly related to neighborhood quality. Thus, owning a home in a
well-off neighborhood exposes a teenager to a set of social norms about
having children outside marriage that are quite different from the
norms in an economically devastated, inner-city community.

ASSETS AND WELFARE

Much recent research on welfare use has focused on the intergenerational transmission of economic dependency. During the early 1980s,
scholars began to worry that an "underclass" was developing within
American society. This group, first depicted in the public imagination
by journalist Ken Auletta, was characterized by persistent poverty, high
rates of unemployment, and, most controversially, deviance from mainstream American values.[45] Some argued that this underclass had developed attitudes and life practices that defied those held by the majority
of society, such as thrift, hard work, self-reliance, and honesty; this
growing moral divergence could be seen in the rising crime rates of
inner-city neighborhoods and the patterns of long-term welfare dependency that sometimes spanned generations.

Over the course of the 1980s and early 1990s, scholars debated
whether such a unified group existed beyond the imagination of jour-
nalists and moral polemicists. One line of research examined the intergenerational transmission of welfare dependency. Several studies in this
vein found that, net of other background factors, there was an increased likelihood of an individual using public assistance as an adult
if he or she had grown up in a household that received welfare.[46] The
connection to parental wealth is manifold. One aspect is legal: although
many regulations regarding welfare were loosened during the 1960s
and 1970s, the ones pertaining to asset ownership were not. Thus, by
definition, those individuals who grew up in welfare-dependent households also grew up in families that had no net worth. Previous research

has not adequately teased out these two intergenerational dynamics to determine which has more causal impact.

Parental net worth may also affect an individual's likelihood of receiving welfare in other very direct ways. When income flows stop for a period of time, parental assets can act as a personal safety net, preventing or at least delaying reliance on the governmental safety net. The ability to draw on a pool of resources to ride out rough financial times serves as an economic buffer, promoting stable, economically self-sufficient families across generations. Conversely, a lack of parental or self-owned assets can put a strain on a family that may lead to welfare dependency after a particularly rough time. As Michael Sherraden explains:

> Let us take the most common type of income shock—the loss of a regular job. When unemployment strikes, the family first relies on unemployment insurance if it is available. . . . When unemployment insurance runs out, the family turns to primary assets, first spending accumulated savings, then cash from the sale of insurance policies, and later cash from the sale of the family car or home. When primary assets are exhausted, the family typically turns to various forms of borrowing from relatives, thereby accumulating liabilities (negative assets), financial or personal. These include loans from parents or other family members, and eventually moving into the residence of other family members.[47]

Sherraden argues that "those with limited primary and secondary resources become economically desperate much faster."[48] For young adults, secondary resources (those of family members) are probably more salient than primary resources (their own assets, which may be more limited in nature). The most logical source of secondary resources is parents—if they have assets, that is. Those without parental aid will become "economically desperate" sooner, and one of the more severe manifestations of economic desperation is the use of public assistance (welfare).

Recall the data presented in Chapter 2, in Figure 2.1 (p. 27), which showed that the poorest African Americans have essentially no assets (also see Table A2.1). About 50 percent of African American families who made below $15,001 in 1994 (approximately the poverty line for a family of four) had no assets or were in debt. By contrast, the median net worth for whites in this category was around $10,000. Thus, when one speaks of coming from a poor family, it means two very different things for blacks and for whites. The resources to prevent economic dependency in rough times are simply not available to poor black families or their adult children. Even within the new African American middle class that has been so often cited as a sign of racial progress,[49] a family's grip on middle-class status is often rather tenuous. As Figure 2.1 demonstrated, the median white family whose annual income was between $35,000 and $50,000 had assets of approximately $72,000, enough to permit its members to endure financial hardship such as unemployment for several months without compromising their daily level of consumption (even assuming that the family could liquidate only a portion of its assets). The comparable middle-income black family has only about $16,000 of net worth (most of which is tied up in home and vehicle); this household could survive without major adjustments only for a relatively short period.

In addition to the role of assets as an insurance mechanism to prevent reliance on public assistance, wealth may also have social-psychological aspects that relate to welfare. Poor whites with assets have a stake in the economy; they have something to lose financially. This is not the case for the typical poor black family who enjoys no wealth. In other words, if you own a house, a farm, or a small side business into which you have poured sweat or financial equity, you have more incentive to reduce expenditures or to make do somehow in order not to lose the house, farm, or business when unemployment or some other income shock hits the family. Conversely, if you have nothing to lose or, worse yet, are already immersed in the world of debt, there is less incentive to avoid sliding into rent arrears or welfare dependency. The drop in lifestyle from losing a home in which one has invested $10,000 of equity is great; by contrast, the lifestyle difference between being $5,000 in debt and $15,000 in debt is comparatively less. These effects of assets on a family's economic decisions (whether or not to rely on public assistance, for instance) may also have an impact on the next generation's calculations.

The following sections attempt to address the questions raised here about the possible role of wealth both in premarital childbearing and in the propensity to use public assistance. The analysis looks at the impact of race and class, in an effort to discover whether net racial differences in family structure and welfare use exist between blacks and whites.

IS THERE A "CULTURE OF ILLEGITIMACY" IN THE AFRICAN AMERICAN COMMUNITY?

This part of the analysis follows a group of girls (ages ten to thirteen in 1984) for eight years to determine whether race has a significant

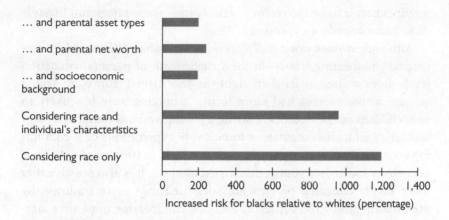

... and parental asset types

... and parental net worth

... and socioeconomic background

Considering race and individual's characteristics

Considering race only

0   200   400   600   800   1,000   1,200   1,400
Increased risk for blacks relative to whites (percentage)

FIGURE 5.1. The effect of being black on premarital childbearing (women only), by model type. Darker bars are statistically discernible from zero. African Americans demonstrate a higher risk of premarital childbearing than whites do. When class background is factored out, this difference is reduced, but race remains significant. (See Table A5.1.)

impact on their risk of having a child before marriage during that time.[50] Figure 5.1 presents in graphical form a comparison of the risk patterns for blacks and whites under various assumptions (also see Table A5.1). The first bar, which merely contrasts blacks to whites without considering any mediating socioeconomic factors, shows that the chance of bearing a child out of wedlock is dramatically higher for African American teenagers—on the order of twelve times as great as for white teenagers. By equalizing the socioeconomic status and family background of blacks and whites (the third bar of Figure 5.1), we find that the racial difference drops in magnitude such that African American girls are slightly more than three times as likely to have a premarital birth as their white counterparts. When wealth differences are factored out, this statistic actually rises slightly, but when assets by type are considered, the black-white difference drops back down to the level shown in the third bar. While the entire effect of race is not explained by class dynamics, this effect declines to about a quarter of what it was when race was considered alone. At the same time, it is clear that large, unexplained differences remain between blacks and whites on this issue. If there were one area where race-based cultural differences mattered—net of economic forces—one might expect it to be the realm of family life, where tastes and lifestyle differences are often expressed.

Although it does not totally account for racial differences in pre- marital childbearing, class—in the specific form of parental education level—does matter in its own right, as shown in Figure 5.2. Young women whose parents had more formal schooling were less likely to bear children out of wedlock. Having a parent who has completed post- secondary education may serve to cultivate expectations of a continu- ing course of study among teenage girls, which, in turn, can lower their propensity to become young, unmarried mothers. It is also possible that more highly educated parents are socialized into more traditionally mainstream family roles (such as delaying childbearing until after mar- riage) and that they pass these values on to their children. More highly educated parents might also be aware of a wider range of birth control options and might be better able to pass this information on to their children.

The reader should note, however, that I have not controlled for the education of the respondent herself because, among this age cohort, it is not at all likely that these girls have finished their schooling. Further, the direction of the effect would not have been clear: does dropping out of school lead to premarital childbearing, or does hav- ing a baby call to a halt educational pursuits? These decisions could also be simultaneous. In addition, many teenage girls who have chil- dren take a "sabbatical" from their role as students, only to return later.

While net worth is insignificant in the asset model (see the fifth bar of Figure 5.2), examining the influence of different types of as- sets on the rate of premarital childbearing indicates that primary res- idence equity does have an effect, as shown in Figure 5.3 (although it is a less powerful predictor than race). Since housing values are so intimately linked to the social and economic capital of neighbor- hoods, this finding adds support to the literature on neighborhood effects.

The only other factors that appear to matter are the age of the girl (girls who were older at the initial time of the survey were more likely to have had a baby out of wedlock during the following eight-year pe- riod) and whether the respondent's mother was married at the time of the respondent's birth. This effect holds strong even when we factor out a whole host of socioeconomic variables and wealth, implying the

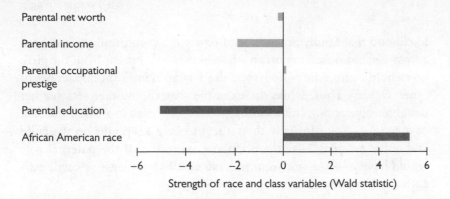

FIGURE 5.2. The relative effects of race and class on premarital childbearing (women only). Darker bars are statistically discernible from zero; lighter bars are statistically equivalent to zero. Of these background variables, race and parental education have a significant impact on teenage childbearing. (See Table A5.1.)

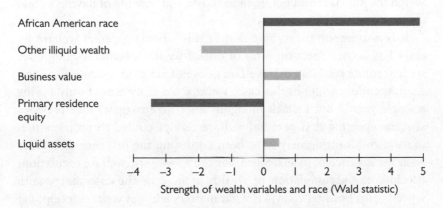

FIGURE 5.3. The relative effects of wealth by type on premarital childbearing (women only). Darker bars are statistically discernible from zero; lighter bars are statistically equivalent to zero. Of the various asset types, only primary residence equity has a significant effect in reducing the rate of premarital childbearing. This effect is smaller than that of race, however. (See Table A5.1.)

likelihood that family practices and patterns are culturally transmitted across generations. By contrast, the absence of a parent from the girl's household during the period 1980–84 has no significant impact net of other factors. Thus, while the example that the mother sets for her daughter concerning childbearing patterns appears to matter, the lack of a second parent (usually the father) to help keep tabs on the child and enforce "rules"—as the popular conception of the paternal role would have it—does not seem to have an effect (at least as single parenthood is measured here).

Other variables that do not have a significant impact in this model include parents' permanent income. Of the class variables, only parental education and housing equity matter, pointing to the importance of social-psychological dynamics in the household and the community, such as future expectations and peer influences. There are relatively few immediate financial issues related to whether or not a teenage girl bears a child. Abortion, if readily available, is usually economically feasible. Rather, the economic issues lie in the longer-term consequences of having a child—and whether a girl has adequate information to weigh the financial and nonfinancial costs and benefits of having a child as an unmarried teen.

It is also important to note that in this schema parental welfare receipt has no net effect on rates of out-of-wedlock births. I cannot say with absolute certainty that welfare does not act as an incentive for premarital childbearing; in this case, welfare use is measured only during a single year.[51] But its lack of significance here suggests that previous studies reporting that parental welfare receipt tended to promote premarital childbearing may have been confusing the presence of welfare with the absence of assets. Since, for the most part, welfare regulations preclude the accumulation of wealth, it may be the case that wealth (specifically, housing equity) is what matters and not welfare receipt *per se*. Table 5.1 summarizes my findings about the factors that do and do not predict premarital childbearing among this cohort of young women.

ARE AFRICAN AMERICANS MORE LIKELY TO RELY ON WELFARE?

Along with higher rates of out-of-wedlock births among African Americans (or as a result of this fact), research has also documented

TABLE 5.1

VARIABLES PREDICTING THE RISK OF
PREMARITAL CHILDBEARING BY
DESCENDING ORDER OF
PREDICTIVE IMPORTANCE

1. *Respondent's age*
2. *African American race*
3. *Parent's education (head of household)*
4. *Equity of parents' primary residence*
5. *Mother not married at birth of respondent*
6. Net value of parents' other illiquid assets
7. Parents' permanent income
8. Net value of parents' business
9. Parents' liquid assets
10. Parent's age (head of household)
11. Female-headed parental household (1980–84)
12. Parents received welfare in 1984
13. Parent's occupational prestige (head of household)

NOTE: Italic type indicates statistical significance at the $p < .10$ level; see Table A5.1.

higher rates of welfare use in the black community. Is this propensity primarily economic in nature, or is it racially based in some ethnic, cultural sense? To answer this question, I examined men and women who were children of low-income parents in 1984.[52] Because welfare use is concentrated among the poor and the near-poor, including the children of middle- and upper-income families would obscure the pattern of results, and I have consequently restricted the sample to the low-income population.[53]

In predicting the odds of welfare use among this group, the results mimic the patterns found elsewhere: even when the sample is restricted to the low-income population, African Americans are, in fact, 2.2 times more likely to receive public assistance, as shown in the first bar of Figure 5.4 (a comparison based only on race). But by taking into account differences in socioeconomic status and family background (which exist even within a constrained group such as this one), the disparity is reduced to a level that is not statistically significant (see the third bar of Figure 5.4, which indicates that blacks are only 10 percent more likely to receive government transfers). When we factor out parental wealth in 1984, the racial difference flips: in this case, African Americans have lower odds of welfare receipt (only 86 percent as likely to receive welfare as their white counterparts), although this difference is not statistically significant. Thus, taking into consideration economic

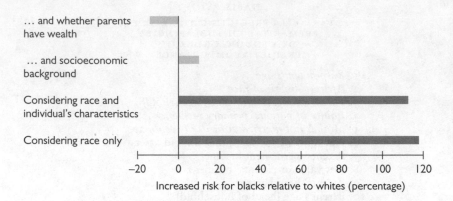

FIGURE 5.4. The effect of being black on the odds of welfare receipt in 1992 for sons and daughters of 1984 low-income families, by model type. Darker bars are statistically discernible from zero; lighter bars are statistically equivalent to zero. When welfare use among blacks and whites is considered on the basis of race alone, there is a significant difference, with African Americans more likely to receive public assistance. But when class background is taken into account, this difference disappears. (See Table A5.2.)

factors, the black-white difference in the risk of welfare use is completely eliminated.

Examining the relative strengths of the racial and economic variables, shown in Figure 5.5 (also see Table A5.2), reveals that the presence of parental assets is the second strongest class variable, reducing the likelihood of using welfare. The strongest class predictor, by far, is parental occupational prestige: children raised in families where the head of the household received more social status from his or her job were less likely to resort to welfare when they became young adults. This effect may be social-psychological, relating to the valuation of work in these families and the transmission of such values to the next generation. If a child sees that a parent is respected for occupational achievements, the child may see a job not only as an income source but also as an important component of social identity and therefore may be more reluctant to rely on income from other sources (such as the government).

Table 5.2 summarizes the factors that do or do not matter in predicting welfare receipt among this group of eighteen- to thirty-year-olds. Completing high school reduces one's likelihood of receiving public assistance (since, as we already know, high school graduation betters

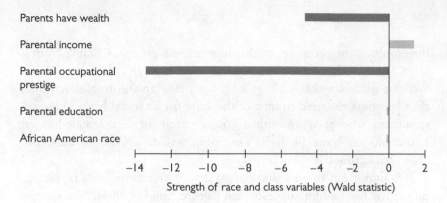

Parents have wealth

Parental income

Parental occupational
prestige

Parental education

African American race

−14 −12 −10 −8 −6 −4 −2 0 2

Strength of race and class variables (Wald statistic)

FIGURE 5.5. The relative effects of race and class on the odds of welfare receipt in 1992 for sons and daughters of 1984 low-income families. Darker bars are statistically discernible from zero; lighter bars are statistically equivalent to zero. African American race has no significant impact on welfare receipt. The presence of parental wealth reduces the likelihood of using public assistance, as does higher parental occupational prestige. (See Table A5.2.)

TABLE 5.2

VARIABLES PREDICTING THE USE OF
WELFARE BY DESCENDING ORDER OF
PREDICTIVE IMPORTANCE

1. *Parent's occupational prestige (head of household)*
2. *Number of siblings*
3. *Respondent graduated from high school*
4. *Parent's age (head of household)*
5. *Female-headed parental household (1980–84)*
6. *Parents had assets in 1984*
7. Respondent graduated from college
8. Female respondent
9. Parents' permanent income
10. Parents received welfare in 1984
11. African American race
12. Parent's education (head of household)
13. Respondent's age

NOTE: Italic type indicates statistical significance at the $p < .10$ level; see Table A5.2.

the employment prospects of this low-income group). Coming from a large family reduces the likelihood of receiving government transfers. We can speculate that siblings might provide an informal safety net, thus lessening the need to turn to the state for financial help. Those respondents who grew up with a young parent or in a female-headed household are more likely to use public assistance, net of class and racial background.

It is important to note that parental welfare receipt itself is not significant. This finding suggests that future pundits should be careful when they speak of families who stay on welfare across generations, creating a legacy of dependency. It may not be the values of dependency that are transmitted across generations, but rather the lack of a stake in the American dream and a dearth of family economic resources in the form of wealth. Such distinctions are very difficult to make, however, since most current welfare regulations prevent those families with assets from becoming eligible; therefore, welfare eligibility and having assets are intricately linked. Given this fact and the patterns of intergenerational transmission presented here, the interconnectedness of wealth (or lack of wealth) and welfare receipt merits further research attention.

IT TAKES A NATION: WEALTH, WELFARE, AND FAMILY STRUCTURE

My analysis documents that social class in general and wealth in particular do indeed have an impact on premarital childbearing and welfare dependency. Housing wealth serves to reduce the risk of having children before marriage among young women. Having any parental assets at all also lowers the risk of welfare use. It may be that those with parental assets are more likely to marry and remain married, thus lowering their likelihood of needing or qualifying for public assistance. It may also be that one does not need to rely on the government when one's own family of origin has some resources to spare.

As for the effect of parental housing wealth on premarital childbearing, it is possible that this coefficient is picking up the neighborhood effects discussed earlier in the chapter. Future researchers might examine the extent to which the housing asset variable works on childbearing behavior through community-level dynamics. This possibility is implied by work that documents a relationship between neighborhood quality, homeownership, and housing values. In addition, if parents own a home, children are more likely to own a home themselves, as we saw in Chapter Two. Since the transition to marriage (and the ordering of marriage and childbearing) may be related to the transition to home-ownership, anything that has a positive effect on filial homeownership may serve to promote marriage (and nuclear family structure) and thereby discourage premarital childbearing.

Although this chapter has demonstrated important links between wealth and family structure, the revision of family process models to include assets does not adequately account for racial differences in all outcomes measured. Including social class in statistical models does eliminate racial differences in welfare use, but the racial disparity in out of wedlock childbearing persists, albeit at a greatly reduced magnitude. Perhaps some race-based cultural differences do indeed remain from generations of economic insecurity. In order to test this hypothesis as it relates to wealth and the racial difference, it would be necessary to gather income and wealth data on several generations of the same family to determine whether this legacy is predictive of the racial gap in the current generation's family processes. Alternatively, even accounting for the economic legacy of previous generations may not explain racial differences. It is possible that an ethnic cultural component is critical to the ordering of childbearing and marriage, just as ethnic differences are manifest in many areas of life ranging from musical taste to cuisine.

It is important, however, to keep in mind the findings from Chapter Three. As that chapter's analysis demonstrated, the deleterious effects of nontraditional family structures (such as out-of-wedlock births to a young parent) on life chances as indicated by educational attainment are not a result of culture or values but rather are merely a statistical reflection of the lower levels of economic resources found in these families. Thus, while racial differences in family structure are not totally accounted for by eliminating the *apparent* differences resulting from parental economic circumstances, in a certain sense the most damaging aspects of certain family structure differences *have* been factored out—that is, their association with lower wealth levels. Perhaps these findings will help to move the debate away from discussion of the values of single parents—either black or white—and toward a discussion of how to foster wealth accumulation among nonnuclear family units. For instance, such a discussion might consider expanding paternal support requirements, which now include only a set level of income support for children, to encompass the development of an asset fund as well.

Future researchers should also examine the impact of parental or individual wealth on other family-related measures such as marital conflict, satisfaction, and divorce. Some research has already hinted that wealth may play an important role in determining racial differences in these measures of marital quality. For example, one study found that the anxiety felt by many African American husbands over their ability to provide for their families was one of the best predictors of marital instability;[54] if African American families had more of an asset reserve, these husbands might feel less such anxiety.

Another study that hints at the role of wealth in determining marital quality comes from the work of Patricia Clark-Nicholas and Bernadette Gray-Little, who found that, for African Americans, "frequently used measures of socio-economic status such as education and occupation were unrelated to marital quality. . . . Income did predict some aspects of marital quality, but, on the whole, was less relevant than perceived economic adequacy."[55] The fact that objective measures of class status were not as robust as subjective ones suggests that traditional measures of socioeconomic status do not adequately reflect the resources available to a family. If wealth were more important than income to family happiness and stability, this would explain the paradox of different effects for objective and subjective class measures among African Americans. Clark-Nicholas and Gray-Little suggest as much when they conclude, "The shortcoming of income . . . is that it assesses only resources and not liabilities."[56] Net worth would correct for this deficiency of income-based measures and thus should be considered by future students of the family.

CHAPTER SIX

Getting into the Black

Conclusions and Policy Implications

Property has its duties as well as its rights.
        Benjamin Disraeli, 1805–81

Taken in its entirety, the research presented in this book can go a long way toward showing that dynamics previously seen as rooted in an alternative or "underclass" culture among African Americans should in fact be viewed as a result of economic inequality. In most cases, the effects of race are dramatically obscured by the impact of class dynamics and economic resources.

For example, if we simply contrast blacks and whites without regard to socioeconomic background, we find that African Americans are more likely to drop out of high school and less likely to complete college, that they are employed for fewer hours and earn less money per hour than whites, that they have lower levels of wealth, and that they are more likely to have a child out of wedlock or to use welfare as young adults. But if we statistically compare blacks and whites who are similar in terms of their individual characteristics (age, gender, number of siblings, and, in some analyses, education and income levels), their family backgrounds (parents' age, whether they grew up in a female-headed household or one that used welfare), and their class origins (parents' education level and occupational prestige, as well as their family's permanent income, net worth, and types of assets), we find that these racial differences change significantly in magnitude and sometimes even in direction. For instance, when class background is equalized, blacks are just as likely as whites to have completed college. When we take into consideration parental assets, we find that the black-white wealth gap among young adults disappears. Racial differences in the chance of using welfare among this age group also vanish.

In certain analyses, race remains a significant predictor of life outcomes, sometimes in the same direction we would expect from anecdotal evidence or summary statistics. For instance, even when we control for class background, African Americans still tend to be employed for fewer hours and are still more likely to have children outside marriage—although these differences are greatly reduced in magnitude. For other outcome measures, race has a counterintuitive net effect when class differences are taken into consideration: in certain class-based models, black workers who are employed full time enjoy a wage advantage over whites; additionally, net of family background, the latest cohorts of African Americans are more likely to graduate from high school than are their white counterparts.

While the impact of race varies depending on which outcome we examine, in almost all instances presented in this book socioeconomic variables have a much greater impact in predicting outcomes than does skin color or racial identity for this recent cohort (young adults who have grown up since the landmark civil rights legislation of the 1960s). These findings represent both good and bad news for policymakers since, on the one hand, money is a lot more transferable than race. On the other hand, the important racial gap in wealth that stems from generations of black-white inequality is not easily remediable because it largely results from past dynamics rather than from a dearth of "equal opportunity" in the post-1960s world. If wealth differences could be rectified by providing equal access in housing and credit markets, a policy solution would be clear. But class differences that result from the wealth of one's parents are not so easy to redress.

I do not argue that culture plays no role in determining the life chances of black and white Americans. Rather, my intent is merely to shift the focus away from race-based discussions of cultural dynamics and toward a better understanding of how economic circumstances work to help determine cultural practices. Although this book has demonstrated the basic relationships between property and other life outcomes, it has not explicated the processes through which these relationships hold or the institutions that perpetuate them. Several ways in which property may have its effects have been mentioned (financing elite education, engendering neighborhood effects, and fostering an

ethic of responsibility and deferred gratification, to name only a few),
but further research, in both the quantitative and qualitative traditions,
is needed to document the cultural practices and institutions that translate wealth into other outcomes.[1] There is much room for future academic research regarding the role of wealth in the transmission of socioeconomic inequality across generations. Armed with a redefinition
of social class that includes assets, empirical researchers can readdress
the race-class debate in other areas—for example, health outcomes.[2]
For now, however, it is important to turn to some of the policy implications of the current study.

RACIAL POLICY IN THE UNITED STATES: LESSONS FROM RECENT HISTORY

Over the course of the twentieth century, African Americans have oc-
cupied a precarious position in the realm of social policy. The origins
of the American welfare system lie in the Social Security Act, signed
into law by President Franklin D. Roosevelt in 1935. This piece of legislation bifurcated the welfare state—not coincidentally—along racial
lines. One part included insurancelike programs geared toward workers who had "paid" for their benefits over the course of their working
careers. Programs of this type include Old Age Insurance (Social
Security), unemployment insurance, and Medicare health insurance
(which was added during the 1960s). These programs became sac-
rosanct, with almost unanimous support because of their universal
nature. But they were not so universal when it came to African
Americans. To a great extent, blacks were initially excluded from these
programs because the programs did not cover the agricultural or service industries in which African Americans were predominantly represented. These industries were excluded in part as an attempt to keep
southern Democrats in the New Deal coalition.[3]

The other half of the New Deal system consists of what we com-
monly call "welfare." Under the assumption of full employment—an assumption upon which the New Deal architects based their legislation—
this portion of the safety net would serve only those who could not
work, such as widows or the disabled. Since full employment was never
achieved, however, either through the free market or by government fiat,
welfare programs ended up as the source of support for the chronically
poor. Aid to Dependent Children (ADC), which later became Aid to

Families with Dependent Children (AFDC) and is now Temporary Assistance to Needy Families (TANF), is the main income-support component of welfare. As a result of economic inequality, blacks find themselves overrepresented among the recipients of TANF and Medicaid (the health insurance component of welfare that was added during the 1960s). These welfare programs—nonuniversal and disproportionately nonwhite—have always been the target of political budget-cutters and the site of highly moralistic political debates.

At the same time that welfare became implicitly racialized, a semi-explicit racial policy was emerging in the form of affirmative action. I call this policy "semi-explicit" because it is not really a coherent policy as much as it is a series of executive orders and Supreme Court rulings that hold together as a federal statement about race. The seeds of affirmative action were planted by Executive Order 8802, signed by Franklin Roosevelt, which "outlawed segregationist hiring policies by defense-related industries that held federal contracts."[4] As Manning Marable describes, President Harry S Truman later directed the Bureau of Employment Security "to act positively and affirmatively to implement the policy of nondiscrimination."[5] It was not until the Kennedy administration, however, that the actual phrase "affirmative action" was used, in Executive Order 10925. Surprisingly, it was under the Republican Nixon administration that affirmative action became particularly aggressive. In 1969, the federal government instituted what later became known as the Philadelphia Plan. This was the first program that specified explicit quotas for minority hiring. It targeted federal contractors and resulted in the percentage of racial minorities in the construction industry rising from 1 percent to 12 percent. Richard Nixon also tried to promote minority business ownership through set-asides of government contracts for minority-owned businesses. His administration also placed Federal Reserve funds in black-owned banks.[6]

Targeted goals for minority representation—that is, quotas—were struck a serious blow by a 1978 Supreme Court ruling, however. In the *Bakke* decision, Justice Lewis Powell wrote that it was unconstitutional for the University of California at Davis to set aside sixteen slots for minorities in its medical school (although the university was in fact permitted to use race as a factor in its admissions policy).[7] A series of court decisions following *Bakke* further curtailed affirmative action. The most serious challenge came at the state level in the form of California's Proposition 209, the California Civil Rights Initiative

(CCRI). This ballot measure, which passed 54.6 percent to 45.4 percent in November 1996, banned the use of race or gender preferences in state employment, contracting, and education. It has so far withstood court challenges.

The consequences of this initiative were felt almost immediately. In the state's premier public law school, Boalt Hall School of Law at U.C. Berkeley, admissions of African Americans dropped by 80 percent, to a paltry fourteen offers following the passage of Proposition 209. Reports from other campuses suggest that black and Latino enrollment has decreased across the entire University of California system. The effect of Proposition 209 on hiring has yet to be detailed. While nationwide public support for affirmative action varies depending on how survey questions are worded, it is clear from events in California that the policy as it now stands will not stand for long. Even its supporters concede that it needs reform, for it tends to provide the most help to upper-class and middle-class members of minority groups, the individuals within those groups who need it least.[8]

As indicated by welfare's recent reincarnation, if affirmative action is to survive at all, it will likely be in a different form, under a different name. One alternative to the current policy, which has also been suggested elsewhere, is *class-based affirmative action.*[9] Such a program could maintain set-asides for certain government contractors, demonstrate preferential hiring practices, and facilitate quotas for college admissions—but these decisions would be based on socioeconomic background rather than on race. In trying to remedy the situation at the University of California, for example, officials have now added a questionnaire regarding class background to the admissions packet for law school; it is yet unclear how much of an impact this change will have on the composition of the student body.

But to be successful in achieving its goal of fostering racial and class equality, such a policy must entail a very specific type of class-based affirmative action. Given the mountain of evidence documenting the importance of wealth in the conception of social class and its particular relevance to issues of racial inequality, any policy that is designed to address the issue of social class must not rely solely on the traditional measures of socioeconomic status (income, occupation, and education) but must take assets into account. In fact, a composite of income and wealth could be constructed by "annuitizing" family net worth (converting it from a stock to an income flow using a specific formula involving the interest rate). By adding this figure to annual parental income, for instance, institutions might be able to construct an appropriate measure on which to judge the resources a student brings to college. Policymakers must, however, be alert to the dangers of using only income, educational, or occupational measures of social class in a system of class-based affirmative action, for this would result in a situation that merely reproduces, if not exacerbates, existing inequalities between African Americans and whites (as well as within those two communities). In lieu of class-based affirmative action, another alternative might entail race-based asset policy.

RACE-BASED ASSET POLICY

In the wake of the urban riots of the late 1960s, a thirteen-year-old African American boy told a reporter in Detroit, "There's nothing the matter . . . that money can't solve."[10] There is much wisdom in the diagnosis offered by this adolescent. In order to fully understand the impact of property ownership on a community, it might prove worthwhile to imagine what could have happened during the hot summers of 1965 in Watts or 1968 in Detroit if the majority of businesses in these areas had been black-owned—or, for that matter, what might (or might not) have occurred in Los Angeles in 1992. Although this link between civil unrest and property ownership is pure speculation, perhaps it merits serious consideration.

During the late 1960s, Detroit's automobile industry provided the highest average wages for African Americans anywhere in the United States—yet the city proved to be one of the urban areas most devastated by the civil unrest of the period.[11] This juxtaposition may point to the inadequacy of focusing exclusively on wages and labor market issues when trying to assess the economic situation of African Americans (or any group in society). Would a community have set fire to businesses or homes owned by its brothers and sisters? Whether or not this inverse association between entrepreneurship and civil disorder exists, many commentators in the 1960s and 1970s certainly pointed to the important role of wealth in determining the quality of life in minority communities. "By the highest estimates," according to William K. Tabb, writing in the late 1960s, "blacks service 10 to 15 percent of the black market. . . . While estimates vary, blacks are represented one-tenth as often in ownership roles as their numbers would warrant if ownership was . . . randomly distributed without regard to race."[12]

Even in the case of New York, which was relatively more equitable than other cities, black business ownership was limited to small-scale enterprises. "One million blacks live in the New York City ghettos of South Bronx, Harlem and Bedford-Stuyvesant," wrote Theodore Cross in his 1969 book *Black Capitalism,* "yet those slums are presently operating only twelve registered Negro-owned businesses hiring ten or more people. The most deprived and undeveloped economies of Latin America have greater elements of entrepreneurial affluence."[13] Medium- and large-scale businesses are the types most likely to raise the economic prospects of many members of a community; businesses hiring fewer than ten individuals are most likely family-owned and family-operated and thus have limited ability to provide direct employment opportunities to others beyond immediate kin.

Consequences of this lack of business ownership extend beyond employment opportunities. Because of a dearth of businesses serving ghetto areas, black residents pay higher prices for consumer goods. "As blacks become the dominant residential group (succession), the business community will generally decline in absolute size," notes Karen Stein in the *Journal of Consumer Affairs,* "due to the loss in white-owned businesses and the difficulties inherent in establishing black-owned businesses."[14] The decline in the number of competing enterprises leads to a situation of oligopoly and thus to higher prices for consumers, through the laws of supply and demand. "Hindered by poor transportation systems to outlying shopping centers and a low level of automobile ownership," Stein continues, "the poor are restricted to shopping in their immediate neighborhood."[15] In addition, local merchants often offer credit, which can prove to be a crucial factor in shopping decisions for people in precarious economic circumstances.[16] This scenario is eerily similar to the situation of sharecroppers trapped by their reliance on credit a hundred years earlier in the South. Thus, a dearth of community business proprietorship, a low incidence of family vehicle ownership, and a lack of cash on hand all interact to hurt the efforts of urban black consumers to make it on their given income levels.

In the wake of the urban unrest of the late 1960s, there was much talk of fostering "black capitalism." As described by Tabb, "black capitalism includes programs for minority group members in financing and marketing, and in bolstering self-confidence and business skills."[17] Underlying such proposals to foster entrepreneurship in the African American community is the assumption that a lack of *human* capital (in this case, business acumen) causes the lack of black business ownership. If society could only teach African Americans about credit markets and give them a dose of "self-confidence," the problem would be solved, dictated the logic of the time.

Black capitalism programs never took off, however. Instead, "community development" became the most prevalent strategy to foster black wealth accumulation during the 1970s. In this strategy, a nonprofit group called a community development corporation (CDC) acts to attract capital and "funnel it to individual businesses privately or co-operatively owned."[18] Today's equivalents are the community development banks that form part of the "enterprise" or "empowerment" zones proposed by Jack Kemp, former HUD secretary (and 1996 vice-presidential candidate) and implemented on a limited basis by George Bush (and continued by Bill Clinton). The enterprise zone strategy works by giving economically depressed communities special tax incentives and a limited amount of capital, in some cases, to foster business development. But this approach does not discriminate between seeding capitalism within the community and luring it from elsewhere. This is a result of the single-minded obsession with creating jobs, rather than fostering business growth, in the black community. Thus, in the end, it is a job-growth program, not "black capitalism."

"In the past, we have made only passing efforts to build wealth and equities in the ghettos of America," summarizes Cross. "Influenced by reformers such as Jacob Riis, we have taken profits out of the slum when the real objective should have been to build profits into it."[19] He argues that the insistence on control of capital by nonprofit organizations such as CDCs has been a guarantee for failure and, furthermore, sends the wrong message and fosters inappropriate skills in the community. For example, with respect to housing policy, Cross writes, "We have insisted that Federal Housing Administration projects for low-income housing be owned by non-profit churches or charitable corporations. Real estate entrepreneurs, with the agility to make low-cost housing actually work, have been charged by Congress with unconscionable profits." It is worth noting that the same federal agency ran programs to promote suburban (predominantly white) homeownership after World War II, with no such stipulations on the management of credit and capital. In these programs, FHA and VA loans went through commercial banks, thus providing a measure of profit and business development as a side benefit to the intended goal of promoting homeownership. "Speculation, the essential lubricant for production of wealth in the normal economy," continues Cross, "has been banished by law from Federally subsidized real estate projects in the slums. To keep the 'quick buck' speculators out of low-income housing, we have adopted strict and impractical safeguards against corruption, which assure us that the legitimate wealth-makers will not participate."[20]

A more radical policy alternative to fostering black capitalism, perhaps inspired by the Nation of Islam and separatist movements of the 1960s, calls for reparations for African Americans. Typically, reparations, such as those paid by Germany after World War I, consist of cash payments made by the losing side to the winning side after a war, as compensation for the losing side's "guilt." The argument for paying reparations to African Americans became particularly refined during the 1970s. One researcher used 1790–1860 slave prices as proxies for the value of slave capital. He then annuitized the prices into an income stream to which he applied compound interest, calculated since the slavery era. The figures he generated under different assumptions ranged from $448 billion to $995 billion at the time he wrote (the early 1970s), "a range which, coincidentally, would encompass the indemnification being demanded by the black nationalist Republic of New Africa (RNA), a prominent black separatist group."[21] It should be noted, however, that the RNA demanded $400 billion in addition to five southern states: Alabama, Georgia, Louisiana, Mississippi, and South Carolina (which this researcher estimated to be valued at $350 billion at the time).

In discussing the movement for reparations, Robert Browne laid out a more general framework for calculation of the "proper" amount: "The development of a minimal reparations formula, then, must encompass at least three elements . . . (a) a payment for unpaid slave labor prior to 1863; b) a payment for underpayment of black people since 1863; and c) a payment to compensate for the black man's being denied the opportunity to acquire a share of America's land and natural resources when they were widely available to white settlers."[22] Implicit in these arguments is the assumption that the major problem in wealth accumulation by African Americans lies in the past exploitation of black labor and past obstacles to equity accumulation and inheritance.

During the 1970s, the implementation of a reparations plan was discussed in terms of direct cash payments to those of African ancestry,
similar to the model of reparations for Japanese Americans interned
during World War II (with the obvious distinction that while the payments for Japanese Americans were made only to those who were actually alive during the period, payments to African Americans would
necessarily be to the descendants of black slaves). Such ideas have even
been advocated by conservative pundits as a method of abrogating a societal responsibility to continue affirmative action policies in education
and the labor market. As Charles Krauthammer argued in *Time* magazine, "It is time for a historic compromise: a monetary reparation to
blacks for centuries of oppression in return for the total abolition of all
programs of racial preference. A one-time cash payment in return for a
new era of irrevocable color blindness. . . . Reparations focus the issue
most sharply. They acknowledge the crime [slavery]. They attempt
restitution. They seek to repay some of the 'bondsman's 250 years of
unrequited toil.'"[23] Krauthammer's call for reparations appears to be
motivated solely by guilt over white enslavement of blacks in the antebellum South and thus does not acknowledge the extent of racial oppression and economic disenfranchisement since that time in the areas
of property accumulation and labor market relations.

In a cautionary note regarding such a reparations strategy, Tabb ob-
serves that "the demand for further redistribution of resources from the
larger society to the black minority depends to a large extent on the degree of solidarity in the black community."[24] This solidarity is limited by
the internal class cleavages that exist among African Americans, particularly since the distribution of income and wealth is more uneven in the
black community than it is among whites. Therefore, the focus on race-
based redistribution "has led to a de-emphasis of class differences internal
to that community."[25] These class differences are important to the issue of
reparations for the same reason they are important to affirmative action
as it currently stands: well-off individuals would stand to gain as much as
impoverished ones. Although this might be an improvement over current
policy, in which middle-class African Americans benefit to a greater extent
than working-class and poor individuals, it still ignores the particular
needs of the most disadvantaged. Further, while the "black capitalism"
programs of the 1970s focused on developing business skills within the
African American community without facing up to the reality of a severe
deficit in financial capital, a simple reparations strategy commits the op-

posite error. Simply giving cash payments to Americans of African descent ignores the social and human capital needed in order to put that money to work within the community. Such a flood of money would create a situation of anomie (normlessness) and would not necessarily lead to more stable community development. Instead, programs are needed that bring both financial *and* social capital into the black community.

Returning to the example of urban civil unrest, we might pose another wealth-based question: if residential integration were a reality, would there have even been a "ghetto" to be looted? How likely would riots have been if the African American community had been dispersed evenly among whites and other races, constituting 10 to 20 percent of each neighborhood? Even without residential integration, if the majority of African Americans had owned the homes in which they resided, how likely would a riot have been, thereby lowering the property values of the resident-owners? The answer to all these questions is that if owning businesses and homes were a part of African American life, the risk of civil unrest would be dramatically lowered. The counterpoint to this conclusion is that as long as African Americans face major institutional obstacles to property ownership, the risk of such conflict remains.

As in the case of business proprietorship—where increased competition for small-business formation from new immigrants may keep rates of black business ownership low—obstacles to black homeownership may be more formidable now than they have ever been. While interest rates are lower than they were in the 1970s and early 1980s, housing price inflation during the 1980s priced many middle-class African American families out of the market. "Thus," as Melvin Oliver and Thomas Shapiro explain, "in a housing market where access to housing is becoming more and more difficult because of price inflation, younger middle-class blacks may be entering the market later and at a much lower level than their white counterparts."[26] Even if they do manage to acquire a home, it may be at a lower equity level, since African Americans have fewer assets to begin with, resulting in smaller down payments.

Further, "because homes in all-black areas increase in equity at a slower rate than comparable homes in white neighborhoods [or may even decrease in value], young blacks may not receive the same rate of return and thus secure the wealth accumulation of similarly situated whites in all-white neighborhoods," according to Oliver and Shapiro.[27]

Their prognosis is grim as well: "Forced to buy housing in black neighborhoods because of racial discrimination or lower housing prices, the black middle class actually falls farther behind in the search for true economic security."[28] In other words, incentives to increase black homeownership will do little to narrow the racial gap in net worth if African Americans cannot buy their homes in racially integrated neighborhoods.

This situation leads to an even grimmer reality. Much of the discussion of residential segregation focuses on the deleterious effects this pattern has on African Americans. Often left out of the debate, however, is the beneficial effect that segregation has for whites. Although the housing system is racially segregated in terms of choices, it remains one market system for blacks and whites, and thus housing value outcomes for whites are not independent of those for African Americans. Housing owned by whites is worth more precisely because it is *not* situated in black neighborhoods. As Chapter Two discussed, researchers have documented how black housing appreciates at a slower rate (or even depreciates) when compared to similar white housing, but little work has focused on systematic economic analysis of residential patterns to generate an overall estimate of the equity gained by whites as a result of segregation in housing markets (as, for instance, estimates of the value of slave labor have been generated).

Property has the particular attribute of quantifying the social value of ideas or objects. Reading a log of prices assigned to various objects can be viewed as akin to an archaeologist digging through strata of earth to follow the development of a civilization. In this vein, when a neighborhood's housing values precipitously decline as the percentage of black residents increases, the situation provides a record of the social value of "blackness" on the part of society. In this way, the social-psychological realm of racist ideology may be directly linked to the economic arena in the valuation of property.

This devaluation of black neighborhoods is partially a result of white fears of a decline in property values and the "white flight" that ensues. In other words, there is a loop: as long as whites are a significant majority and have the ability to decide where they will live, they will have an economic incentive to flee integrated neighborhoods, thus continuing the vicious cycle. Aside from any personal ideology, it is in the economic interest of white homeowners to sell off when they anticipate that the neighborhood has reached a racial tipping point, for fear others will make the same calculation and sell off first, causing a gen-

eral loss of value before they have had a chance to sell (give〔
rash of selling depresses prices). Soon, all the neighborhood
also believe that they need to sell because they are anticipating
ers will do so. This "expectation of expectations" is how Ger.
tems theorist Niklas Luhmann defines social structure.[29] Thus, both
blacks and whites are trapped by this social structure into reproducing
current residential patterns. As a result, even if African Americans were
allowed equal access to the home buying market and if interest rates
were prescribed by law to be the same for blacks and whites, African
Americans would still be at a disadvantage in terms of housing values,
since whites could still flee and thereby depress housing values for
blacks. Remedies for this situation are difficult to come by. Politically,
any policy limiting the market (restricting the ability of white homeowners to sell, for instance) would fly in the face of the notion of individual choice that is so central to American ideology; economically, it
would not be in the immediate interest of whites, whose housing is generally worth more precisely because it is not in a black neighborhood.
In this way, race and class can reinforce each other.

Currently, given the difficulties they face in purchasing homes, when
African Americans do find a desirable community that will sell to them,
large numbers of black potential homeowners are drawn to that area
(in the long term, perpetuating the dynamic of race and property inequality). One recent study shows that blacks are reluctant to move out
of predominantly white housing tracts and that new construction increases the likelihood of African Americans moving into a predominantly white development tract.[30] In other words, black families usually—and understandably—take whatever limited opportunities are
available to live in integrated neighborhoods. Ironically, however, if
white homeowners were given a guarantee that the percentage of black
residents would not exceed, say, 15 percent in a given community, they
might be less likely to flee because they would not fear a complete racial
turnover of the community. But such ironic constraints on the residential choices of African Americans are no more a feasible alternative
than limiting the market decisions of whites. In short, the challenge is
to achieve a balanced distribution of black and white residential patterns without resorting to draconian encroachments on the property
rights of either group.

In this vein, there may be ways to structure incentives into the
property tax code to foster integrated communities. For example,

some policy analysts have proposed the development of "social insurance."[31] As applied to the issue of integrated housing, this form of
insurance would protect property owners from any rundown in prices
resulting from selling sprees as a neighborhood "tips" from white to
black. With this insurance in place, the economic incentive to pull out
when a neighborhood starts to integrate would be eliminated; ideally,
the insurance "policy" would never need to be cashed in. The difficulty lies in the details, of course, especially the task of factoring out
changes in prices that may be occurring as the result of other exoge-
nous forces.

In order to better develop policy options to address the racial gap
in housing wealth, it might be useful to study communities such as
Columbia, Maryland—an integrated community where owner occu-
pancy is the norm—using ethnographic or other more detailed method-
ologies. It would be interesting to compare this community to ones that
are predominantly white and ones that are predominantly black (such
as Silver Springs, Maryland) where homeownership is also the norm to
determine the relative effects of integration *per se* and those of property
values on life outcomes.

While it is difficult to be optimistic about the possibility of change in
the realm of race and real estate, another development initially appears
more promising for the future of wealth equality. Specifically, as a result of rapid price gains in the securities markets, stocks now outpace
real estate as the primary investment vehicle for American families.
Although "there are no definitive current numbers about how many
American households have more money in stocks than in real estate,"
according to Brett D. Fromson, "the value of stocks held by Americans
now exceeds $5 trillion."[32] This 1995 statistic edged out the estimated
$4.5 trillion that Americans held as home equity. These statistics may
be misleading, however, since the distribution of wealth in liquid assets
such as stocks is more unequal than that in real estate—that is, since a
relatively small number of individuals own huge amounts of securities,
the modal (most common) American family may still have a greater net
investment in its home. Nonetheless, Fromson reports that many economists and market analysts agree that this represents a historic shift.

What does this mean for African Americans? On the one hand, stock
certificates know no skin color. An African American's purchase of IBM
or DuPont stock does not affect a white individual's decision about
which security to buy (as purchases by blacks might have affected a

white person's real estate decision). The anonymity of stock certificates means that there is much less potential for the emergence of a vicious cycle such as that encountered in the housing market. On the other hand, African Americans are currently much less likely to invest in the stock market, and those who do will generally reap lower returns in absolute terms since they are starting with less. Also, given the recent run in stock market prices, if blacks are to enter the stock market in greater numbers, they will be doing so at a time when prices may already be inflated, and therefore they will find themselves in a precarious situation and at a disadvantage compared to whites, who have enjoyed a head start. Further, with limited assets to begin with, African Americans may be more hesitant to put their nest eggs in such risky investment instruments as common stock or corporate bonds.

Therefore, short of radical policy interventions such as reparations or government-dictated residence patterns, it is likely that the black-white asset gap will continue to widen. This is true because of the cruel fact that wealth begets greater wealth. Starting with a few hundred dollars at 10 percent compounded interest, an individual will end up with a thousand dollars after a decade or two. Starting with a thousand dollars, however, another individual will end up with several thousand dollars, and the wealth gap will have grown in absolute terms despite equal access to investments. (This calculation does not even take into consideration the greater yields available to individuals with more money to invest.) Thus, as long as the economy grows at a decent pace, thereby creating wealth for all Americans, the asset gap between blacks and whites will grow wider. This fact dictates an ultimate trade-off in policy choices. The more universal an asset development policy is, the more politically popular it becomes, but the less it will do to reduce racial inequalities in wealth (and therefore other outcomes).

An even more potentially dangerous situation may be engendered if the move to privatize Social Security becomes law. In an effort to increase the nation's personal savings rate (which hovers around 5 percent) and at the same time save the Social Security trust fund from bankruptcy as the "baby boomers" move into retirement, many conservative lawmakers are arguing for the conversion of Social Security from a defined-benefit program that invests in government bonds (debt) to a defined-contribution program that invests in the stock market (assets)—akin to a corporate 401k or Individual Retirement Account. A defined-benefit, or fixed-benefit, pension (Social Security's current structure) guarantees participants a set return during their retirement, in the form of a monthly check. Changing to a defined-contribution, or fixed-contribution, plan would mean that individuals contribute a set amount from their paychecks (as they do now) but that the returns they receive when they retire depend on how the investments performed during the interim. In essence, the transition to this new system represents a shifting of the risk from the government to the individual, albeit with the possibility of greater returns. Proponents argue that the average rate of return on the stock market would make the privatized system much more lucrative for the individuals regardless of whether they choose the investments themselves or whether the fund is administered by a federal trustee. These proponents also claim that the infusion of this new capital into the securities markets would stimulate the economy, creating jobs and better asset growth for all.

At least one scholar has argued that wealth inequality between blacks and whites is overstated when it does not take into consideration Social Security pension wealth.[33] By providing a better return to Social Security, a privatization plan might serve to help equalize wealth holdings between the races. On the other hand, such a fixed-contribution system might also put the retirement funds of many Americans for whom Social Security is their only pension plan (a group in which African Americans are disproportionately represented) at the mercy of the ups and downs of the stock market.

While this change would have important implications for racial differences in wealth holdings, it would have even greater implications for the class structure of the United States. The future economic well-being of workers—in terms of their retirement nest egg—would depend directly on the performance of the corporations in which their Social Security funds were invested. How can workers argue for an increase in wages if they know that their retirement fund (as reflected by the company's stock price) may suffer? This arrangement puts employees in the position of making a trade-off between future and current income. It also gives managers a rhetorical advantage in their efforts to keep wages depressed. This may already be taking place to a certain extent with the widespread investment in the stock market through private pension funds, but it would become all the more prevalent if the largest pension fund in the country (Social Security) became entwined with the stock market.

Some may argue that having the long-term economic interests of workers directly tied to the prospects of the firm helps to create common incentives for workers and owners and thus creates a more efficient site of production. They may also argue that workers would benefit by having greater control over the actions of corporations (through their privileges as shareholders). But a more pessimistic view holds that the current inequality of wages and asset ownership in the context of the modern corporation provides a gravely unequal starting position for workers and owners to voice their interests. Workers would be even more powerless in their negotiations with management for higher wages if not only their current standard of living but their future lifestyle as well depended on the largess of the corporation.

Within this tricky context of the nature of wealth and inequality, a sound policy to foster property equity between the races is difficult to implement. The simplest idea would be to implement a national wealth tax. At the end of each fiscal or calendar year, each individual would use a checklist to assess his or her assets and liabilities and would be required to pay the government a certain percentage of that net worth if it exceeded a given deduction. These funds would be redistributed to the asset-poor. While tax-based transfers are the most efficient way to remedy inequities (and also have the benefit of being color-blind), they are also politically risky. Political scientist Harold Wilensky has demonstrated that voter uprisings against taxes—such as Proposition 13 in California—are most likely to occur with respect to property taxes."[34]

Given these political risks, lawmakers may have to be inventive in developing asset-based policies. One place to start might be slackening the strict asset tests that current welfare policy enforces. If welfare recipients were able to save without being penalized for their asset accumulation, public assistance might come closer to serving the role for which it was intended: that of a temporary safety net. Likewise, by selling public housing to its residents (who are predominantly black) in a program not unlike the VA or FHA programs instituted after World War II, the government could create a whole new class of urban homeowners with a stake in the American dream. Another interesting idea that has been proposed is the creation of Individual Development Accounts (IDAs) that foster savings among the asset-poor (who are disproportionately minorities).[35] Perhaps tax incentives could be implemented for these parents to save for their children's future expenses in much the same way that IRAs now act for retirement savings.

In an even more aggressive option, the government could institute child development savings accounts (akin to Social Security), with the government acting as custodian until the child reaches age eighteen. The money would then be released only for educational or occupational expenses such as tuition, licenses, fees, or capital investments. If asset-based policy were geared directly toward children, it might become more politically palatable to lawmakers who prefer not to "reward" poor adults. (It is important to keep in mind, however, that every policy intervention has unintended consequences. For instance, if the government saved for children, parents might be more reluctant to do this themselves.)

The bigger challenge may lie in designing a program that will sufficiently entice economically disadvantaged families to participate. Experience has shown that fostering savings among the poor is not easy. In an impoverished area of rural Kentucky, a foundation sponsored a program that matched the savings of individuals by contributing $6 for each $1 the participants put up themselves. Only eight people chose to participate. The program administrator, Jennifer Hart, explained why so few individuals enrolled: "They don't think they have a future. If they did, they would think about it and delay instant gratification. But they have no reason to. And they can't. They can only think about how they are going to feed the children this week and pay the rent this month."[36] These are significant obstacles. Nevertheless, policies that encourage the values of savings and thrift might be able to garner support from the political right as well as the left. Self-sufficiency and asset accumulation are effective rallying calls in the search for racial equity.

RACE, CLASS, AND PROPERTY IN AMERICA: SUMMARY AND CONCLUSIONS

The classical economist and moral philosopher Adam Smith recognized that social classes arose when humans were able to accumulate and store resources. Before this development—when people were hunter-gatherers, or even during the early agricultural stages of development when people could not preserve what they did not consume—humankind existed in a classless society (though there were other forms of inequality). When individuals became able to store resources, class inequalities were generated, along with a corresponding change in social relations. At the end of the day, not everyone was equal, and those who had more could preserve that advantage. In fact, the word "asset" comes from an Anglo-French legal term, *aver assetz,* to have enough.[37] Individuals traded these accumulated goods—these assets—for other goods or for a guarantee of remittal in the future when times were not so rosy, when they did *not* have enough.

Since the genesis of social class through this act of accumulating and saving, property relations and labor market issues have been intimately linked throughout history. For example, in sixteenth-century England, the common grazing land was parceled into privately held farms, creating newly formed private property. This Enclosure Movement, as it was called, set the stage for the agricultural revolution and the development of new technologies such as the seed drill and the cotton gin. These changes generated new inequities as well. First, land was not distributed equally; second, once new technologies emerged as a response to this nascent private market in the agricultural arena, inequalities sprouted up with respect to who owned and distributed these new means of production and who could afford to use them. In this manner, changes in the organization of land ownership engendered changes in the way agricultural work was organized.

The same relation between property laws, technology, and the organization of work can be seen in the Industrial Revolution. Specifically, the introduction of limited liability in the form of corporations allowed the collectivization of capital, thus providing the appropriate legal environment. Corporations were given the same legal rights as individuals to enter into contracts and incur obligations. Most important, when people pooled their property in this way, they insulated themselves from the debts and responsibilities of these institutions, using the corporation as a "front" for their business. This is why the owners of Exxon, for instance, are not subject to liens against their personal fortunes in the wake of the Valdez oil spill. The main societal benefit of this protection is that, with limited liability, individuals are more likely to take risks with their assets, thereby stimulating the development and production of new goods and services. Even as changes in property law can spur the development of new technologies and inequalities, the emergence of new technologies, such as the printing press, also generate new forms of property, such as copyrights.

Although property has been central to the history of stratification, and although the founding fathers of the social sciences such as Adam Smith, Karl Marx, and Max Weber were intimately concerned with property analysis, the role of wealth has been largely absent from the empirical tradition of research on inequality. This is even more the case with respect to the debate over racial inequality. From the initial wresting of soon-to-be slaves from their families and possessions along the western coast of Africa, to the failed promise of land redistribution after Emancipation, to the dynamics of residential segregation and differential credit access that continue relatively unabated today, African Americans have been systematically prevented from accumulating property. It should be said, however, that the link between property inequity and racial division is not unique to this country or even to the Western world. Property law has formed the centerpiece of race-based policies in countries as disparate as Germany under the Third Reich (dispossessing Jews from their wealth) and imperial Japan (which barred *burakumin* from ownership for several centuries). In fact, it could be plausibly argued that unequal property relations are a necessary (but not sufficient) prerequisite for racial divisions.

By including property in the conception of social class, the empirical analysis presented throughout this book has shifted, but not ended, the race-class debate. Although race becomes insignificant in predicting a number of important outcomes for young adults when asset levels are included in causal models, wealth itself is nevertheless distributed unequally by race. Thus, one may conclude that the locus of racial inequality no longer lies primarily in the labor market but rather in class and property relations that, in turn, affect other outcomes. While young African Americans may have the *opportunity* to obtain the same education, income, and wealth as whites, in actuality they are on a slippery slope, for the discrimination their parents faced in the housing and credit markets sets the stage for perpetual economic disadvantage.

On the policy side, this study shows the importance of shifting the debate about race from the traditional focus on the labor market to one geared toward rectifying wealth differences. Wealth, not occupation or education, is the realm in which the greatest degree of racial inequality lies in contemporary America. The implications of this finding for social policy are twofold. The first possibility involves shifting race-based affirmative action policy from the areas of education and occupation to a focus on asset inequality. The second argues for a shift to a class-based affirmative action policy—that is, implementing educational, hiring, and contracting preferences that are based on class and not skin color; such a policy must, however, include net worth in its definition of class if we are to avoid worsening black-white inequities. The political obstacles to any such policy changes are indeed great. But the potential benefits to society are even greater.

Appendix

TABLE AI.I

NONSTUDENT RESPONDENTS AGES 18–30 WHO WERE SONS OR
DAUGHTERS OF HEADS OF 1984 PSID FAMILIES, 1992–95 ($N = 1,285$)

	Total	Blacks	Whites
Respondent Characteristics			
Black	.111 (.314)	—	—
Latino	.002 (.140)	—	—
Other racial group	.004 (.059)	—	—
Female	.490 (.500)	.526 (.499)	.494 (.500)
Age in 1992	25.012 (2.981)	25.015 (3.209)	29.014 (2.947)
Number of siblings	2.757 (2.129)	3.503 (2.749)	2.666 (2.019)
High school graduate	.888 (.315)	.840 (.367)	.898 (.303)
College graduate	.211 (.408)	.078 (.269)	.225 (.418)
Held back a grade	.128 (.334)	.091 (.288)	.134 (.340)
Expelled from school	.178 (.383)	.255 (.436)	.171 (.376)
Not working in 1992	.235 (.262)	.396 (.489)	.058 (.234)
Used welfare in 1992	.148 (.355)	.187 (.390)	.144 (.351)
Hours worked in 1992 (workers only)	1,837.67 (774.401)	1,621.03 (890.495)	1,861.27 (756.973)
Working full time in 1992	.582 (.493)	.402 (.490)	.608 (.488)
Hourly wage in 1992 (full time only)	9.742 (5.251)	7.800 (4.324)	9.893 (5.287)
Income in 1992	38,177.9 (38,502.1)	23,515.2 (18,516.8)	40,410.9 (40,292.3)
Net worth in 1994 (individuals who headed households only)	55,292.8 (354,685)	14,014.4 (28,490.9)	60,196.4 (374,732)

Parental Characteristics			
Age of head of household in 1984	45.49 (8.02)	44.04 (9.33)	45.71 (7.78)
Number of years female-headed household, 1980–84	.140 (.317)	.393 (.452)	.104 (.274)
Welfare receipt in 1984	.025 (.157)	.084 (.278)	.016 (.125)
Parental Class Measures			
Education of head of household in 1984	12.452 (2.775)	1▪.519 (2.733)	12.715 (2.642)
Occupational prestige of head of household	40.608 (13.387)	30.283 (10.258)	41.959 (13.063)
Income, 1980–84 (constant 1995 dollars)	62,031.3 (47,031.8)	36,02▪.9 (22,205.9)	65,804.8 (48,674.7)
No wealth in 1984	.050 (.219)	.175 (.380)	.031 (.172)
Net worth in 1984	151,115 (459,174)		170,836 (490,192)
Primary residence equity	45,405.4 (50,867.1)	26,250.4 (35,817.4)	49,360.4 (52,626.0)
Business equity	38,106.0 (190,468)	15,518.7 (20,791.5)	43,936.0 (204,135)
Net value of other illiquid assets	34,605.3 (140,841)	71▪,669 (6,077.58)	39,161.1 (150,818)
Net value of liquid assets	32,997.4 (324,881)	5,332.72 (20,396.8)	38,378.1 (348,487)

NOTE: Mean values shown, with standard deviations in parentheses; analysis weighted by the 1992–95 core sample individual-level weight assigned by the PSID.

1994 MEDIAN AND MEAN FAMILY
NET WORTH AND PERCENTAGE
WITH ZERO OR NEGATIVE NET WORTH, BY
RACE AND 1992 YEARLY
FAMILY INCOME (IN 1994 DOLLARS)
(N = 7,324)

Yearly Income	Total Net Worth		
	White	Black	Total
Median Values			
<$15,001	$10,000	$0	$6,000
$15,001–$35,000	45,700	11,000	36,600
$35,001–$50,000	81,000	40,000	76,925
$50,001–$75,000	140,200	54,000	135,000
>$75,000	308,000	114,600	300,000
Total	$72,000	$9,771	$58,000
Mean Values			
<$15,001	$47,214	$15,959	$38,941
$15,001–$35,000	96,530	58,146	86,850
$35,001–$50,000	166,185	74,834	157,067
$50,001–$75,000	250,334	79,073	244,124
>$75,000	567,749	229,006	555,749
Total	$183,207	$38,993	$163,042
Percentage in the Red			
<$15,001	22.91%	50.16%	30.12%
$15,001–$35,000	10.82	17.86	11.89
$35,001–$50,000	5.68	13.40	6.45
$50,001–$75,000	3.31	6.69	3.44
>$75,000	1.86	1.23	1.84
Total	9.91%	30.34%	12.76%

NOTE: Data from the 1994 PSID; analysis weighted by the 1992 family weight.

1994 MEDIAN AND MEAN FAMILY NET WORTH (EXCLUDING HOME EQUITY) AND HOME EQUITY, BY RACE AND 1992 YEARLY FAMILY INCOME (IN 1994 DOLLARS) (N = 7,324)

Yearly Income	Net Worth (Excluding Home Equity)			Home Equity		
	White	Black	Total	White	Black	Total
Median Values						
<$15,001	$3,400	$0	$1,400	$0	$0	$0
$15,001–$35,000	17,000	6,000	13,300	14,000	0	10,000
$35,001–$50,000	37,000	15,800	35,000	35,000	15,400	31,000
$50,001–$75,000	74,500	31,200	72,000	50,208	20,000	50,000
>$75,000	181,000	60,000	179,800	90,000	43,000	90,000
Total	$28,816	$2,000	$22,000	$30,000	$0	$23,000
Mean Values						
<$15,001	$26,633	$5,273	$20,979	$20,580	$10,686	$17,961
$15,001–$35,000	61,023	17,327	54,380	35,506	15,534	32,470
$35,001–$50,000	112,976	45,474	106,238	53,209	29,359	50,829
$50,001–$75,000	178,707	48,406	173,982	71,627	30,668	70,142
>$75,000	447,060	148,580	436,486	20,690	80,425	109,383
Total	$130,991	$21,123	$115,628	$52,216	$17,870	$47,414

NOTE: Data from the 1994 PSID; analysis weighted by the 1992 family weight.

TABLE A2.3

1994 MEAN HOMEOWNERSHIP AND SELF-EMPLOYMENT RATES,
BY RACE AND 1992 YEARLY FAMILY INCOME (IN 1994 DOLLARS) (N = 7,324)

	Homeownership			Self-Employment		
Yearly Income	White (%)	Black (%)	Total (%)	White (%)	Black (%)	Total (%)
<$15,001	53.41	44.31	55.93	11.25	9.26	10.82
$15,001–$35,000	57.38	50.25	56.44	9.66	12.09	9.98
$35,001–$50,000	56.78	47.27	55.99	10.02	21.30	10.96
$50,001–$75,000	52.58	53.04	52.59	8.35	12.94	3.44
>$75,000	58.13	30.00	57.23	10.63	2.64	10.38
Total	56.42	46.78	55.32	9.99	12.05	10.23

NOTE: Data from the 1994 PSID; analysis weighted by the 1992 family weight.

TABLE A2.4

HOME FINANCING DATA, BY RACE

	White (%)	Black (%)	Total (%)
Refinanced mortgage (N = 1,071)	40.40	30.45	39.76
Turned down for financing (N = 871)	1.10	4.41	1.36
Had previous business with bank (N = 2,701)	11.82	2.39	10.88
Pays mortgage insurance (N = 1,205)	61.91	47.43	48.35
Pays mortgage tax (N = 1,206)	56.22	64.40	56.74
Has fixed-interest mortgage (N = 1,159)	77.70	81.86	77.96
Has government-sponsored loan (N = 1,051)	21.71	46.86	23.29
Median 1996 monthly rent for tenants: $400			
Median 1996 monthly mortgage costs for owners: $279			

NOTE: Data from the 1994 PSID; analysis weighted by the 1992 family weight.

TABLE A2.5

NATURAL LOGARITHM OF 1994 NET WORTH FOR 1992–94 RESPONDENTS AGES 18–30 WHO WERE SONS OR DAUGHTERS OF HEADS OF 1984 PSID FAMILIES

	Model A (Base)	Model B (Background)	Model C (SES)	Model D (Net Worth)	Model E (Asset Type)
Respondent Characteristics					
Black	−1.625** (.558)	−1.001+ (.562)	.011 (.604)	.321 (.609)	.392 (.625)
Latino	−3.247** (1.159)	−2.300* (1.151)	−2.092+ (1.140)	−1.789 (1.141)	−1.617 (1.186)
Other racial group	3.401 (3.472)	2.468 (3.380)	2.199 (3.331)	2.147 (3.305)	2.344 (3.321)
Female		−.725* (.366)	−.790* (.402)	−.741+ (.401)	−.666 (.405)
Age in 1992		.053 (.064)	.046 (.072)	.049 (.071)	.051 (.072)
Number of siblings		−.078 (.081)	.015 (.093)	.016 (.093)	.007 (.093)
High school graduate		.202 (.572)	−.244 (.583)	−.363 (.579)	−.365 (.582)
College graduate		.106 (.423)	−.233 (.440)	−.324 (.437)	−.350 (.444)
Income in 1992 (natural logarithm)		.742*** (.146)	.634*** (.147)	.611*** (.146)	.621*** (.148)
Parental Characteristics					
Age of head of household in 1984			−.032 (.029)	−.043 (.029)	−.035 (.029)
Number of years female-headed household, 1980–84			−1.442* (.601)	−.994 (.614)	−.968 (.630)
Welfare receipt in 1984			−.442 (1.155)	.005 (1.157)	.077 (1.171)
Parental Class Measures					
Education of head of household in 1984			−.101 (.083)	−.096 (.083)	−.079 (.084)
Occupational prestige of head of household, 1980–84			.028+ (.016)	.025 (.016)	.025 (.016)

Natural logarithm of income, 1980–84 (constant 1995 dollars)			1.050** (.359)	.619 (.377)	.673+ (.391)
Has wealth in 1984				−2.893+ (1.535)	.178 (.854)
Natural logarithm of net worth in 1984				.423** (.139)	
Natural logarithm of primary residence equity					.062 (.047)
Natural logarithm of business equity					.038 (.041)
Natural logarithm of net value of other illiquid assets					.131 (.086)
Natural logarithm of net value of liquid assets					.036 (.050)
Constant	7.840*** (.184)	−.739 (1.917)	−8.860* (3.668)	−8.077* (3.665)	−6.783+ (3.910)
R^2	.026	.092	.135	.151	.150
N	625	625	625	625	625

NOTE: Standard errors in parentheses; analysis weighted by the 1992 individual weight. The interaction effects between parental wealth variables and number of siblings are not significant; neither are interactions between race and wealth variables.

$^+p < .10$ $^*p < .05$ $^{**}p < .01$ $^{***}p < .001$

TABLE A3.1

LOG-ODDS OF HIGH SCHOOL GRADUATION FOR 1995 RESPONDENTS AGES 18-30
WHO WERE SONS OR DAUGHTERS OF 1984 HEADS OF PSID FAMILIES

	Model A (Base)	Model B (Background)	Model C (SES)	Model D (Net Worth)	Model E (Asset Type)
Respondent Characteristics					
Black	−.030 (.283)	.133 (.290)	.960** (.326)	.983** (.336)	.941** (.335)
Latino	−1.114** (.450)	−.980* (.419)	−.247 (.462)	−.357 (.459)	−.254 (.452)
Other racial group	4.061 (8.168)	3.613 (7.986)	1.728 (8.046)	1.691 (8.059)	1.585 (8.087)
Female		.567** (.188)	.611** (.200)	.600** (.201)	.615** (.203)
Age in 1992		.148*** (.028)	.122*** (.033)	.114*** (.033)	.127*** (.034)
Number of siblings		−.122** (.044)	−.031 (.058)	−.020 (.058)	−.030 (.059)
Parental Characteristics					
Age of head of household in 1984			−.005 (.016)	−.009 (.016)	−.015 (.016)
Number of years female-headed household, 1980–1984			−.537+ (.314)	−.365 (.331)	−.439 (.336)
Welfare receipt in 1984			−.213 (.375)	.030 (.404)	−.125 (.405)
Parental Class Measures					
Education of head of household in 1984			.264*** (.045)	.261*** (.045)	.252*** (.045)
Occupational prestige of head of household, 1980–84			.012 (.009)	.012 (.009)	.008 (.010)
Natural logarithm of income, 1980–84 (constant 1995 dollars)			.510* (.211)	.425+ (.218)	.350 (.242)

	(1)	(2)	(3)	(4)	(5)
Has wealth in 1984				-.383 (.664)	.129 (.403)
Natural logarithm of net worth in 1984				.098 (.066)	
Natural logarithm of primary residence equity					.020 (.025)
Natural logarithm of business equity					.065+ (.037)
Natural logarithm of net value of other illiquid assets					-.035 (.055)
Natural logarithm of net value of liquid assets					.082** (.027)
Constant	3.597 (4.091)	.191 (4.056)	-8.349 (4.526)	-7.827+ (4.550)	-6.554 (4.646)
L^2_{df}	8.023_3	49.521_6***	153.256_{12}***	156.843_{14}***	170.998_{17}***
N	1,290	1,290	1,290	1,290	1,290

NOTE: Standard errors in parentheses; an analysis weighted by the 1995 individual weight.
+$p < .10$ *$p < .05$ **$p < .01$ ***$p < .001$

TABLE A3.2

LOG-ODDS OF COLLEGE GRADUATION FOR 1995 RESPONDENTS AGES 18–30 WHO HAD
COMPLETED HIGH SCHOOL AND WERE SONS OR DAUGHTERS OF 1984 HEADS OF PSID FAMILIES

	Model A (Base)	Model B (Background)	Model C (SES)	Model D (Net Worth)	Model E (Asset Type)
Respondent Characteristics					
Black	−.958*** (.274)	−.816** (.281)	.017 (.314)	.161 (.318)	.210 (.319)
Latino	.060 (.457)	.165 (.475)	.575 (.579)	.751 (.561)	.752 (.594)
Other racial group	4.751+ (2.566)	4.474+ (2.565)	2.927 (2.570)	2.849 (2.571)	2.748 (2.572)
Female		.104 (.141)	.021 (.155)	.031 (.156)	.043 (.157)
Age in 1992		.187*** (.025)	.146*** (.030)	.146*** (.031)	.142*** (.031)
Number of siblings		−.198*** (.044)	−.202*** (.050)	−.189*** (.051)	−.202*** (.051)
Parental Characteristics					
Age of head of household in 1984			.032* (.013)	.025+ (.013)	.026* (.013)
Number of years female-headed household, 1980–84			−.175 (.340)	−.034 (.346)	.176 (.354)
Welfare receipt in 1984			.103 (.731)	.206 (.763)	.278 (.748)
Parental Class Measures					
Education of head of household in 1984			.326*** (.046)	.327*** (.046)	.328*** (.047)
Occupational prestige of head of household, 1980–84			.007 (.007)	.006 (.007)	.006 (.008)
Natural logarithm of income, 1980–84 (constant 1995 dollars)			.522** (.171)	.132 (.192)	.198 (.198)

	(1)	(2)	(3)	(4)	(5)
Has wealth in 1984				2.745^{**} (.192)	.754 (.535)
Natural logarithm of net worth in 1984				$.295^{***}$ (.072)	
Natural logarithm of primary residence equity					$.092^{***}$ (.026)
Natural logarithm of business equity					.000 (.018)
Natural logarithm of net value of other illiquid assets					.057 (.046)
Natural logarithm of net value of liquid assets					$.051^{*}$ (.023)
Constant	-2.356^{+} (1.283)	-3.418^{*} (1.455)	-14.224^{***} (2.192)	-11.412^{***} (2.267)	-11.535^{***} (2.349)
L^2_{df}	32.160_{3}	109.186_{6}	275.171_{12}	293.635_{14}	300.587_{17}
N	1,113	1,113	1,113	1,113	1,113

NOTE: Standard errors in parentheses; analysis weighted by the 1995 individual weight. College graduation is defined as receipt of a bachelor's degree.
$^{+}p < .10$ $^{*}p < .05$ $^{**}p < .01$ $^{***}p < .001$

TABLE A3.3

LOG-ODDS OF BEING HELD BACK A GRADE FOR 1995 RESPONDENTS AGES 18–30 WHO WERE SONS OR DAUGHTERS OF 1984 HEADS OF PSID FAMILIES

	Model A (Base)	Model B (Background)	Model C (SES)	Model D (Net Worth)	Model E (Asset Type)
Respondent Characteristics					
Black	−.242 (.280)	−.335 (.286)	−.820** (.308)	−.827** (.311)	−.851** (.314)
Latino	−.421 (.606)	−.549 (.611)	−1.123+ (.633)	−.958 (.628)	−1.093+ (.628)
Other racial group	−4.330 (8.168)	−4.067 (8.000)	−2.713 (8.033)	−2.661 (8.047)	−2.658 (8.059)
Female		−.833*** (.179)	−.867*** (.184)	−.865*** (.184)	−.870*** (.186)
Age in 1992		−.089* (.026)	−.062* (.030)	−.050* (.030)	−.061* (.030)
Number of siblings		.037 (.045)	−.014 (.054)	−.031 (.054)	−.024 (.055)
Parental Characteristics					
Age of head of household in 1984			−.012 (.014)	−.006 (.014)	−.003 (.015)
Number of years female-headed household, 1980–84			.278 (.304)	−.005 (.323)	.068 (.325)
Welfare receipt in 1984			−.290 (.403)	−.711 (.432)	−.517 (.427)
Parental Class Measures					
Education of head of household in 1984			−.196*** (.041)	−.189*** (.041)	−.185* (.042)
Occupational prestige of head of household, 1980–84			−.013 (.008)	−.012 (.008)	−.010 (.008)

Natural logarithm of income, 1980–84 (constant 1995 dollars)			−.135 (.190)	.026 (.203)	.149 (.221)
Has wealth in 1984				1.051+ (.638)	.013 (.191)
Natural logarithm of net worth in 1984				−.178** (.062)	
Natural logarithm of primary residence equity					−.032 (.022)
Natural logarithm of business equity					−.058* (.029)
Natural logarithm of net value of other illiquid assets					−.027 (.048)
Natural logarithm of net value of liquid assets					−.072** (.024)
Constant	−4.366 (4.097)	−2.288 (4.062)	−1.960 (4.416)	.846 (4.459)	−.812 (4.530)
L^2_{df}	3.276_3 ***	39.026_6 ***	92.049_{12} ***	102.150_{14} ***	113.863_{17} ***
N	1,288	1,288	1,288	1,238	1,288

NOTE: Standard errors in parentheses; analysis weighted by 1995 individual weight.
$^+ p < .10$ $^* p < .05$ $^{**} p < .01$ $^{***} p < .001$

LOG-ODDS OF SCHOOL EXPULSION OR SUSPENSION FOR 1995 RESPONDENTS AGES 18–30 WHO WERE SONS OR DAUGHTERS OF 1984 HEADS OF PSID FAMILIES

	Model A (Base)	Model B (Background)	Model C (SES)	Model D (Net Worth)	Model E (Asset Type)
Respondent Characteristics					
Black	.475* (.203)	.454* (.210)	.176 (.228)	.169 (.229)	.119 (.116)
Latino	-.027 (.460)	-.126 (.466)	-.392 (.477)	-.347 (.472)	-.481 (.476)
Other racial group	-4.696 (8.168)	-4.523 (7.982)	-3.985 (7.990)	-3.958 (8.002)	-3.978 (8.003)
Female		-.989*** (.154)	-.996*** (.156)	-.993*** (.156)	-.997*** (.156)
Age in 1992		-.056* (.022)	-.030 (.026)	-.024 (.026)	-.031 (.026)
Number of siblings		-.008 (.038)	-.017*** (.046)	-.027 (.046)	-.025 (.046)
Parental Characteristics					
Age of head of household in 1984			-.014 (.012)	-.010 (.012)	-.009 (.012)
Number of years female-headed household, 1980–84			.222 (.261)	.072 (.272)	.105 (.275)
Welfare receipt in 1984			.209 (.336)	-.009 (.352)	.076 (.352)
Parental Class Measures					
Education of head of household in 1984			-.079* (.035)	-.075* (.036)	-.076* (.036)
Occupational prestige of head of household, 1980–84			-.004 (.007)	-.003 (.007)	-.002 (.007)

	Model 1	Model 2	Model 3	Model 4	Model 5
Natural logarithm of income, 1980–84 (constant 1995 dollars)			−.074 (.163)	.042 (.174)	.150 (.185)
Has wealth in 1984				.684 (.555)	.053 (.339)
Natural logarithm of net worth in 1984				−.112* (.053)	
Natural logarithm of primary residence equity					−.011 (.019)
Natural logarithm of business equity					−.033 (.018)
Natural logarithm of net value of other illiquid assets					−.037 (.039)
Natural logarithm of net value of liquid assets					−.048* (.020)
Constant	−3.628 (4.084)	−2.267 (4.037)	−.323*** (4.286)	−1.156 (4.315)	−2.402 (4.355)
L^2_{df}	8.297^*_3	60.004^{***}_6	77.259^{***}_{12}	82.440^{***}_{14}	89.855^{***}_{17}
N	1,285	1,285	1,285	1,285	1,285

NOTE: Standard errors in parentheses; analysis weighted by 1995 individual weight.
$^+ p < .10$ $^* p < .05$ $^{**} p < .01$ $^{***} p < .001$

LOG-ODDS OF UNEMPLOYMENT/LABOR FORCE NONPARTICIPATION FOR 1992 RESPONDENTS AGES
18–30 WHO WERE SONS OR DAUGHTERS OF 1984 HEADS OF LOW-INCOME PSID FAMILIES

	Model A (Base)	Model B (Background)	Model C (SES)	Model D (Net Worth)
Respondent Characteristics				
Black	.428 (.366)	.372 (.405)	.521 (.513)	.141 (.564)
Latino	7.920 (13.461)	8.516 (13.473)	9.548 (22.206)	10.276 (22.210)
Other racial group	—	—	—	—
Female		2.012*** (4.76)	2.066*** (.520)	2.022*** (.534)
Age in 1992		.004 (.064)	-.029 (.085)	.002 (.086)
Number of siblings		-.051 (.075)	-.163 (.100)	-.192+ (.102)
High school graduate		-.907* (.420)	-.582 (.477)	-.192+ (.102)
College graduate		-.566 (.824)	-.333 (.868)	-.073 (.871)
Parental Characteristics				
Age of head of household in 1984			.039** (.036)	.026 (.039)
Number of years female-headed household, 1980–84			.118 (.608)	-.366 (.686)
Welfare receipt in 1984			1.501** (.578)	1.462* (.614)
Parental Class Measures				
Education of head of household in 1984			-.196* (.082)	-.228** (.087)
Occupational prestige of head of household, 1980–84			.044* (.019)	.059** (.021)

Natural logarithm of income, 1980–84 (constant 1995 dollars)				-1.689^{**} (.594)
Has wealth in 1984			$-.395$ (.459)	$-.355$ (.477)
Constant	2.453 (6.732)	2.387 (6.944)	7.314 (11.954)	7.510 (12.030)
L^2_{df}	10.894^{**}_{2}	40.757^{***}_{7}	68.389^{***}_{13}	77.062^{***}_{14}
N	250	250	250	250

NOTE: Standard errors in parentheses; analysis weighted by 1992 individual weight. Low-income families are defined here as families whose 1984 annual income was less than 185 percent of the official poverty threshold for a family of four. The category "Other racial group" displayed no unique variation in these models.

$^+p < .10$ $^*p < .05$ $^{**}p < .01$ $^{***}p < .001$

HOURS WORKED BY 1992 RESPONDENTS AGES 18–30 WHO WERE EMPLOYED AT LEAST ONE HOUR IN 1992 AND WERE SONS OR DAUGHTERS OF 1984 HEADS OF PSID FAMILIES

	Model A (Base)	Model B (Background)	Model C (SES)	Model D (Net Worth)	Model E (Asset Type)
Respondent Characteristics					
Black	−245.397** (88.549)	−210.816* (86.634)	−182.651* (91.402)	−151.831+ (91.777)	−171.052+ (97.114)
Latino	−120.909 (155.138)	−101.554 (153.149)	−71.107 (155.792)	−10.329 (158.119)	−42.826 (161.974)
Other racial group	−845.239* (359.828)	−847.488* (352.587)	−899.473* (352.954)	−909.789** (351.957)	−887.525* (352.629)
Female		−277.535*** (46.521)	−260.448*** (46.819)	−256.504*** (46.716)	−252.474*** (46.837)
Age in 1992		20.319* (8.599)	29.461* (9.561)	28.341* (.077)	27.078** (9.588)
Number of siblings		12.523 (11.573)	23.700+ (12.682)	26.547 (12.654)	25.182 (12.696)
High school graduate		401.983*** (392.262)	363.689*** (82.446)	357.169*** (82.243)	355.494*** (82.538)
College graduate		11.479 (58.843)	−1.309 (61.969)	−7.056 (61.966)	−17.371 (63.072)
Parental Characteristics					
Age of head of household in 1984			−2.293 (3.684)	−2.784 (3.678)	−3.098 (3.737)
Number of years female-headed household, 1980–84			−248.081 (88.374)	−212.392* (89.016)	−195.558* (90.114)
Welfare receipt in 1984			−214.486 (219.398)	−156.172 (220.098)	−137.359 (222.177)
Parental Class Measures					
Education of head of household in 1984			33.599** (12.020)	33.537** (12.017)	33.084** (12.175)
Occupational prestige of head of household, 1980–84			1.528 (2.258)	1.486 (2.255)	1.454 (2.271)

	(1)	(2)	(3)	(4)	(5)
Natural logarithm of income, 1980–84 (constant 1995 dollars)			−211.083*** (49.602)	−262.480*** (52.987)	−255.610*** (54.317)
Has wealth in 1984				−182.039 (222.605)	−125.745 (143.385)
Natural logarithm of net worth in 1984				41.021* (17.862)	
Natural logarithm of primary residence equity					14.286* (6.414)
Natural logarithm of business equity					6.989 (5.520)
Natural logarithm of net value of other illiquid assets					−8.390 (12.341)
Natural logarithm of net value of liquid assets					8.682 (8.682)
Constant	1875.369*** (24.953)	1102.285*** (219.597)	2808.999*** (493.450)	2972.968*** (495.882)	3276.302*** (533.646)
R^2	.012	.071	.092	.099	.102
N	1,084	1,084	1,084	1,084	1,084

NOTE: Standard errors in parentheses; analysis weighted by 1992 individual weight.

*$p < .10$ **$p < .05$ ***$p < .01$ ****$p < .001$

HOURLY WAGES OF 1992 RESPONDENTS AGES 18–30 WHO WERE EMPLOYED FULL TIME IN 1992 AND WERE SONS OR DAUGHTERS OF 1984 HEADS OF PSID FAMILIES

	Model A (Base)	Model B (Background)	Model C (SES)	Model D (Net Worth)	Model E (Asset Type)
Respondent Characteristics					
Black	−.431 (.972)	.987 (.837)	1.415+ (.832)	1.281 (.831)	.601 (.493)
Latino	1.316 (1.327)	.761 (1.123)	1.240 (1.148)	1.169 (1.238)	1.393 (1.294)
Other racial group	1.912 (4.703)	−2.030 (3.951)	−1.817 (3.727)	−1.739 (3.714)	−1.993 (3.705)
Female		−.945* (.366)	−1.488*** (.353)	−1.530*** (.352)	−1.527*** (.352)
Age in 1992		.534*** (.070)	.512*** (.074)	.520*** (.074)	.515*** (.074)
Number of siblings		−.033 (.090)	.029 (.093)	.028 (.094)	.062 (.094)
High school graduate		2.627*** (.762)	1.929** (.742)	1.982** (.740)	1.756* (.745)
College graduate		4.306*** (.439)	2.851*** (.453)	2.877*** (.452)	2.918*** (.458)
Parental Characteristics					
Age of head of household in 1984			−.037 (.029)	−.033 (.029)	−.039 (.030)
Number of years female-headed household, 1980–84			.282 (.681)	.250 (.680)	.072 (.687)
Welfare receipt in 1984			−.368 (1.734)	−1.151 (1.781)	−1.547 (1.816)
Parental Class Measures					
Education of head of household in 1984			.269** (.089)	.280** (.089)	.284** (.090)
Occupational prestige of head of household, 1980–84			−.027* (.016)	−.025 (.016)	−.030+ (.016)
Natural logarithm of income, 1980–84 (constant 1995 dollars)			2.387*** (.343)	2.770*** (.376)	2.602*** (.376)
Has wealth in 1984				4.045* (1.901)	1.523 (1.172)

Natural logarithm of net worth in 1984				−.376* (.148)	
Natural logarithm of primary residence equity					−1.26* (.050)
Natural logarithm of business equity					.003 (.039)
Natural logarithm of net value of other illiquid assets					−.192* (.095)
Natural logarithm of net value of liquid assets					.027 (.049)
Constant	9.958*** (.217)	−6.727** (1.856)	−31.868*** (3.535)	−32.515*** (3.551)	−31.434*** (3.822)
R^2	.002	.306	.393	.399	.406
N	649	649	649	649	649

NOTE: Standard errors in parentheses; analysis weighted by 1992 individual weight.

$^+p < .10$ $^*p < .05$ $^{**}p < .01$ $^{***}p < .001$

TABLE A5.1

COX PROPORTIONAL-HAZARD REGRESSION FOR RISK OF PREMARITAL CHILDBEARING BY 1992 RESPONDENTS AGES 18–21 WHO WERE DAUGHTERS OF 1984 HEADS OF PSID FAMILIES

	Model A (Base)	Model B (Background)	Model C (SES)	Model D (Net Worth)	Model E (Asset Type)
Respondent Characteristics					
Black	2.573*** (.348)	2.351*** (.366)	1.152* (.530)	1.247* (.541)	1.152* (.518)
Latino	1.689** (.622)	1.541* (.629)	1.154 (.729)	1.258+ (.764)	1.914* (.768)
Age 10		−.965+ (.518)	−1.210* (.584)	−1.326* (.602)	−1.418* (.610)
Age 11		−.614 (.434)	−1.311* (.521)	−1.453** (.531)	−1.562** (.541)
Age 12		−.744 (.492)	−.948+ (.506)	−1.287* (.549)	−1.392* (.559)
Age 13 (suppressed)	—			—	—
Parental Characteristics					
Age of head of household in 1984			−.007 (.037)	.004 (.038)	.010 (.037)
Mother not married at birth of respondent			.694 (.552)	.892 (.603)	.952+ (.556)
Number of years female-headed household, 1980–84			.296 (.612)	.603 (.632)	.192 (.688)
Welfare receipt in 1984			.275 (.740)	.583 (.860)	.149 (.786)
Parental Class Measures					
Education of head of household in 1984			−.250* (.102)	−.229* (.105)	−.203+ (.105)
Occupational prestige of head of household, 1980–84			.002 (.017)	.007 (.018)	.000 (.018)

Natural logarithm of income, 1980–84 (constant 1995 dollars)			$-.766$ (.481)	$-.752$ (.544)	$-.656$ (.526)
Has wealth in 1984				-2.745 (1.825)	-1.304^{*} (.783)
Natural logarithm of net worth in 1984				$.084$ (.178)	
Natural logarithm of primary residence equity					$-.082^{+}$ (.044)
Natural logarithm of business equity					$.069$ (.064)
Natural logarithm of net value of other illiquid assets					$-.152$ (.110)
Natural logarithm of net value of liquid assets					$.038$ (.054)
L^2_{df}	43.972^{***}_{2}	49.004^{***}_{5}	155.151^{***}_{12}	168.792^{***}_{14}	168.078^{***}_{17}
N	236	236	236	236	236

NOTE: Standard errors in parentheses; analysis weighted by 1992 individual weight (rounded to the nearest integer for the Cox regression).

$^{+}p < .10$ $^{*}p < .05$ $^{**}p < .01$ $^{***}p < .001$

TABLE A5.2

LOG-ODDS OF WELFARE RECEIPT BY 1992 RESPONDENTS AGES 18–30 WHO WERE SONS OR DAUGHTERS OF 1984 HEADS OF LOW-INCOME PSID FAMILIES

	Model A (Base)	Model B (Background)	Model C (SES)	Model D (Net Worth)
Respondent Characteristics				
Black	.770* (.312)	.748* (.336)	.091 (.450)	-.153 (.485)
Latino	7.606 (13.460)	6.567 (13.466)	5.500 (13.476)	5.194 (13.477)
Other racial group	—	—	—	—
Female		.662* (.318)	.700+ (.358)	.559 (.364)
Age in 1992		.090 (.110)	.008 (.074)	.012 (.074)
Number of siblings		-.076 (.124)	-.264 (.059)	-.286*** (.086)
High school graduate		-1.246*** (.350)	-1.168** (.385)	-1.099** (.390)
College graduate		-2.710 (1.692)	-2.812+ (1.706)	-2.708 (.852)
Parental Characteristics				
Age of head of household in 1984			.087** (.030)	.081** (.031)
Number of years female-headed household, 1980–84			1.422** (.502)	1.285* (.524)
Welfare receipt in 1984			-.291 (.572)	-.378 (.294)

Parental Class Measures

	Model 1	Model 2	Model 3	Model 4
Education of head of household in 1984				−.020 (.073)
Occupational prestige of head of household, 1980–84			−.060*** (.016)	−.063*** (.017)
Natural logarithm of income, 1980–84 (constant 1995 dollars)			.294 (.393)	.494 (.411)
Has wealth in 1984				−1.027* (.478)
Constant	2.781 (6.731)	−.734 (6.934)	−4.534 (7.775)	−5.723 (7.830)
L^2_{df}	13.708**$_2$	37.581***$_{17}$	70.769***$_{13}$	75.428***$_{14}$
N	264	264	264	264

NOTE: Standard errors in parentheses; analysis weighted by 1995 individual weight. Low-income families are defined here as families whose 1984 annual income was less than 185 percent of the official poverty threshold for a family of four. The category "Other racial group" displayed no unique variation in these models.

*p < .10   **p < .05   ***p < .01   ****p < .001

Notes

CHAPTER ONE

1. Data from the Panel Study of Income Dynamics (PSID), 1994 Wealth Supplement. The PSID is an ongoing study conducted by the Survey Research Center, Institute for Social Research, at the University of Michigan; see the PSID Web site at *www.isr.umich.edu/src/psid*. For further statistics on median and mean net worth at various income levels, see Table A2.1 in the Appendix of this book.

2. These family descriptions were extrapolated from profiles of specific families who were interviewed for this study. The age, racial, income, family size, wealth, housing tenure, and divorce descriptions of these families come directly from cases 4348 and 1586 of the PSID 1984 wave (inflation-adjusted to 1996 dollars). The names and other details are fictitious but are in line with previous research that would suggest such profiles.

3. Neither family received health insurance from an employer. Since the Smiths' income was under 185 percent of the poverty line, their children were eligible for Medicaid. (In most states, the Joneses' children would also have been eligible for Medicaid since that family's wealth was in the form of a home, which is excluded from the asset limits of many states.)

4. See, e.g., G. Levinger and O. Moles, eds., *Divorce and Separation: Contexts, Causes, and Consequences* (New York: Basic Books, 1979); and R. Conger, G. H. Elder, et al., "Linking Economic Hardship to Marital Quality and Instability," *Journal of Marriage and the Family* 52 (1990): 643–56.

5. Throughout this book, the terms "black" and "African American" are used interchangeably, as are the terms "Hispanic" and "Latino." Black people of Caribbean origin make up a negligible portion of the data sample.

6. M. Oliver and T. Shapiro, *Black Wealth/White Wealth: A New Perspective on Racial Inequality* (New York: Routledge, 1995).

7. W. J. Wilson, *The Declining Significance of Race: Blacks and Changing American Institutions* (Chicago: University of Chicago Press, 1978).

8. J. L. Hochschild, *Facing Up to the American Dream: Race, Class, and the Soul of the Nation* (Princeton, N.J.: Princeton University Press, 1995), p. 55.

9. Ibid.

10. S. Danziger and P. Gottschalk, *America Unequal* (New York and Cambridge: Russell Sage Foundation and Harvard University Press, 1995), p. 90.

11. P. Blau and O. D. Duncan, *The American Occupational Structure* (New York: Free Press, 1967).

12. Ibid., p. 239.

13. Much of this betterment can be traced to geographic mobility. In fact, the major explanation for black socioeconomic advancement during the 1940s and 1950s was the movement of African Americans from the rural South to the industrial North with its higher wages. See, e.g., M. A. Fosset, O. R. Galle, and J. A. Burr, "Racial Occupational Inequality, 1940–1980: A Research Note on the Impact of Changing Regional Distribution of the Black Population," *Social Forces* 68 (1989): 415–27.

14. S. J. Ventura, J. A. Martin, S. C. Curtin, and T. J. Mathews, "Report of Final Natality Statistics, 1996," *Monthly Vital Statistics Report* 46 (1997): suppl. 2.

15. See National Center for Children in Poverty, *One in Four: America's Youngest Poor* (New York: Columbia University School of Public Health, 1995).

16. Statistics are from K. DeBarros and C. Bennett, "The Black Population in the United States: March 1997 (Update)," *Current Population Reports,* Series P-20, No. 508 (Washington, D.C.: U.S. Government Printing Office, 1998).

17. See, e.g., J. Bound and R. B. Freeman, "What Went Wrong? The Erosion of the Relative Earnings and Employment of Young Black Men in the 1980s," *Quarterly Journal of Economics* 107 (1992): 201–32; P. Moss and C. Tilly, "A Turn for the Worse: Why Black Men's Labour Market Fortunes Have Declined in the United States," *Sage Race Relations Abstracts* 18 (1993): 5–45.

18. C. Jencks, "Is the American Underclass Growing?" in *The Urban Underclass,* ed. C. Jencks and P. Peterson (Washington, D.C.: Brookings Institution, 1991).

19. DeBarros and Bennett, "The Black Population in the United States: March 1997."

20. Ibid.

21. Ibid.

22. W. J. Wilson, *The Truly Disadvantaged: The Inner City, the Underclass, and Public Policy* (Chicago: University of Chicago Press, 1987).

23. See, e.g., S. Thernstrom and A. Thernstrom, *America in Black and White: One Nation, Indivisible* (New York: Simon and Schuster, 1997).

24. Wilson, *Declining Significance of Race,* p. 1.

25. M. Hout, "Occupational Mobility of Black Men: 1962 to 1973," *American Sociological Review* 49 (1984): 308–22; I. S. Son, S. W. Model, and G. A. Fisher, "Polarization and Progress in the Black Community: Earnings and Status Gains for Young Black Males in the Era of Affirmative Action," *Sociological Forum* 4, no. 3 (1989): 309–27.

26. See two articles by C. Link, E. Ratledge, and K. Lewis: "Black-White Differences in Returns to Schooling: Some New Evidence," *American Economic Review* 66 (1976): 221–23; and "The Quality of Education and Cohort Variation in Black-White Earnings Differentials: Reply," *American Economic Review* 70 (1980): 196–203.

27. J. C. Henretta, "Race Differences in Middle-Class Lifestyle: The Role of Home Ownership," *Social Science Research* 8 (1979): 63–78.

28. J. Feagin and H. Vera, *White Racism: The Basics* (New York: Routledge, 1995); C. West, *Race Matters* (New York: Vintage, 1994).

29. Influential authors K. Davis and W. E. Moore acknowledged as much in their 1945 article "Some Principles of Stratification" (*American Sociological Review* 10 [1945]: 242–49).

30. C. Fischer, M. Hout, M. Sanchez-Jankowski, S. R. Lucas, A. Swidler, and K. Voss, *Inequality by Design: Cracking the Bell Curve Myth* (Princeton, N.J.: Princeton University Press, 1996), p. 3.

31. T. Veblen, *The Theory of the Leisure Class* (New York: Penguin, 1979).

32. Shils paraphrased in M. E. Sobel, "Lifestyle Differentiation and Stratification in Contemporary U.S. Society," *Research in Social Stratification and Mobility* 2 (1983):116. Also see the original article: E. Shils, "Deference," in *The Logic of Social Hierarchies,* ed. E. O. Laumann, P. M. Siegal, and R. M. Hodge (Chicago: Markham, 1970), pp. 420–48.

33. Abrams cited in D. L. Kirp, J. P. Dwyer, and L. A. Rosenthal, *Our Town: Race, Housing, and the Soul of Suburbia* (New Brunswick, N.J.: Rutgers University Press, 1995), p. 83.

34. R. Sennett and J. Cobb, *The Hidden Injuries of Class* (New York: Basic Books, 1972), p. 36.

35. Because the PSID follows each child from the original family, there are in some cases multiple children from the same family of origin (39.1 percent of respondents under the broadest sample parameters have at least one sibling or cousin from the same 1968 household). To correct for the possibility of nonindependence within families, which might bias the standard errors, I tested models that randomly selected one individual from each family of origin. Results were not significantly different; thus, I have chosen to keep the larger, original sample since many of my arguments depend on the insignificance of the race variable and I wanted the larger sample size upon which to base my claims. Generalized linear models (random effects models) also yield the same pattern of results.

36. There are two general exceptions to this statement. First, Native Americans, who make up a very small portion of the population, tend to be more socioeconomically disadvantaged than blacks (although this varies by nation/tribe). Second, educational data show that some Latino groups (particularly those with limited English literacy on average) do more poorly than blacks on some measures.

37. For a discussion of skin tone and stratification, see, e.g., V. M. Keith and C. Herring, "Skin Tone and Stratification in the Black Community," *American Journal of Sociology* 97 (1991): 760–78.

38. A. Hacker, *Two Nations: Black and White, Separate, Hostile, and Unequal* (New York: Ballantine, 1992).

39. I. Light and C. Rosenstein, *Race, Ethnicity, and Entrepreneurship in Urban America* (New York: Aldine de Gruyter, 1995), p. 17.

40. Ibid., p. 18.

41. R. L. Boyd, "Black and Asian Self-Employment in Large Metropolitan Areas: A Comparative Analysis," *Social Problems* 37 (1990): 258–73.

42. Light and Rosenstein, *Race, Ethnicity, and Entrepreneurship.*

43. H. W. Aurand, "Self-Employment: Last Resort of the Unemployed," *International Social Science Review* 58 (1983): 7–11.

44. Light and Rosenstein, *Race, Ethnicity, and Entrepreneurship.*

45. G. J. Borjas and S. G. Bronars, "Consumer Discrimination and Self-Employment," *Journal of Political Economy* 97 (1989): 581–605.

46. Ibid.

CHAPTER TWO

1. C. Anderson, *Black Labor, White Wealth: The Search for Power and Economic Justice* (Edgewood, Md.: Duncan and Duncan, 1994).

2. S. Spilerman, M. Semyonov, and N. Lewin-Epstein, "Wealth, Intergenerational Transfers, and Life Chances," in *Social Theory and Social Policy: Essays in Honor of James Coleman*, ed. A. Sorensen and S. Spilerman (New York: Praeger, 1993).

3. These figures include housing and vehicle equity.

4. M. Oliver and T. Shapiro, *Black Wealth/White Wealth: A New Perspective on Racial Inequality* (New York: Routledge, 1995).

5. J. L. Hochschild, *Facing Up to the American Dream: Race, Class, and the Soul of the Nation* (Princeton, N.J.: Princeton University Press, 1995), p. 72.

6. F. D. Blau and J. W. Graham, "Black-White Differences in Wealth and Asset Composition," *Quarterly Journal of Economics* 105 (1990): 321–39.

7. Also see A. Brimmer, "Income, Wealth, and Investment Behavior in the Black Community," *A.E.A. Papers and Proceedings* 78 (1988): 151–55.

8. Oliver and Shapiro, *Black Wealth/White Wealth.*

9. In the case of the PSID, the amount of savings is imputed through the difference between 1984 and 1989 net worth, adjusted for inheritances received, value changes in 1984 assets, and changes in household composition (people moving in or out with assets or debts). I then take that as a percentage of the inflation-adjusted, five-year average income for that period. However, windfalls and gifts may appear to be savings in this case. Alternative measures include self-reported savings as a percentage of annual income.

10. W. Hrung, "The Permanent Income Hypothesis and Black/White Savings Differentials" (Department of Economics, University of California at Berkeley, 1997).

11. C. D. Carroll, B.-K. Rhee, and C. Rhee, "Are There Cultural Effects on Saving? Some Cross-Sectional Evidence," *Quarterly Journal of Economics* 109 (1994): 695–99.

12. See, e.g., K. C. Land and S. T. Russell, "Wealth Accumulation Across the Life Course: Stability and Change in Sociodemographic Covariate Structures of

Net Worth Data in the Survey of Income and Program Participation, 1984–1991," *Social Science Research* 25 (1996): 423–62.

13. Brimmer, "Income, Wealth, and Investment Behavior," p. 153.

14. D. Massey and N. Denton, *American Apartheid: Segregation and the Making of the Underclass* (Cambridge, Mass.: Harvard University Press, 1993).

15. J. C. Henretta, "Race Differences in Middle-Class Lifestyle: The Role of Home Ownership," *Social Science Research* 8 (1979): 63–78; also see M. R. Jackman and R. W. Jackman, "Racial Inequalities in Home Ownership," *Social Forces* 58 (1980): 1221–34.

16. T. Parcel, "Wealth Accumulation of Black and White Men: The Case of Housing Equity," *Social Problems* 30 (1982): 199–211.

17. Oliver and Shapiro, *Black Wealth/White Wealth*, p. 9.

18. M. Sherraden, *Assets and the Poor: A New Direction for Social Policy* (Armonk, N.Y.: Sharpe, 1991), p. 131.

19. Oliver and Shapiro, *Black Wealth/White Wealth*, p. 37.

20. Ibid.

21. Ibid.

22. E. F. Frazier, *The Free Negro Family* (Nashville: Fisk University Press, 1932), p. 35.

23. P. Kolchin, *American Slavery, 1619–1877* (New York: Hill and Wang, 1993), p. 16.

24. C. F. Oubre, *Forty Acres and a Mule: The Freedman's Bureau and Black Land Ownership* (Baton Rouge: Louisiana State University Press, 1978).

25. P. Cimbala, "A Black Colony in Dougherty County: The Freedman's Bureau and the Failure of Reconstruction in Southwest Georgia," *Journal of Southwest Georgia History* 4 (1986): 72.

26. Du Bois quoted in Sherraden, *Assets and the Poor,* p. 133.

27. P. Cimbala, "The Freedman's Bureau, the Freedmen, and Sherman's Grant in Reconstruction Georgia, 1865–1867," *Journal of Southern History* 55 (1989): 597–98.

28. Oubre, *Forty Acres and a Mule,* p. xiii.

29. P. S. Peirce, *The Freedman's Bureau: A Chapter in the History of Reconstruction* (New York: Haskell House, 1904), p. 22.

30. N. Lemann, *The Promised Land: The Great Black Migration and How It Changed America* (New York: Vintage, 1991), p. 11.

31. "From Field to Factory: Afro-American Migration, 1915–1940," Smithsonian Institution exhibition, Museum of American History, Washington, D.C., 1994.

32. Oliver and Shapiro, *Black Wealth/White Wealth*, p. 38.

33. Ibid.

34. Sherraden, *Assets and the Poor,* p. 133.

35. M. Marable, *How Capitalism Underdeveloped Black America: Problems in Race, Political Economy, and Society* (Boston: South End Press, 1983), pp. 142–43.

36. Sherraden, *Assets and the Poor.*

37. A. Meier and E. Rudwick, *From Plantation to Ghetto* (New York: Hill and Wang, 1970).

38. Lemann, *Promised Land*, p. 6.

39. Oliver and Shapiro, *Black Wealth/White Wealth*, p. 38.

40. Massey and Denton, *American Apartheid*, p. 52.

41. D. L. Kirp, J. P. Dwyer, and L. A. Rosenthal, *Our Town: Race, Housing, and the Soul of Suburbia* (New Brunswick, N.J.: Rutgers University Press, 1995), p. 7.

42. Massey and Denton, *American Apartheid*, p. 54.

43. Kirp, Dwyer, and Rosenthal, *Our Town*, p. 26.

44. F. S. Levy and R. Michel, *The Economic Future of American Families* (Washington, D.C.: Urban Institute Press, 1991); and Spilerman, Semyonov, and Lewin-Epstein, "Wealth, Intergenerational Transfers, and Life Chances."

45. Joint Center for Housing Studies, *The State of the Nation's Housing: 1997* (Cambridge: Harvard University, 1998). The Luxembourg Income Study is a dataset housed at the Centre d'Etudes de Populations, de Pauvreté et de Politiques Socio-Economiques (CEPS), Difrerdange, Luxembourg; see *http://lissy.ceps.lu/access.htm.*

46. K. DeBarros and C. Bennett, "The Black Population in the United States: March 1997 (Update)," *Current Population Reports*, Series P-20, No. 508 (Washington, D.C.: U.S. Government Printing Office, 1998).

47. Joint Center for Housing Studies, *State of the Nation's Housing, 1997.*

48. F. Stutz and A. E. Kartman, "Housing Affordability and Spatial Price Variation in the United States," *Economic Geography* 58 (1982): 221–35; J. Adams, "Growth of U.S. Cities and Recent Trends in Urban Real Estate Values," in *Cities and Their Vital Systems,* ed. J. H. Ausubel and R. Herman (Washington, D.C.: National Academy Press, 1988), pp. 108–45.

49. G. Duncan and J. L. Aber, "Neighborhood Structure and Conditions," in *Neighborhood Poverty: Context and Consequences for Child and Adolescent Development,* ed. G. Duncan, J. Brooks-Gunn, and J. L. Aber (New York: Russell Sage Foundation, 1997).

50. E. Rosenbaum, "Racial/Ethnic Differences in Home Ownership and Housing Quality, 1991," *Social Problems* 43 (1997): 403–26.

51. See, e.g., R. Alba and J. Logan, "Variations on Two Themes: Racial and Ethnic Patterns in the Attainment of Suburban Residence," *Demography* 28 (1991): 431–53; Massey and Denton, *American Apartheid;* R. Farley and W. H. Frey, "Changes in the Segregation of Whites from Blacks," *American Sociological Review* 59 (1994): 23–45; E. Rosenbaum, "The Structural Constraints on Minority Housing Choices," *Social Forces* 72 (1994): 725–47.

52. S. McKinney and A. B. Schnare, "Trends in Residential Segregation by Race: 1960–1980," *Journal of Urban Economics* 26 (1989): 269–80.

53. Farley and Frey, "Changes in the Segregation of Whites from Blacks."

54. Massey and Denton, *American Apartheid*, p. 11.

55. R. E. Weink, C. E. Reid, J. C. Simonson, and F. J. Eggers, *Measuring Racial Discrimination in American Housing Markets: The Housing Market Practices Survey* (Washington, D.C.: Department of Housing and Urban Development, 1979); M. Fix and R. Struyk, eds., *Clear and Convincing Evidence: Measurement of Discrimination in America* (Washington, D.C.: Urban Institute Press, 1993).

56. J. Yinger, G. Galster, B. Smith, and F. Eggers, *The Status of Research into Racial Discrimination and Segregation in American Housing Markets* (Washington, D.C.: U.S. Department of Housing and Urban Development, 1978).

57. D. Massey and E. Fong, "Segregation and Neighborhood Quality: Blacks, Hispanics, and Asians in the San Francisco Metropolitan Area," *Social Forces* 69 (1990): 15–32; A. Gross and D. Massey, "Spatial Assimilation Models: A Micro-Macro Comparison," *Social Science Quarterly* 72 (1991): 349–59; L. Stearns and J. Logan, "The Racial Structuring of the Housing Market and Segregation in Suburban Areas," *Social Forces* 65 (1986): 29–42; D. Massey and N. Denton, "Suburbanization and Segregation in U.S. Metropolitan Areas," *American Journal of Sociology* 94 (1988): 592–626.

58. D. Massey and N. Denton, "Trends in the Residential Segregation of Blacks, Hispanics, and Asians: 1970–1980," *American Sociological Review* 52 (1987): 802–25.

59. Rosenbaum, "Racial/Ethnic Differences in Home Ownership and Housing Quality," p. 3.

60. U.S. National Advisory Commission on Civil Disorders, *The Kerner Report* (New York: Pantheon, 1988), p. 1.

61. W. J. Wilson, *The Truly Disadvantaged: The Inner City, the Underclass, and Public Policy* (Chicago: University of Chicago Press, 1987); Massey and Denton, *American Apartheid*. Also see C. Jencks and P. Peterson, eds., *The Urban Underclass* (Washington, D.C.: Brookings Institution, 1991).

62. Massey and Denton, *American Apartheid*, p. 2; emphasis added.

63. Rosenbaum, "Racial/Ethnic Differences in Home Ownership and Housing Quality."

64. Massey and Denton define hypersegregation as the condition of being "very highly segregated [having a black-white index of dissimilarity greater than 60 percent] on at least four of the five dimensions at once" (*American Apartheid*, p. 74). The five dimensions are unevenness, isolation, clustering, concentration, and urban centralization. For a technical discussion, see D. Massey and N. Denton, "Hypersegregation in U.S. Metropolitan Areas: Black and Hispanic Segregation Along Five Dimensions," *Demography* 26 (1989): 378–79.

65. Oliver and Shapiro, *Black Wealth/White Wealth*, p. 205.

66. Joint Center for Housing Studies, *The State of the Nation's Housing: 1996* (Cambridge: Harvard University, 1997).

67. Keister and Caldwell attempt to *simulate* the change in distribution of wealth by race since the 1960s under various assumptions of discrimination; see L. A. Keister and S. B. Caldwell, "A Dynamic Analysis of the Micro-foundations of Wealth Distribution in the United States" (paper presented at the annual meeting of the American Sociological Association, Washington, D.C., 1995).

68. Spilerman finds that in Israel intergenerational (parental) assistance is one of the most powerful predictors of whether young adults become home-owners; see S. Spilerman, "Intergenerational Assistance, Home Ownership, and Wealth Inequality in Israel" (paper presented at the Conference on Inequality at the Center for Social Policy Studies, Jerusalem, 1996).

69. Oliver and Shapiro, *Black Wealth/White Wealth.*

70. See, e.g., S. Mayer, *What Money Can't Buy: Family Income and Children's Life Chances* (Cambridge: Harvard University Press, 1997).

71. See Land and Russell, "Wealth Accumulation Across the Life Course."

72. The rankings correspond to the beta statistics of the regression results of Table A2.5.

73. When I rerun the series of models without the possibly biasing effect of income, the race coefficient shows the same pattern.

74. Brimmer, "Income, Wealth, and Investment Behavior."

CHAPTER THREE

1. P. Blau and O. D. Duncan, *The American Occupational Structure* (New York: Free Press, 1967). Also see T. Parsons, *The Social System* (Glencoe, Ill.: Free Press, 1951).

2. See J. S. Coleman, *Equality of Educational Opportunity (Summary Report)* (Washington, D.C.: U.S. Department of Health, Education, and Welfare, Office of Education, 1966). For reanalysis of this report and further research, see, e.g., C. Jencks, M. Smith, H. Acland, M. Bane, D. Cohen, H. Gintis, B. Heyns, and S. Michelson, *Inequality: A Reassessment of the Effect of Family and Schooling in America* (New York: Basic Books, 1972).

3. R. Farley, *Blacks and Whites: Narrowing the Gap?* (Cambridge: Harvard University Press, 1984).

4. K. DeBarros and C. Bennett, "The Black Population in the United States: March 1997 (Update)," *Current Population Reports,* Series P-20, No. 508 (Washington, D.C.: U.S. Government Printing Office, 1998).

5. Unless otherwise noted, educational statistics in this chapter come from the U.S. Department of Education, *Digest of Education Statistics* (Washington, D.C.: National Center for Education Statistics, Office of Educational Research and Improvement, 1995).

6. DeBarros and Bennett, "The Black Population in the United States: March 1997."

7. U.S. Bureau of the Census, *Statistical Abstract of the United States* (Washington, D.C.: U.S. Government Printing Office, 1995), p. 189.

8. Ibid., p. 192.

9. See, e.g., L. M. Wolfle, "Postsecondary Educational Attainment Among Whites and Blacks," *American Educational Research Journal* 22 (1985): 501–25.

10. U.S. Bureau of the Census, *Statistical Abstract,* p. 170.

11. R. H. Bradley, D. J. Mundfrom, and L. Whiteside, "A Factor Analytic Study of the Infant-Toddler and Early Childhood Versions of the HOME Inventory Administered to White, Black, and Hispanic American Parents of Children Born Preterm," *Child Development* 65 (1994): 880–88.

12. U.S. Department of Education, *The Condition of Education: 1996* (Washington, D.C.: National Center for Education Statistics, Office of Education Research and Improvement, 1996) p. 64.

13. Ibid.

14. J. C. Hearn, "Academic and Nonacademic Influences on the College Destinations of 1980 High School Graduates," *Sociology of Education* 64 (1991): 158–71.

15. P. Leonard, C. Dolbeare, and E. Lazere, *A Place to Call Home: The Crisis in Housing for the Poor* (Washington, D.C.: Center on Budget and Policy Priorities and Low Income Housing Information Service, 1989).

16. F. K. Goldscheider and C. Goldscheider, "The Intergenerational Flow of Income: Family Structure and the Status Of Black Americans," *Journal of Marriage and the Family* 53 (1991): 499–508.

17. R. D'Amico, "Does Employment During High School Impair Academic Progress?" *Sociology of Education* 57 (1984): 152–64.

18. J. Kane and L. Spizman, "Race, Financial Aid Awards, and College Attendance: Parents and Geography Matter," *American Journal of Economics and Sociology* 53 (1994): 85–97.

19. See W. J. Wilson, *The Truly Disadvantaged: The Inner City, the Underclass, and Public Policy* (Chicago: University of Chicago Press, 1987).

20. S. Dornbusch, "Community Influences on the Relation of Family Statuses to Adolescent School Performance: Differences Between African Americans and Non-Hispanic Whites," *American Journal of Education* 99 (1991): 543–67.

21. See, e.g., L. Datcher, "Effects of Community and Family Background on Achievement," *Review of Economics and Statistics* 64 (1982): 32–41; J. Crane, "The Epidemic Theory of Ghettos and Neighborhood Effects on Dropping Out and Teenage Childbearing," *American Journal of Sociology* 96 (1991): 1226–59; and M. Corcoran, R. Gordon, D. Laren, and G. Solon, "The Association Between Men's Economic Status and Their Family and Community Origins," *Journal of Human Resources* 27 (1992): 575–601.

22. J. Brooks-Gunn, G. Duncan, P. Klebanov, and N. Sealand, "Do Neighborhoods Influence Child and Adolescent Development?" *American Journal of Sociology* 99 (1993): 353–95. This study has been criticized for not accounting for the correlation of error terms between the family and neighborhood-level measures. By contrast, some scholars have argued the opposite dynamic: namely, that relative deprivation (for instance, living in a well-off neighborhood if one's family is poor) is worse for children. For this line of reasoning, see, e.g., R. Haveman and B. Wolfe, *Succeeding Generations: On the Effects of Investments in Children* (New York: Russell Sage Foundation, 1994).

23. R. Dreeben, "Race, Instruction, and Learning," *American Sociological Review* 51 (1986): 660–69.

24. U.S. Bureau of the Census, *Statistical Abstract*, p. 150.

25. For the view that school expenditures do not make much difference, see E. A. Hanushek, "The Impact of Differential Expenditures on School Performance," *Education Researcher* 18 (1989): 45–51, 62.

26. S. E. Mayer, "The Effect of Schools' Racial and Socioeconomic Mix on High School Students' Chances of Dropping Out" (Harris School of Public Policy, University of Chicago, 1991).

27. J. R. Harris, *The Nurture Assumption* (New York: Free Press, 1998). Also see classic urban ethnographies such as William F. Whyte's *Street Corner*

Society (Chicago: University of Chicago Press, 1943) for a rich description of the effects of peer groups and communities on the lifestyles and life chances of teenagers.

28. Haveman and Wolfe, *Succeeding Generations,* p. 36.

29. See Crane, "Epidemic Theory of Ghettos."

30. J. L. Aber, J. Brooks-Gunn, and M. Gephart, "The Effects of Neighborhoods on Children, Youth, and Families: A Developmental Contextual Framework," in *Neighborhood Poverty: Context and Consequences for Child and Adolescent Development,* ed. G. Duncan, J. Brooks-Gunn, and J. L. Aber (New York: Russell Sage Foundation, 1997).

31. L. G. Humphreys, "Trends in Levels of Academic Achievement of Blacks and Other Minorities," *Intelligence* 12 (1988): 231–60.

32. R. Herrnstein and C. Murray, *The Bell Curve: Intelligence and Class Structure* (New York: Free Press, 1995), p. 319.

33. K. Vincent, "Black/White IQ Differences: Does Age Make the Difference?" *Journal of Clinical Psychology* 47 (1991): 266–70.

34. J. Ogbu, "Minority Coping Responses and School Experience," *Journal of Psychohistory* 18 (1991): 433–56.

35. A. W. Smith, "Educational Attainment as a Determinant of Social Class Among Black Americans," *Journal of Negro Education* 58 (1989): 416.

36. P. J. Burke, "Identity and Sex-Race Differences in Educational and Occupational Aspirations Formation," *Social Science Research* 17 (1988): 29–47.

37. R. Frank and P. Cooke, *The Winner Take All Society* (New York: Viking Penguin, 1995).

38. Moynihan cited in M. Sherraden, *Assets and the Poor: A New Direction for Social Policy* (Armonk, N.Y.: Sharpe, 1991), p. 161.

39. J. C. Henretta, "Race Differences in Middle-Class Lifestyle: The Role of Home Ownership," *Social Science Research* 8 (1979): 63–78.

40. E. Rosenbaum, "Racial/Ethnic Differences in Home Ownership and Housing Quality, 1991," *Social Problems* 43 (1997): 403. Also see J. Adams, *Housing America in the 1980s* (New York: Russell Sage Foundation, 1987); and D. Foley, "The Sociology of Housing," *American Review of Sociology* 6 (1980): 457–78.

41. J. B. Calhoun, "Population Density and Social Pathology," *Scientific American* 206 (1962): 139–48.

42. W. R. Gove, M. Hughes, and O. R. Galle, "Overcrowding in the Home: An Empirical Investigation of Its Possible Pathological Consequences," *American Sociological Review* 44 (1979): 59.

43. See ibid.; I. Altman, *The Environment and Social Behavior: Privacy, Personal Space, Territory, and Crowding* (Monterey, Calif.: Brooks/Cole, 1975); M. Baldassare, *Residential Crowding in Urban America* (Berkeley: University of California Press, 1978); O. R. Galle and W. R. Gove, "Overcrowding, Isolation, and Human Behavior: Exploring the Extremes in Population Distribution," in *Social Demography,* ed. K. Tauber and J. Sweet (New York: Academic Press, 1978), pp. 95–132; O. R. Galle and W. R. Gove, "Crowding and Human Behavior in Chicago, 1940–1970," in *Residential Crowding and Design,* ed. J. R. Aiello and A. Baum (New York: Plenum Press, 1979).

Some past research on the effects of household crowding has used aggregate-level data to look at such outcome variables as rates of drug use and crime. Such studies have been criticized for the high level of co-linearity between independent variables. When using household—rather than aggregate—data, this problem is eliminated. For the debate, see A. Booth, S. Welch, and D. R. Johnson, "Crowding and Urban Crime Rates," *Urban Affairs Quarterly* 11 (1976): 291–308; and P. C. Higgins, P. J. Richards, and J. H. Swan, "Crowding and Urban Crime Rates: Comment," *Urban Affairs Quarterly* 11 (1976): 309–16.

44. Gove, Hughes, and Galle, "Overcrowding in the Home."

45. H. Hawkins, "Urban Housing and the Black Family," *Phylon* 37 (1976): 73–84. Analysis of the 1989 wave of the Panel Study of Income Dynamics (PSID) shows that African Americans on average have 1.41 times more persons per room than whites.

46. Altman, *The Environment and Social Behavior.*

47. B. M. Caldwell and R. H. Bradley, *Manual for the Home Observation for the Measurement of the Environment* (Little Rock: University of Arkansas Press, 1984).

48. D. Conley, "Separate and Unequal? Household Level Effects of Segregated Housing Markets: Evidence from Two Generations" (paper presented at the annual meeting of the American Sociological Association, Washington, D.C., 1996).

49. Ibid.

50. See Foley, "Sociology of Housing."

51. K. R. Mahaffey, J. L. Annest, and J. Roberts, "National Estimates of Blood Lead Levels: United States, 1976–1980: Association with Selected Demographic and Socio-Economic Factors," *New England Journal of Medicine* 307 (1982): 573–79.

52. National Center for Children in Poverty, *Five Million Children: A Statistical Portrait of America's Youngest Poor* (New York: Columbia University School of Public Health, 1990), p. 54; also see L. V. Klerman and M. Parker, *Alive and Well? A Review of Health Policies and Programs for Young Children* (New York: National Center for Children in Poverty, 1990), p. 24.

53. D. M. Heer, "Effects of Sibling Number on Child Outcome," *Annual Review of Sociology* 11 (1985): 27–47.

54. L. C. Steelman and B. Powell, "Acquiring Capital for College: The Constraints of Family Configuration," *American Sociological Review* 54 (1989): 844–55.

55. These variables may be more subject to misspecification bias than the high school and college completion indicators since they are retrospective. Respondents are asked in 1995 about their entire primary and secondary school careers, and thus the events themselves may have occurred prior to 1984, which is when wealth is measured.

56. While it would have been extremely desirable to have been able to examine differences in school quality (partially to directly address the Coleman findings), in the social capital of neighborhoods, and in the selectivity of post-secondary institutions attended, the PSID data, which had such rich wealth

measures, lacked more detail on the type of postsecondary educational institution attended, the level of resources belonging to that institution, and the social capital in local communities. Since such a strong overall effect of wealth has been presented here, future researchers may want to fill in these contextual issues and map out the specific causal mechanisms by which wealth has its impact.

CHAPTER FOUR

1. A. Hacker, *Two Nations: Black and White, Separate, Hostile, and Unequal* (New York: Ballantine, 1992), p. 113.

2. K. DeBarros and C. Bennett, "The Black Population in the United States: March 1997 (Update)," *Current Population Reports,* Series P-20, No. 508 (Washington, D.C.: U.S. Government Printing Office, 1998).

3. Ibid.

4. Hacker, *Two Nations*, p. 109.

5. C. A. Valentine, *Culture and Poverty, Critique and Counterproposals* (Chicago: University of Chicago Press, 1968); O. Lewis, *La Vida: A Puerto Rican Family in the Culture of Poverty—San Juan and New York* (New York: Random House, 1966).

6. Valentine, *Culture and Poverty.*

7. Ibid.

8. L. Rainwater, *Behind Ghetto Walls: Black Families in a Federal Slum* (Chicago: Aldine, 1970).

9. L. C. Thurow, *Generating Inequality: Mechanisms of Distribution in the U.S. Economy* (New York: Basic Books, 1975).

10. D. L. Hiestand, *Economic Growth and Employment Opportunities for Minorities* (New York: Columbia University Press, 1964); S. Lieberson, *A Piece of the Pie: Blacks and White Immigrants Since 1880* (Berkeley: University of California Press, 1980).

11. C. Murray, *Losing Ground: American Social Policy, 1950–1980* (New York: Free Press, 1984).

12. W. J. Wilson, *The Truly Disadvantaged: The Inner City, the Underclass, and Public Policy* (Chicago: University of Chicago Press, 1987).

13. Ibid.

14. Recent ethnographic work suggests that many dynamics are at work in explaining chronic unemployment in persistently impoverished areas, including a lack of jobs, perverse incentives, and low wages as well as cultural factors and survival strategies. See, e.g., D. Dohan, "Making Cents in Urban Barrios: Survival Strategies of Immigrants and Natives in Low Wage Labor Markets" (paper presented at the annual meeting of the American Sociological Association, San Francisco, 1998).

15. Data from the U.S. Bureau of Labor Statistics, "Labor Force Statistics from the Current Population Survey," Table 2; published on the Internet at *http://www.bls.gov/news.release/wkyeng.t02.htm.*

16. Hacker, *Two Nations*, p. 102.

17. J. L. Hochschild, *Facing Up to the American Dream: Race, Class, and the Soul of the Nation* (Princeton, N.J.: Princeton University Press, 1995), p. 103.

18. C. Jencks, "Is the American Underclass Growing?" in *The Urban Underclass,* ed. C. Jencks and P. Peterson (Washington, D.C.: Brookings Institution, 1991); C.W. Reimers, "Sources of the Family Income Differentials Among Hispanics, Blacks, and White Non-Hispanics," *American Journal of Sociology* 89 (1984): 889–903.

19. See, e.g., M. A. Fossett, O. R. Galle, and J. A. Burr, "Racial Occupational Inequality, 1940–1980: National and Regional Trends," *American Sociological Review* 51 (1989): 421–29.

20. P. Doeringer and M. J. Piore, *Internal Labor Markets and Manpower Analysis* (Lexington, Mass.: Heath, 1971).

21. S. Spilerman, "Careers, Labor Market Structure, and Socio-Economic Achievement," *American Journal of Sociology* 83 (1977): 551–93.

22. R. L. Kaufman and T. N. Daymont, "Racial Discrimination and the Social Organization of Industries," *Social Science Research* 10 (1981): 225–55.

23. C. M. Tolbert, P. M. Horan, and E. M. Beck, "The Structure of Economic Segmentation: A Dual Economy Approach," *American Journal of Sociology* 85 (1980): 299–323; G. Wilson, "Pathways to Power: Racial Differences in the Determinants of Job Authority" (paper presented at the annual meeting of the American Sociological Association, New York City, 1996).

24. Kaufman and Daymont, "Racial Discrimination and the Social Organization of Industries." Other recent work along these lines has focused on the disproportionate concentration of African Americans in the public sector during a period of retrenchment—i.e., the 1980s—as an explanation for a widening earnings gap. See, e.g., J. F. Zipp, "Government Employment and Black-White Earnings Inequality, 1980–1990," *Social Problems* 41 (1994): 363–82.

25. E. O. Wright, "Race, Class, and Income Inequality," *American Journal of Sociology* 83 (1978): 1368–97.

26. G. Wilson, "Payoffs to Power Among the Middle Class: Has Race Declined in Significance?" (University of Miami, Department of Sociology, 1996).

27. A. Cherlin, *Marriage, Divorce, Remarriage,* rev. ed. (Cambridge: Harvard University Press, 1992).

28. See two articles by J. D. Kassarda: "City Jobs and Residents on a Collision Course: The Urban Underclass Dilemma," *Economic Development Quarterly* 4 (1990): 313–19; and "Structural Factors Affecting the Location and Timing of Urban Underclass Growth," *Urban Geography* 11 (1990): 234–64.

29. C. Link, E. Ratledge, and K. Lewis, "Black-White Differences in Returns to Schooling: Some New Evidence," *American Economic Review* 66 (1976): 221–23.

30. J. Akin and I. Garfinkel, "The Quality of Education and Cohort Variation in Black-White Earnings Differentials: Comment," *American Economic Review* 70 (1980): 186–91.

31. S. A. Cancio, D. T. Evans, and D. J. Maume, "Reconsidering the Declining Significance of Race: Racial Differences in Early Career Wages," *American Sociological Review* 61 (1996): 541–56; G. Farkas and K. Vicknair,

"Appropriate Tests of Racial Wage Discrimination Require Controls for Cognitive Skill: Comment on Cancio, Evans, and Maume," *American Sociological Review* 61 (1996): 557–60; D. J. Maume, S. A. Cancio, and D. T. Evans, "Cognitive Skills and Racial Wage Inequality: Reply to Farkas and Vicknair," *American Sociological Review* 61 (1996): 561–64.

32. J. Kirschenman and K. M. Neckerman, "We'd Love to Hire Them But. . . : The Meaning of Race for Employers," in *The Urban Underclass*, ed. C. Jencks and P. Peterson (Washington D.C.: Brookings Institution, 1991).

33. Wilson, *The Truly Disadvantaged*.

34. C. Jencks, *Rethinking Social Policy: Race, Poverty, and the Underclass* (Cambridge: Harvard University Press, 1992), p. 123.

35. R. Price and E. Mills, "Race and Residence in Earnings Determination," *Journal of Urban Economics* 17 (1985): 1–18; D. Ellwood, "The Spatial Mismatch Hypothesis: Are There Jobs Missing in the Ghetto?" in *The Black Youth Employment Crisis*, ed. R. Freeman and H. Holzer (Chicago: University of Chicago Press, 1986); K. Ihlanfeldt and D. Sjoquist, "Job Accessibility and Racial Differences in Youth Employment Rates," *American Economic Review* 80 (1990): 267–79.

36. M. Semyonov, D. R. Hoyt, and R. I. Scott, "Place, Race, and Differential Occupational Opportunities," *Demography* 21 (1984): 259–70.

37. R. W. Rumberger, "The Influence of Family Background on Education, Earnings, and Wealth," *Social Forces* 61 (1983): 755–73.

38. R. Hodge, "Occupational Mobility as a Probability Process," *Demography* 3 (1966): 19–34; P. Blau and O. D. Duncan, *The American Occupational Structure* (New York: Free Press, 1967); D. Featherman and R. Hauser, *Opportunity and Change* (New York: Basic Books, 1978).

39. C. Jencks, M. Smith, H. Acland, M. Bane, D. Cohen, H. Gintis, B. Heyns, and S. Michelson, *Inequality: A Reassessment of the Effect of Family and Schooling in America* (New York: Basic Books, 1972); C. Jencks, S. Bartlett, M. Corcoran, J. Crouse, D. Eaglesfield, G. Jackson, K. McLelland, P. Meuser, M Olneck, J. Schwartz, S. Ward, and J. Williams, *Who Gets Ahead? The Determinants of Economic Success in America* (New York: Basic Books, 1979); W. H. Sewell and R. Hauser, *Education, Occupation, and Earnings: Achievement in Early Career* (New York: Academic Press, 1975).

40. J. A. Brittain, *The Inheritance of Economic Status* (Washington, D.C.: Brookings Institution, 1977).

41. M. P. Massagli and R. Hauser, "Response Variability in Self- and Proxy Reports of Paternal and Filial Socio-Economic Characteristics," *American Journal of Sociology* 89 (1983): 420–31.

42. P. Taubman, "The Determinants of Earnings: Genetics, Family, and Other Environments: A Study of White Male Twins," *American Economic Review* 66 (1976): 858–70.

43. G. Solon, "Intergenerational Income Mobility in the United States," *American Economic Review* 82 (1992): 393–408.

44. Some research has revealed a higher intergenerational correlation for wealth than for income. Kotlicoff and Summers estimate that only 20 percent of capital accumulation can be attributed to life-cycle savings and thus 80 per-

cent is heritable; see L. J. Kotlicoff and L. Summers, "The Role of Intergenerational Transfers in Aggregate Capital Accumulation," *Journal of Political Economy* 89 (1981): 706–32. Modigliani questions the 80 percent figure but not the basic principle that a substantial portion of net worth can be attributed to intergenerational transmission; see F. Modigliani, "The Role of Intergenerational Transfers and Life Cycle Saving in the Accumulation of Wealth," *Journal of Economics and Sociology* 49 (1988): 129–51.

45. R. M. Fernandez and N. Weinberg, "Sifting and Sorting: Personal Contacts and Hiring in a Retail Bank," *American Sociological Review* 62 (1997): 883–902.

46. M. S. Granovetter, "The Strength of Weak Ties," *American Journal of Sociology* 78 (1973): 1360–80.

47. J. Gross, "Poor Without Car Find Trek to Work Is Now a Job," *New York Times,* November 18, 1997, p. A1.

48. Hacker, *Two Nations,* p. 113.

49. Ibid.

50. Ibid.

51. H. Ishida, S. Spilerman, and K. H. Su, "Educational Credentials and Promotion Chances in Japanese and American Organizations," *American Sociological Review* 62 (1997): 866.

52. J. T. Cook and J. L. Brown, "Asset Development Among America's Poor: Trends in the Distribution of Income and Wealth," research in progress, working paper, CHPNP-WP No. AD-121595, Center on Hunger, Poverty, and Nutrition Policy, Tufts University, Medford, Mass., 1995.

53. I use a dichotomous variable alone for this low-income population because it is assumed that, for low-income families, having any assets at all is the critical factor in keeping them successfully linked to the labor market. I did test models with the continuous wealth function, and they were not as robust.

54. DeBarros and Bennett, "The Black Population in the United States: March 1997."

55. Jencks, *Rethinking Social Policy,* p. 33.

56. T. Sowell, *Markets and Minorities* (New York: Basic Books, 1981).

CHAPTER FIVE

1. A. Hacker, *Two Nations: Black and White, Separate, Hostile, and Unequal* (New York: Ballantine, 1992), p. 73.

2. See, e.g., S. McLanahan and G. Sandefur, *Growing Up with a Single Parent: What Hurts and What Helps* (Cambridge: Harvard University Press, 1994).

3. N. G. Bennett, D. Bloom, and C. Miller, "The Influence of Nonmarital Childbearing on the Formation of First Marriages," *Demography* 32 (1995): 41–62.

4. See, e.g., the following two articles by A. T. Geronimus and S. Korenman: "The Socioeconomic Consequences of Teen Childbearing Reconsidered," *Quarterly Journal of Economics* 108 (1992): 1187–1214; and "The

Socioeconomic Costs of Teenage Childbearing: Evidence and Interpretation," *Demography* 30 (1993): 281–90.

5. See, e.g., the following two articles by S. A. Hoffman, M. Foster, and F. F. Furstenberg: "Reevaluating the Costs of Teen Childbearing," *Demography* 30 (1993): 1–13; and "Reevaluating the Costs of Teen Childbearing: Response to Geronimus and Korenman," *Demography* 30 (1993): 291–96.

6. D. Hogan and E. Kitagawa, "The Impact of Social Status, Family Structure, and Neighborhood on the Fertility of Black Adolescents," *American Journal of Sociology* 90 (1985): 825–55.

7. R. Haveman and B. Wolfe, *Succeeding Generations: On the Effects of Investments in Children* (New York: Russell Sage Foundation, 1994), p. 190.

8. Ibid.

9. T. Skocpol, *Social Policy in the United States: Future Possibilities in Historical Perspective* (Princeton, N.J.: Princeton University Press, 1995), p. 214.

10. Haveman and Wolfe, *Succeeding Generations,* pp. 72–73.

11. See the following works by W. E. B. Du Bois: *The Philadelphia Negro* (Philadelphia: University of Pennsylvania Press, 1899); and *The Negro American Family* (New York: New American Library, 1908).

12. E. F. Frazier, *The Negro Family in the United States* (New York: Dryden Press, 1948); S. Elkins, *Slavery: A Problem in American Institutional and Intellectual Life* (Chicago: University of Chicago Press, 1963); G. Myrdal, *An American Dilemma: The Negro Problem and Modern Democracy* (New York: Harper and Brothers, 1944).

13. S. P. Morgan, A. McDaniel, A. T. Miller, and S. H. Preston, "Racial Differences in Household and Family Structure at the Turn of the Century," *American Journal of Sociology* 98 (1993): 799.

14. D. Moynihan, *The Negro Family: The Case for National Action* (Washington, D.C.: U.S. Department of Labor, Office of Policy Planning and Research, 1965).

15. R. W. Fogel and S. L. Engerman, *Time on the Cross: The Economics of American Negro Slavery* (Boston: Little, Brown, 1974).

16. E. D. Genovese, *The Political Economy of Slavery: Studies in the Economy and Society of the Slave South* (New York: Pantheon, 1965).

17. H. G. Gutman, *The Black Family in Slavery and Freedom, 1750–1925* (New York: Pantheon, 1976).

18. B. Duncan and O. D. Duncan, "Family Stability and Occupational Success," *Social Problems* 16 (1969): 262–306; S. McLanahan and L. Bumpass, "Intergenerational Consequences of Family Disruption," *American Journal of Sociology* 94 (1988): 130–52.

19. R. Staples, "Changes in Black Family Structure: The Conflict Between Family Ideology and Structural Conditions," *Journal of Marriage and the Family* 47 (1985): 1005–13.

20. L. Gary, L. Beatty, G. Berry, and M. Price, "Stable Black Families: Final Report" (Institute for Urban Affairs and Research, Howard University, Washington, D.C., 1983).

21. See, e.g., H. P. McAdoo, ed., Black Families, 3d ed. (Thousand Oaks, Calif.: Sage, 1997).

22. R. Angel and M. Tienda, "Determinants of Extended Household Structure: Cultural Pattern or Economic Need?" *American Journal of Sociology* 87 (1982): 1360–83.

23. C. Stack, *All Our Kin: Strategies for Survival in a Black Community* (New York: Harper and Row, 1974), p. 43.

24. S. Ruggles, "The Origins of African-American Family Structure," *American Sociological Review* 59 (1994): 139.

25. C. Murray, *Losing Ground: American Social Policy, 1950–1980* (New York: Free Press, 1984).

26. Z. Qian and S. H. Preston, "Changes in American Marriage, 1972 to 1987: Availability and Forces of Attraction by Age and Education," *American Sociological Review* 58 (1985): 492.

27. It is interesting to note, however, that neither the extent of sex education nor knowledge about birth control has a significant effect on the odds of teenage, premarital childbearing for either blacks or whites; see S. L. Hanson, D. E. Myers, and A. L. Ginsburg, "The Role of Responsibility and Knowledge in Reducing Teenage Out-of-Wedlock Childbearing," *Journal of Marriage and the Family* 49 (1987): 241–56. Easily available contraception and abortion services reduce rates of teenage, out-of-wedlock childbearing among whites but have no effect among African Americans; see Haveman and Wolfe, *Succeeding Generations,* p. 74.

28. Haveman and Wolfe, *Succeeding Generations,* p. 11.

29. Ellwood and Bane did find, however, that higher benefits resulted in a greater likelihood that a single mother would move out of her own parents' household when she had a child; see D. Ellwood and M. J. Bane, "The Impact of AFDC on Family Structure and Living Arrangements," working paper, U.S. Department of Health and Human Services, Grant no. 92A–82, 1984.

30. See, e.g., M. Guttentag and P. F. Secord, *Too Many Women? The Sex Ratio Question* (Beverly Hills, Calif.: Sage, 1983).

31. N. G. Bennett, D. E. Bloom, and P. H. Craig, "The Divergence of Black and White Marriage Patterns," *American Journal of Sociology* 95 (1989): 692–722.

32. K. J. Kiecold and M. A. Fossett, "Mate Availability and Marriage Among African Americans: Aggregate- and Individual-Level Analyses," in *The Decline in Marriage Among African Americans: Causes, Consequences, and Policy Implications,* ed. M. B. Tucker and C. Mitchell-Kernan (New York: Russell Sage Foundation, 1995), pp. 121–35.

33. D. T. Lichter, D. K. McLaughlin, G. Kephart, and D. J. Landy, "Race and the Retreat from Marriage: A Shortage of Marriageable Men?" *American Journal of Sociology* 98 (1993): 781.

34. W. J. Wilson, *The Truly Disadvantaged: The Inner City, the Underclass, and Public Policy* (Chicago: University of Chicago Press, 1987), chap. 3, "Poverty and Family Structure: The Widening Gap Between Evidence and Public Policy Issues," pp. 63–92.

35. M. Testa and M. Krogh, "The Effect of Employment on Marriage Among Black Males in Inner-City Chicago," in *The Decline in Marriage*

Among African Americans: Causes, Consequences, and Policy Implications, ed. M.B. Tucker and C. Mitchell-Kernan (New York: Russell Sage Foundation, 1995), p. 90.

36. M. Testa, "Male Joblessness, Nonmarital Parenthood, and Marriage" (paper presented at the Chicago Urban Poverty and Family Life Conference, Chicago, 1991).

37. R. Schoen, "The Widening Gap Between Black and White Marriage Rates: Context and Implications," in *The Decline in Marriage Among African Americans: Causes, Consequences, and Policy Implications*, ed. M.B. Tucker and C. Mitchell-Kernan (New York: Russell Sage Foundation, 1995), pp. 103–16.

38. N. Marks and S. McLanahan, "Gender, Family Structure, and Social Support Among Parents," *Journal of Marriage and the Family* 55 (1993): 481–93; L. Hao, "Family Structure, Private Transfers, and the Economic Well-Being of Families with Children," *Social Forces* 75 (1996): 269–92.

39. Hao, "Family Structure, Private Transfers, and Economic Well-Being."

40. D.P. Hogan, D.J. Eggebeen, and C.C. Clogg, "The Structure of Exchange in American Families," *American Journal of Sociology* 98 (1993): 1428–58; Marks and McLanahan, "Gender, Family Structure, and Social Support."

41. Haveman and Wolfe, *Succeeding Generations,* p. 35.

42. Hanson, Myers, and Ginsburg, "The Role of Responsibility and Knowledge in Reducing Teenage Out-of-Wedlock Childbearing."

43. Hogan and Kitagawa, "Impact of Social Status, Family Structure, and Neighborhood."

44. J. Crane, "The Epidemic Theory of Ghettos and Neighborhood Effects on Dropping Out and Teenage Childbearing," *American Journal of Sociology* 96 (1991): 1226–59; J. Brooks-Gunn, G. Duncan, P. Klebanov, and N. Sealand, "Do Neighborhoods Influence Child and Adolescent Development?" *American Journal of Sociology* 99 (1993): 353–95.

45. K. Auletta, *The Underclass* (New York: Random House, 1982).

46. See, e.g., M. Hill and M. Ponza, "Does Welfare Dependency Beget Welfare Dependency?" (Survey Research Center, Institute for Social Research, University of Michigan, 1984); G. Duncan, M. Hill, and S. Hoffman, "Welfare Dependence Within and Across Generations," *Science* 231 (1988): 467–71; G. Duncan and S. Hoffman, "Teenage Welfare Receipt and Subsequent Dependence Among Black Adolescent Mothers," *Family Planning Perspectives* 22 (1990): 16–20; G. Solon, M. Corcoran, R. Gordon, and D. Laren, "A Longitudinal Analysis of Sibling Correlations in Economic Status," *Journal of Human Resources* 26 (1991): 509–34.

47. M. Sherraden, *Assets and the Poor: A New Direction for Social Policy* (Armonk, N.Y.: Sharpe, 1991), p. 149.

48. Ibid.

49. See, e.g., B. Landry, *The New Black Middle Class* (Berkeley: University of California Press, 1987).

50. By "risk," I mean hazard rate in a proportional-hazards, event-history framework.

51. Haveman and Wolfe found that growing up (through age fifteen) in a household that ever received AFDC benefits had no impact on a woman's chance of subsequently using welfare (*Succeeding Generations,* p. 210).

52. Most of the previous studies included only women; however, in many states men were also eligible for public assistance in forms such as home relief during this period.

53. This is the same strategy used by Peter Gottschalk; see P. Gottschalk, "The Intergenerational Transmission of Welfare Participation: Facts and Possible Causes," *Journal of Policy Analysis and Management* 11 (1992): 254–72.

54. S. Hatchett, J. Veroff, and E. Douvan, "Marital Instability Among Black and White Couples in Early Marriage," in *The Decline of Marriage Among African Americans: Causes, Consequences, and Policy Implications,* ed. M. B. Tucker and C. Mitchell-Kernan (New York: Russell Sage Foundation, 1995), pp. 177–218.

55. P. Clark-Nicholas, and B. Gray-Little, "Effect of Economic Resources on Marital Quality in Black Married Couples," *Journal of Marriage and the Family* 52 (1991): 650.

56. Ibid., p. 653.

CHAPTER SIX

1. Similarly, by better measuring economic resources, future researchers will be equipped to answer a number of other questions that have yet to be resolved. For instance, there has been a spirited debate regarding the extent to which family structure has its impact through the psychological milieu of the household (the confluence model) and the extent to which absence of a parent or large sibling cohorts, for example, have their effects as a result of different resource availability and requirements in such households (the resource dilution model). With a more comprehensive definition of economic resources, this debate can be addressed more rigorously by modeling interactions between income/wealth and family structure variables.

2. For an introduction to this line of research, see, e.g., P. F. Short and G. R. Wilensky, *Household Wealth and Health Insurance as Protection Against Medical Risks* (Rockville, Md.: U.S. Department of Health and Human Services, Public Health Service, Office of the Assistant Secretary for Health, National Center for Health Services Research, 1984).

3. T. Skocpol, *Social Policy in the United States: Future Possibilities in Historical Perspective* (Princeton, N.J.: Princeton University Press, 1995), p. 219.

4. M. Marable, "Staying on the Path to Racial Equality," in *The Affirmative Action Debate,* ed. G. E. Curry (Reading, Mass.: Addison-Wesley, 1996), p. 4.

5. Ibid.

6. Ibid., p. 7.

7. For a discussion of the *Bakke* decision, see L. Chavez, *The Color Bind: California's Battle to End Affirmative Action* (Berkeley: University of California Press, 1998).

8. For a discussion of the weaknesses of affirmative action, see G. C. Loury, "Performing Without a Net," in *The Affirmative Action Debate,* ed. G. E. Curry (Reading, Mass.: Addison-Wesley, 1996), pp. 49–76.

9. For instance, see R. D. Kahlenberg, *The Remedy: Class, Race, and Affirmative Action* (New York: Basic Books, 1996).

10. T. L. Cross, *Black Capitalism: Strategy for Business in the Ghetto* (New York: Atheneum, 1969), p. 27.

11. Ibid.

12. W. K. Tabb, *The Political Economy of the Black Ghetto* (New York: Norton, 1970), p. 33.

13. Cross, *Black Capitalism,* p. viii.

14. K. Stein, "Explaining Ghetto Consumer Behavior: Hypotheses from Urban Sociology," *Journal of Consumer Affairs* 14 (1980): 234.

15. Ibid., p. 234.

16. Ibid.

17. Tabb, *Political Economy of the Black Ghetto,* p. 32

18. Ibid., p. 35.

19. Cross, *Black Capitalism,* p. 16

20. Ibid.

21. R. S. Browne, "The Economic Case for Reparations to Black America," *American Economic Review* 62 (1972): 42. Browne discusses research conducted by J. Marketti at the Industrial Relations Research Institute, University of Wisconsin at Madison.

22. Ibid., p. 44.

23. C. Krauthammer, "Reparations for Black Americans," *Time,* December 31, 1990, p. 18.

24. Tabb, *Political Economy of the Black Ghetto,* p. 33.

25. Ibid.

26. M. Oliver and T. Shapiro, "Race and Wealth," *Review of Black Political Economy* 17 (1989): 21.

27. Ibid., p. 23.

28. Ibid., p. 21.

29. N. Luhmann, *Power and Trust* (New York: Columbia University Press, 1979).

30. S. J. South and K. D. Crowder, "Leaving the 'Hood: Residential Mobility Between Black, White, and Integrated Neighborhoods," *American Sociological Review* 63 (1995): 17–26.

31. D. Kirp and E. Davis, "Nothing to Fear But Fear Itself: Insurance Against Social 'Bads'" (Goldman School of Public Policy, University of California at Berkeley, 1997).

32. B. D. Fromson, "Stocks Are Replacing Homes as the Primary Nest Egg for Many American Families, According to Economists and Market Analysts," *Washington Post,* November 27, 1995, p. A1.

33. J. P. Smith, "Racial and Ethnic Differences in Wealth Transfer Behavior," *Journal of Human Resources* 30 (1995): S158–83.

34. H. L. Wilensky, *The "New Corporatism": Centralization and the Welfare State* (Beverly Hills, Calif.: Sage, 1976), pp. 14–23.

35. M. Sherraden, *Assets and the Poor: A New Direction for Social Policy* (Armonk, N.Y.: Sharpe, 1991).

36. M. Janofsky, "Pessimism Retains Grip on Appalachian Poor," *New York Times*, February 9, 1998, pp. A1, A13.

37. Sherraden, *Assets and the Poor,* p. 96.

Index

Dalton Conley is Assistant Professor of
Sociology and African and African American
Studies at Yale University. (Photo by Stephen
Hudner.)

Text:	10/13.25 Sabon
Display:	Sabon
Composition:	Publication Services, Inc.
Printing and binding:	Haddon Craftsmen